# Hollywood's Indies

Classics Divisions, Specialty Labels and the American Film Market

Yannis Tzioumakis

EDINBURGH
University Press

For
Siân Lincoln

© Yannis Tzioumakis, 2012, 2013

First published in hardback in 2012 by
Edinburgh University Press Ltd
22 George Square, Edinburgh EH8 9LF
www.euppublishing.com

This paperback edition 2013

Typeset in 11/13 Ehrhardt
by Servis Filmsetting Ltd, Stockport, Cheshire

A CIP record for this book is available from the British Library

ISBN 978 0 7486 4012 6 (hardback)
ISBN 978 0 7486 8593 6 (paperback)
ISBN 978 0 7486 6451 1 (webready PDF)
ISBN 978 0 7486 6453 5 (epub)

The right of Yannis Tzioumakis
to be identified as author of this work
has been asserted in accordance with
the Copyright, Designs and Patents Act 1988.

# Contents

Acknowledgements iv

Introduction 1

## Section I  Independent
1  United Artists Classics (1980 to 1986) 23
2  Triumph Films (1982 to 1985), Universal Classics (1982 to 1984) and Twentieth Century Fox International Classics (1982 to 1985) 44
3  Orion Classics (1983 to 1997) 65

## Section II  Indie
4  Fine Line Features (1990 to 2005) 87
5  Sony Pictures Classics (1992 to date) 109

## Section III  Indiewood
6  Fox Searchlight (1994 to date) 133
7  Paramount Classics / Paramount Vantage (1997 to 2008) 156
8  Focus Features (2002 to date) 177
9  Warner Independent Pictures (2003 to 2008) and Picturehouse (2005 to 2008) 199

Index 227

# Acknowledgements

The genesis of this book began in April 2007 during a discussion on independent cinema with Geoff King, following his Liverpool research seminar on Charlie Kaufman, *Adaptation* and American independent cinema's move to indiewood. For that reason, he is the first person I would like to thank, especially as, in the four years that have elapsed since then, we have regularly exchanged our views on many issues related to independent film and his work has certainly influenced mine.

Then I would like to thank Edinburgh University Press (EUP) for commissioning this book, as well as for supporting American independent cinema as a field of research. EUP has also supported the 'American Indies' series and has commissioned several relevant titles that have advanced knowledge on the subject greatly. Specifically, I would like to thank Esme Watson, who commissioned this volume; Vicki Donald, who supported its development; and Gillian Leslie, who oversaw the final stages. Many thanks also to the rest of the EUP team, including Anna Glazier, James Dale and Rebecca Mackenzie. They have been a real pleasure to work with, as was Wendy Lee, who sorted out many issues with the manuscript during the copy-editing process.

The research for this book took several years to complete and involved a number of trips to the Margaret Herrick Library in Los Angeles. I would like to thank the library staff for all their help in locating relevant material on the studios' specialty labels, and especially Sandra Archer, who spent huge amounts of time helping me identify the less obvious sources. I would also like to thank the staff at the British Film Institute Library, where I spent the last few days of my research, chasing references and bringing the manuscript to scratch.

The book benefits immensely from interviews and email exchanges with filmmakers and industry executives who were involved with these divisions in various capacities. In particular, I would like to thank Mike Medavoy, former

Head of Production at Orion Pictures, and Eric Pleskow, former President and Chief Executive Officer of Orion Pictures, for providing me with information on Orion Classics; Ira Deutchman, former Executive at United Artists Classics and former President of Fine Line Features; James Schamus, Chief Executive Officer of Focus Features; and David Burton Morris, co-writer and director of Sundance-winner *Purple Haze*, which was distributed by Triumph Films. Besides it being a real privilege to talk to them about the respective companies with which they were/are involved, they also helped me understand the industry's point of view in terms of the role these companies play in contemporary US independent cinema.

This book would have taken far more time to finish, had it not been for Julia Hallam. As Head of the Department of Communication and Media at Liverpool University, Julia arranged for me to take a semester of research leave in 2011, providing me with valuable time to complete the project. Julia also read draft chapters of the work, providing me with feedback, while her overall support over the years as mentor, colleague, boss and friend has been immeasurable. A massive thank you, Julia! I would also like to thank the rest of my colleagues at Liverpool, who were also very supportive: Katia Balabanova, Peter Goddard, Kay Richardson, Adrian Quinn and especially Karen Ross, who has also been a great supporter of my work.

A number of close friends and colleagues deserve a huge thank you for encouraging me to undertake this project: Lydia Papadimitriou, Ruth McElroy, Rigas Goulimaris, Katerina Yanniki, Linda Crane, Nickianne Moody, Hayley Trowbridge and Jim Friel lent me their warm encouragement, while Gary Needham, Claire Molloy, Warren Buckland, Alisa Perren and Peter Krämer read draft chapters and discussed the subject with me in detail. Ben Howarth did a stellar job in transcribing interviews while Louise Wilks helped me immensely with the compilation of the book's index. I thank them both very much.

Family and friends in Greece and the UK have continued to support my research endeavours, and they will be happy to see this book finished. In Greece, I would like to thank Panayiotis and Christina Tzioumakis, Leonidas Tzioumakis, Patroula Vrantza, Panayiotis Koutakis, Dimitra Kavatha, Harris Tlas, Harris Papadopoulos, Maria Goulimari and Eleftheria Thanouli. In the UK, I am grateful to Frank Halligan, Joanne Whiteside, Andy Stockell, Paul Shaughnessy, Yolanda Akil-Perez, Lisa and Jason Bloom, David Oswald, Carys and Alex Damon, and Roger and Maggie Lincoln.

This book would not have been the same and would have taken far more time to complete, if it had not benefited from the input of a most talented and brilliant research assistant. Sarah Wharton went through literally thousands of articles, created bibliographies, took notes, identified issues and pretty much became my right hand in this project. She always submitted the work I asked her to do on time and she maintained her humour and good will throughout this process. She will be much more organised than me when she starts work on her first book in the near future!

Finally, I would like to reserve my greatest thanks for Siân Lincoln; I dedicate this book to her. Siân has been the staunchest supporter of this project right from the start and has worked tirelessly to create the best possible conditions for me to complete it. She has watched films with me, listened to my ideas, offered hers, helped with library research and generally supported me in every way imaginable. This has included looking after our newborn son, Roman, for long stretches of the day so that I could find space to work on the book. I am always humbled by her love, devotion, understanding and support. Thank you, Siân.

# Introduction

## THE COMPLICATIONS OF 'INDEPENDENCE'

Arguably the most defining, and at the same time controversial, characteristic of independent film as a category of filmmaking within the context of US cinema is that it has existed historically both outside the Hollywood film industry and within it. On the one hand, there have been commercial feature film productions that were financed, produced, distributed and exhibited away from the major film studios (in all their incarnations) and their subsidiary companies and divisions, which have firmly controlled American cinema since the 1910s. On the other hand, there have also been countless feature films in which one or more aspects of their finance, production and distribution history took place outside the Hollywood studios, and therefore also claimed the label 'independent', even though other aspects were determined by a wide array of arrangements with the dominant players in the Hollywood industry, to the extent that the label 'independent' has often been strongly questioned. In this respect, filmmakers, film critics, film scholars, the trade press – all the institutions that are authorised to contribute to the definitions of American independent cinema – have always been aware of this distinction and therefore have utilised the label 'independence' with provisos.[1] Indeed, they have habitually talked about 'independence within the industry', 'true independence', 'semi-independence' and, more recently, 'indie' and 'indiewood' filmmaking.[2]

This seemingly fundamental distinction in the field of US independent filmmaking becomes even more complicated when one moves beyond questions of industrial location and examines questions of aesthetics and of political and ideological disposition, which, according to Geoff King, constitute the three key points of orientation in any effort to define independent film.[3] While a large number of films made outside the Hollywood industry avoid utilising the formal strategies associated with Hollywood films and embrace political views firmly removed from the dominant ideological positions that have traditionally been represented in Hollywood films (individualism, capitalism, patriarchy, racism and so on),[4] other 'genuinely independent' films make no effort to engage with alternative aesthetic practices or ideological standpoints. For instance, films produced and distributed by independent companies for the substantial Christian audience or for narrower religious market niches are normally characterised by simplistic narratives and conservative political values that always tend to support the status quo.[5] Conversely, despite being made within the boundaries of the industry and often with resources provided directly by the majors, a number of 'independent' films have made radical aesthetic choices and assumed alternative political perspectives, even though certain key principles that have been a staple of American cinema, such as representation and narrative, remained untouched. For example, a film like Spike Lee's *Do the Right Thing* (1989), which was financed and distributed by Universal, expresses a clear anger towards American society about the predicament of black people, while also utilising two distinct visual styles and sounds that highlight the incompatibility of the assimilationist and separatist political positions that historically have driven race politics in the US.[6]

Not surprisingly, these complications have resulted in intense disagreements among filmmakers, critics, scholars, the press and the cinema-going public about the criteria according to which one could define independent filmmaking in the US. This disagreement took place primarily within the context of a distinct body of independent film production and distribution that sprang up in the late 1970s / early 1980s and, arguably, continues to date. Often labelled as 'contemporary American independent cinema', this body of work was perceived from the beginning as a 'movement',[7] and as a concerted effort to create a sustained alternative paradigm to Hollywood cinema.[8] As such, it was expected to support alternative aesthetic, cultural and political ideologies (in other words, to exist outside the Hollywood film industry and its players), and, importantly, to exclude in the process all other forms of independent filmmaking that had points of contact with Hollywood and its practices. This view can be seen clearly in Annette Insdorf's scene-setting account of the early years of contemporary US independent cinema. Writing for *American Film* in 1981, she argued that what distinguished then-current releases, such as *Northern Lights* (J. Hanson and R. Nilsson, 1981 [1978]), *Heartland* (R. Pearce, 1980) and *Return of the Secaucus Seven* (J. Sayles, 1980) – all films financed, produced and distributed away from the Hollywood studios – were:

> casting, pace, cinematic style and social and moral vision. Countering big stars with fresh faces, big deals with intimate canvasses and big studios with regional authenticity, these filmmakers treat[ed] inherently American

concerns with a primarily European style. Geographically rooted directors resist[ed] Hollywood's priorities and potential absorption.[9]

These films, Insdorf continued, were also separate from other independent productions that mobilised conventions and characteristics associated with Hollywood practices. For instance, despite being produced and distributed by companies other than the majors, films by directors such as George Romero, John Carpenter, Tobe Hooper and David Cronenberg demonstrate a propensity for 'Grand Guignol, violence and sex' and therefore were in a position to attract (and they did attract) 'commercial money'.[10]

The type of film that Insdorf highlighted as a representative example of contemporary American independent cinema, and which the independent film companies themselves dubbed as 'quality film' to convey 'the requisite upscale tone without precluding substantial commercial success',[11] was quickly confirmed as the dominant expression of independent filmmaking in the 1980s. This resulted in the production and distribution outside the major studios of many canonical titles such as *Chan is Missing* (W. Wang, 1982), *El Norte* (G. Nava, 1983), *Stranger than Paradise* (J. Jarmusch, 1984), *The Kiss of the Spider Woman* (H. Babenco, 1985) and *She's Gotta Have It* (S. Lee, 1986). With early titles such as *Return of the Secaucus Seven* registering over $2 million at the US box office, *My Dinner with André* (L. Malle, 1981) grossing $1.9 million, and *Chan is Missing* recording $1 million against extremely low budget and advertising costs,[12] this type of filmmaking seemed to have a solid commercial basis from which it could expand and become a sustained alternative to Hollywood.

The commercial success not only of these films but also of many world cinema arthouse titles, which were also handled in the US theatrical market primarily by the same stand-alone distributors that released many of the independently produced titles mentioned above (New Yorker Films, the Samuel Goldwyn Company, New World Pictures, First Run Features, Pickman Films and many others), inevitably attracted the attention of the major studios to these, until recently marginal, markets. The first company to stake its claim was United Artists. After rebranding an existing generic division, specialising in non-theatrical releases of films from the company's huge library of titles, as a theatrical distributor for 'special markets',[13] United Artists Classics became the first studio division to compete against those independent distributors. Its 'special markets' consisted of the foreign arthouse and homegrown independent film markets, as well as the film reissue market, which in the pre-video era had also proved to be a significant contributor of revenues for the division.

The entry of United Artists (and almost immediately afterwards, Columbia, Twentieth Century Fox and Universal) into the US independent film market was met with mixed reactions. For independent producers, their arrival in the sector was great news, as it meant the presence of several new theatrical distributors who could acquire their product. Furthermore, and compared to the existing independent distributors whose buying and marketing power was limited, the studio divisions had the backing of vast, diversified conglomerates and had established relationships with exhibitors and access to a national distribution network (should a film prove a crossover success), which potentially made for a more commercially promising distribution process. Finally, a distribution contract with one of these companies could also mean a film's exploitation in the nascent cable and home video markets (and therefore better remuneration for the producer and / or filmmaker), even though these deals were still rare for independent or arthouse films in the early 1980s.

For the stand-alone distributors, however, the studios' excursion into the 'special markets' was certainly undesirable. After more than a decade of controlling the arthouse market and competing only against each other, stand-alone distributors suddenly found themselves in a position where they had to compete with companies that had the financial backing of entertainment corporations and access to their resources. With a number of key arthouse and independent producers and filmmakers keen to try the studio divisions in an effort to secure the best possible deal for their films, independent distributors started facing cut-throat competition, especially for the most commercially promising titles. For instance, as Ira Deutchman, Head of Distribution and Marketing at Cinecom between 1982 and 1990, and before that one of the key creative executives at United Artists Classics (1981 to 1982), admitted, Cinecom bid for many of the early US independent films, such as *Lianna* (J. Sayles, 1983) and *Streamers* (R. Altman, 1983), but lost them to UA Classics.[14]

Irrespective of whether one adopts the perspective of the independent producers or the distributors, what is clear is that, right from the very beginning of the American independent cinema movement of the early 1980s, there was a group of films that had direct links with the major studios. Films like *Streamers* and *Lianna* might have been financed and produced outside the industry, but they were acquired and distributed in the theatres by the classics divisions of the main studios. This meant that their 'independence' was necessarily reconfigured from one 'outside' Hollywood to one 'within' it.

This initial blurring of lines in terms of what constitutes independent film in contemporary American cinema, caused by the studio divisions' entry into the independent film market, was, arguably, a continuation of a well-established trend that had made its presence felt for over a decade before critics started talking about contemporary American independent cinema in the early 1980s. The trend involved the habitual acquisition and distribution of genre and exploitation films by the majority of the stand-alone companies, which, in the 1980s, became part of the institutional apparatus that supported the type of 'alternative' independent filmmaking that Insdorf identified in her article. For instance, Pickman Films, which distributed one of the key early examples of contemporary American independent cinema, Richard Pearce's *Heartland*, had also distributed (as Levitt–Pickman) *Death Game* (P. S. Traynor, 1977), a thriller characterised by the elements of 'Grand Guignol, violence and sex' that contributors to the definition of independent cinema in the 1980s wanted excised from the canon. Levitt–Pickman also distributed the blaxploitation film *Super Spook* (Anthony B. Major, 1975) and the softcore feature *Gymslip Lovers* (J.-P. Scardino, 1975), while also releasing the Merchant Ivory production *The Europeans* (J. Ivory, 1979), another 'quality' title. This trend, of course, reveals yet again the pitfalls involved in efforts towards defining independent cinema. If it is not considered problematic for those early definitions of contemporary American independent cinema that stand-alone distributors were in the business of distributing exploitation films alongside their 'quality' independent titles, then why should the majors' entry into the independent film market be objected to? After all, it seems that both the studios and the independents were in the business of releasing primarily 'commercial' titles before 'quality films' started showing clear signs of commercial success.

The complications of what constitutes independent filmmaking took a new and decisive turn later in the decade, when both studio divisions and successful stand-alone companies branched out into film production. Such arrangements in the 'quality' independent sector remained rare, especially for the 1980s classics divisions, which participated in the finance of only a handful of productions (such as *Under the Volcano* [J. Huston, 1985; Universal Classics]), and often in partnership with other investors (*End of the Line* [J. Russell, 1987; Orion Classics]);[15] nevertheless, they signalled the beginning of an American independent cinema that was also financed, produced and distributed by companies with corporate ties to the Hollywood majors. And if the affinities with Hollywood of a film by Orion Classics could be questioned, given that that division's parent company was a successful stand-alone producer–distributor itself and not a major studio or a branch of an entertainment conglomerate,[16] *Under the Volcano* stands as an interesting example of why the classics divisions have been treated with suspicion as ambassadors of independent film. As I discuss in Chapter 2, despite being nurtured and overseen by Universal Classics, the film was produced during a change of management regime in the division and was later 'taken over' by big sister Universal, which was responsible for its release.

These complications are even more noticeable in the 1990s and 2000s, when 'quality' independent cinema reached great heights in terms of popularisation and commercial success. As a result, it became progressively more difficult for critics to discern markers of independence, especially within the Hollywood industry. For accounts of American independent cinema of the 1980s, however, these complications were largely ignored by critics and scholars, for a number of reasons. First, the extent to which United Artists Classics and the rest of the 1980s classics divisions traded in US independent film was relatively low and the number of their film releases of such designation was small. Specifically, the five classics divisions that are discussed in the first three chapters of this study distributed approximately twenty US independent features in total in the 1980s, with Orion Classics releasing a few more in the 1990s. In this respect, complications around a definition of the independent label, which had arisen because of the involvement of these divisions in the independent sector, were not deemed noteworthy.

Second, the role of these early divisions in the finance, production and distribution of those twenty or so independent films has not been examined in any detail by studies of the independent cinema of the period (despite critical interest in some of their titles). In fact, with the exception of *Off-Hollywood: The Making and Marketing of Independent Films*,[17] which offers a detailed examination of the role of the classics divisions in three of these US independent film productions, the rest of the studies make only passing reference to these divisions.[18] But even the welcome detail of *Off-Hollywood* raises no questions about those divisions' position in the independent sector or about the nature of their relationship with their respective parent organisation and mainstream cinema. Commissioned by the Sundance Film Institute and the Independent Feature Project, and written by industry executives and consultants, this study focused on the history of a set of films with the intention of acting as an 'educational tool for filmmakers, producers and professionals' and without the kind of critical perspective that characterises more scholarly works.

Third, and as an extension to the above point, critics and scholars have failed to register a more general interest in these studio divisions as an industry phenomenon. Arguably, the main reason behind this lack of interest has to do with the fact that, for the majority of researchers, the main focus of American independent cinema has been what was labelled in retrospect the 'Sundance–Miramax era',[19] a period in the history of contemporary American independent cinema that commenced with the astonishing success of *sex, lies, and videotape* (S. Soderbergh, 1989). Indeed, despite great activity in the independent film sector throughout the 1980s, book-length studies in the field (all of which were published post-1990) tend to concentrate on more recent independent filmmaking. In this respect, the period before that time has often been perceived as a sort of 'prehistory' of independent cinema, before filmmakers like Soderbergh, Tarantino and Linklater, and companies like Miramax, Fox Searchlight and Focus Features wrote (and some are still writing) its 'history'. Finally, with the exception of Orion Classics, all the other 1980s classics divisions were short-lived companies that lasted between three and five years, which contributed further to perceptions that they were 'insignificant' forces in the shaping of contemporary American independent cinema.

The neglect in terms of a critical examination of the first classics divisions has been largely responsible for a common misconception. Specifically, it allowed the cultivation of a widespread belief in critical and academic circles that contemporary American independent cinema in the 1980s, before the *sex, lies, and videotape* 'revolution' and the emergence of the 'Sundance–Miramax era', was easy (or perhaps easier, compared to later periods) to discern and define, at least when it came to questions of industrial location: it was situated outside the Hollywood studios.[20] And yet, the 'complications' I described above, and which I discuss in detail in Section I (Chapters 1 to 3), tell a different story. Additionally, many practices associated with the better-known studio divisions of the 1990s and 2000s and their relationship to independent cinema also had their origins in the 1980s and in the approaches to US independent filmmaking taken by the first wave of classics divisions.

## 'INDEPENDENT', 'INDIE' AND 'INDIEWOOD'

In 1990, stand-alone distributor New Line Cinema, which had found significant commercial success in the 1980s with the *Nightmare on Elm Street* horror franchise and was enjoying its most profitable year following the runaway success of *Teenage Mutant Ninja Turtles* (S. Barron, 1990), established the first new specialty division in seven years, Fine Line Features. Unlike the earlier divisions, Fine Line set out to focus on 'specialised, hard-to-market films', albeit ones with 'more crossover potential than classics-oriented films'.[21] This meant an almost exclusive emphasis on English-language films, with the lion's share coming from the booming US independent film sector. Furthermore, some of these films would have much higher budgets compared to the low-budget pictures of the previous decade. As Ira Deutchman, Fine Line's first senior executive, admitted, his vision for the company was to concentrate on American films that:

> normally would have been the studios' types of films if you went back 10 years, but were not getting those kinds of releases any more. And the people who I had in my mind were directors like Jonathan Demme and people who at that time were working with Orion. Not Orion Classics, but Orion. And Orion was actually on the rocks at that point . . . and I just kept thinking that was the kind of thing that would really interest me, getting to the next level of slightly more commercially oriented movies but films that were not big-audience types of films . . . At that time, nobody was really doing those kind of mid-level films.[22]

Although Fine Line was involved in only a handful of films like the ones Deutchman describes above – most notably *My Own Private Idaho* (G. Van

Sant, 1991), *The Player* (R. Altman, 1992) and *Short Cuts* (R. Altman, 1993) – what becomes evident in this phase of American independent cinema is the emergence of a particular type of film that often has only a few points of contact with the 'quality' independent films of the 1980s. Indeed, while Miramax, Fine Line and a number of other distributors (and producer–distributors) continued, in the first half of the 1990s, to release low-budget US films that often had difficult subject matter or utilised unusual formal codes, they also ensured that many of these titles were also characterised by a number of commercial elements that could be exploited by these companies' marketing departments. These elements included but were not limited to:

- the presence of recognisable stars, even if stardom was meaningful only within a narrow demographic (the rebranded Matt Dillon in *Drugstore Cowboy* [G. Van Sant, 1989]; James Spader in *sex, lies, and videotape*)
- the use of much stronger generic frameworks than the films of 1980s, which would allow the distributor to sell the movie as a genre picture (the use of obvious con artist and film noir frameworks in *The Grifters* [S. Frears, 1990]; the heist movie in *Reservoir Dogs* [Q. Tarantino, 1992])
- an emphasis on well-defined niche audiences, such as African Americans (*A Rage in Harlem* [B. Duke, 1991])
- the deployment of authorship, once several filmmakers started gaining critical and audience recognition (Hal Hartley, Quentin Tarantino and so on).

More controversially, arguably, the main point of departure for the post-1989 independent film was the inclusion of the themes of sex and / or violence, suspenseful plots and all sorts of other commercial 'content' elements that were treated as anathema in the quality independent films of the previous era. However, in including these elements, the independents of the 1990s did not try to replicate the aesthetics of Romero, Carpenter or Cronenberg. Instead, the elements were reconfigured within a package of hip, filmmaker-driven, quality cinema upon which the industry, the press and the film-going public almost immediately agreed to impress the label 'indie', the 'hip offspring' of independence, as Alisa Perren put it.[23]

Despite this dramatic transformation of independent films on a textual level, the key players in the early years of the 1990s were Miramax and Fine Line, both companies without corporate ties to a Hollywood major. These were followed by smaller independent outfits, such as the Samuel Goldwyn Company and October Films, and Orion Classics, the only 1980s classics arm to have survived to the 'indie era', which was also a division of a company with no corporate links to a major studio. In this respect, questions of industrial location seemed still to provide relatively clear answers about who practised independent filmmaking, despite the fact that the actual independent product had started reaching out towards Hollywood in other obvious (that is, commercial) ways. Furthermore, both Fine Line and the independent companies it competed against did not hesitate to invest in finance and production, especially as this practice would allow them to control the commercial elements of their films more fully and right from the beginning.

In this climate, the Hollywood majors started once again to warm to the idea of establishing specialty film divisions. Within a two-year period, Sony (which had taken over Columbia in 1989) started Sony Pictures Classics in 1992; Turner Broadcasting System (TBS), a cable broadcaster, took over New Line Cinema (and Fine Line) in 1994; and perhaps more importantly, Disney took over market leader Miramax in 1993. Besides complicating anew questions of how to define the 'independent filmmaking' label, these corporate moves highlighted a number of differences in the ways in which this second wave of classics divisions were conceived of by their parent companies, which reflect the polyphonic character of US indie cinema at the time. For instance, unlike Fine Line Features, Sony Pictures Classics retained substantial points of contact with the classics arms of the 1980s, including a focus on world arthouse cinema; a slow and cautious system of platform release that was supported by frugal spending in terms of marketing; and a much larger number of releases (compared to the earlier classics divisions and Fine Line) that emphasised profits from distribution volume rather than from one big hit that could offset losses from the rest of the releases. Furthermore, Sony's division was managed by the trio of executives that had previously been running Orion Classics, which suggests very clear continuity with that particular company. And yet, despite all these points of contact, Sony Pictures Classics released a much higher number of US independent films than Orion Classics, becoming one of the most important suppliers of films of that designation; twenty-five such releases appeared in the first seven years of operations, including such canonical titles as *Safe* (T. Haynes, 1995), *Living in Oblivion* (T. DiCillo, 1995) and *Welcome to the Dollhouse* (T. Solondz, 1996).

While Fine Line's 'relocation' in TBS did not affect its status or philosophy in any substantial way, Miramax's takeover by Disney had far-reaching repercussions. Specifically, the Hollywood major provided its new subsidiary with serious funding and resources, which helped it accelerate an aggressive growth plan that had already been in place before the takeover,[24] and which had helped the company distinguish itself in both the American indie cinema and the world arthouse film markets. This plan included a large annual release schedule, which by 1992 had reached over twenty titles (the highest number of titles of all other divisions and independents in the market); an increasing emphasis on finance and production; a well-executed plan for film acquisitions from the world's most important festivals; two specialty labels within the company – one for genre pictures (Dimension Films) and one for higher quality productions, in the 1980s mould (Prestige); and extremely aggressive marketing practices that always ensured maximum visibility for Miramax titles. With Disney's financial backing, Miramax's domination of these markets reached such an extent that, by the mid-1990s and only a couple of years after the takeover, it had become incredibly difficult to justify the 'specialty division' label that all other studio divisions were carrying. This was also because Miramax had adopted practices that created yet another expression of independent filmmaking, which has been labelled 'indiewood'. This mode of filmmaking had very few similarities with the quality independent cinema of the 1980s, and in many ways enhanced several of the characteristics associated with indie cinema while also depending on increasingly large budgets.

The progenitor of this move to indiewood was *Pulp Fiction* (Q. Tarantino, 1994), a film that, according to Jim Hillier, 'repositioned the goalposts of American cinema blurring the boundary between mainstream Hollywood product and the independent fringe'.[25] Indeed, with the exception of addressing primarily a niche audience, *Pulp Fiction* played up all the other characteristics of 'indie' cinema: stars (much more 'household names' than the norm at the time); genre (very clearly stated in its title and the suggestive pose of Uma Thurman in the poster for the film); authorship (at the time, Tarantino was emerging as one of the most celebrated young filmmakers, firmly associated with independent cinema and Miramax); and, of course, the inclusion of sex and often extreme violence in the several interconnected storylines that comprise the film. Equally importantly, *Pulp Fiction* was distributed using mass release methods, strongly associated with the practices of the Hollywood majors, as the independent distributors (and the rest of the studio labels at that time) could not afford to spend on a nationwide marketing campaign.

This enhanced 'convergence' with Hollywood – complete with box-office grosses on a level also associated with studio films – signalled a further wave of classics divisions that took place progressively during the decade between 1995 and 2005. Twentieth Century Fox, Paramount, Universal and Warner Bros. took their places next to Disney and Columbia through the establishment of Fox Searchlight, Paramount Classics (later Paramount Vantage), Universal Classics (later Focus Features), Warner Independent and Picturehouse (a second Warner label that was instigated by Warner's major divisions HBO and New Line Cinema, and which replaced Fine Line in 2005), respectively. By that time, of course, the label 'classics', which carried connotations of films targeting narrow markets and niche audiences, had become dated. With the exception of Paramount Classics, which a few years later was also rebranded as a non-classics division, all the new studio arms opted for names that did not utilise the classics label. Additionally, with the exception of Warner Independent, none of these new companies' names specified a marketing identity clearly associated with independent filmmaking. Finally, these divisions were accompanied by several new stand-alone companies and subsidiaries of other entertainment corporations that bore little resemblance to older independent distributors such as October Films and the Samuel Goldwyn Company. Backed by investors and hedge funds from around the world, producer–distributors such as Lions Gate (later Lionsgate), USA Films, Artisan, Newmarket Films and a few others were well-capitalised companies in a position to compete for the most commercial properties in the acquisitions market, while also producing their own commercially strong titles.

This particular environment, which started taking shape in the late 1990s, seemingly had very few points of contact with the independent film sector of the previous decade. On the level of industrial location, all major studios had now established subsidiaries to acquire, produce and distribute films for this expanding and reconfigured 'independent' sector. Furthermore, and more controversially, some of the major studios themselves 'experimented' with the finance, production and distribution of a small number of films that seemed to share a large number of characteristics with the key titles handled by their divisions. According to Geoff King, a number of films that were released in 1999, including *Three Kings* (D. O. Russell; Warner Bros.), *Election* (A. Payne; Paramount) and *Fight Club* (D. Fincher; Twentieth Century Fox), were prime examples of 'indiewood' as practised by the Hollywood majors.[26] And while low-budget quality and less obviously commercial 'indie' films continued to be acquired, produced and distributed both by stand-alone distributors and by the studio divisions, these titles found it increasingly difficult to compete against the more clearly indiewood titles for playdates, marketing support, critical notice and, more importantly, audience attention. This was especially the case as the existence of so many new distributors had started clogging the available release dates to the extent that numerous films from the independent sector were often put out on the same date.

On the level of aesthetics, the dominant indiewood mode of filmmaking bridged conventions associated with Hollywood films with an extensive array of stylistic, narrative and thematic approaches that were originally developed in different cinematic traditions (exploitation, art cinema, earlier expressions of independent cinema and so on) and which, according to King, functioned as 'markers of "distinction" designed to appeal to more particular, niche audience constituencies'.[27] This allowed for the production of a number of films that could cross over more easily to the mainstream, compared to other categories of independent filmmaking, as they would normally be more accessible in terms of narrative construction, visual style and / or thematic preoccupation. As a result, and a few years after the *Pulp Fiction* phenomenon, the sector saw an increasing number of $100 million hit films, including *Good Will Hunting* (G. Van Sant, 1997; Miramax), *Shakespeare in Love* (J. Madden, 1998; Miramax), *Traffic* (S. Soderbergh, 2000; USA Films) and, more recently,

*Inglourious Basterds* (Q. Tarantino, 2008; the Weinstein Company) and *Juno* (J. Reitman, 2007; Fox Searchlight). Equally, on an ideological level, indiewood films often engaged with alternative political ideas (anti-corporate capitalism in *Fight Club*) or conveyed clearly pessimistic messages (the futility of action in the war against drugs in *Traffic*); however, these alternative views were often buried under the films' slick production values, star cast, genre expectations and high-quality entertainment.

## FROM INDEPENDENT TO SPECIALTY FILM

At some point in the long voyage from the 'European-style' independent films of the 1980s to the indiewood blockbusters of the late 1990s and 2000s, from the quality films of the pre-Sundance–Miramax era to the infinitely more commercial films of the third wave of the studios' specialty divisions, the notion of 'independence' as a real alternative to Hollywood cinema lost both its appeal and its exegetic power. Although politically and aesthetically daring independent films continued to be made and released outside and within the industry, filmmakers, critics and audiences simply stopped being interested in their status as independent films. In recent research on the ways Internet Movie Database users discuss the films in the IMDb Top 50 independent film chart, which consists of the fifty highest-rated films 'not produced by a major studio' (the Big Six and MGM / UA in this case), Hayley Trowbridge notes that, in 350 reviews of these films by the users of the database, only 1.4 per cent mention the word 'independent' as a useful way to discuss the films in question. Instead, labels such as 'original' (10.3 per cent), 'complex' (7.1 per cent), 'beautiful' (6.8 per cent), 'intelligent' (6 per cent) and a few others take precedence, suggesting that the 'independent' label is of very little significance to the specific online film-fan community that uses this high-web-presence film database.[28]

The reasons for this decline in interest in the concept of 'independence' are varied. First, despite a long history of independent filmmaking in the US, film critics and scholars turned their attention to the subject only from the 1980s onwards, when the body of work that became known as 'contemporary American independent cinema' emerged.[29] This, of course, meant that the definitions that were provided and the agenda that was set were very much determined by the cultural and political landscape of the time. With the New Right having become a major force in American culture and politics by 1978 and with a 'new conservative spirit' permeating many aspects of American popular culture in the late 1970s and early 1980s, including Hollywood cinema,[30] it was clear that independent film was perceived as a vehicle for the articulation of progressive and even radical ideas. It was expected that it would be 'anything

INTRODUCTION 13

Hollywood was not' and engage with issues and concerns that Hollywood films would eschew.³¹ However, when this conservative cycle reached its end in the early 1990s with the election of a Democrat president (Bill Clinton) and with the major studios already releasing aesthetically and thematically daring films that were also questioning the status quo (for instance, the deconstruction of potent American myths in *Unforgiven* [C. Eastwood, 1991] and the exposition of official history as corrupt in *JFK* [O. Stone, 1991]), the type of independent cinema that defined the 1980s inevitably started to lose its rationale. In this sense, irrespective of questions of industrial location and aesthetics, the ideological basis of independence was not fixed but very much time-specific.

Second, in the late 1980s and early 1990s, Hollywood cinema underwent significant changes that would also affect independent film. Although, by the 1980s, all Hollywood studios had become divisions of diversified entertainment conglomerates or had diversified themselves by branching out into other media industries, the seven years between 1989 and 1996 saw a new wave of corporate mergers and takeovers that involved five of the big Hollywood powers: Warner, Columbia, Universal, Paramount and Disney. When the dust settled, all the studios found themselves part of even larger global entertainment corporations with a mandate to develop franchises that could bring profits from multiple sources. The studios' increased emphasis on ultra-expensive event films created a space for smaller pictures, as the excessive production and marketing costs of the studio blockbusters meant that only a few of them could be made every year. With the studios' global distribution pipelines in need of a constant flow of product and with the studios supplying only a fraction of it, smaller films became essential for the healthy operation of the industry. This realisation came at a time when American independent cinema was increasing in popularity following the strong commercial performance of *sex, lies, and videotape* and also of *Wild at Heart* (D. Lynch, 1990), *The Player* and, of course, *Pulp Fiction*. In this respect, what seemed to be important was not so much an opposition between (mainstream) Hollywood and independent cinema but a distinction between expensive franchise and smaller specialised films, irrespective of whether the latter were coming from studios and their subsidiaries or from companies without corporate ties to them.

Finally, public and critical interest in questions of independence declined once the label itself started being utilised for marketing purposes. Indeed, following the popularisation of independent cinema in the early 1990s, studio divisions and stand-alone distributors alike started using the concept of independence (and the hipper 'indie' label) as a marketing hook in an effort to position specific films in the marketplace. For instance, Sony Pictures Classics utilised the participation of *The Spanish Prisoner* (D. Mamet, 1998) in the Sundance Film Festival as a key marketing strategy in both the trailer and the poster for the film in order to position it as an indie title.³² *The Spanish*

*Prisoner* became the most commercially successful film that Mamet had yet released and still ranks at the time of writing as one of Sony Pictures Classics' most successful titles. However, by the late 1990s and early 2000s, this form of marketing and advertising had lost its cachet. After so much appropriation, overuse and abuse, the label was inevitably rendered meaningless for critics and the cinema-going public alike.

Given the problems that surround the use of term 'independent' and its later derivatives, some film industry scholars have often opted for the less controversial 'specialty' or 'specialised' film label. In his classic study *The Hollywood Studio System* (1986), Douglas Gomery distinguishes between the major studios and the specialised companies. The former involved large producing–distributing and producing–distributing–exhibiting organisations that consistently controlled the film industry from the 1920s till the 1950s. Specialised companies, on the other hand, included United Artists, a distributing organisation servicing independent producers; its programme of releases therefore did not resemble the programmes of the studios. The label also included the Poverty Row companies Monogram and Republic, much smaller than the studios, which, despite also being organised as producers–distributors, were not able to compete with the industry leaders. For that reason, they had to concentrate their business on the 'specialised markets', areas in which the studios had little or no interest as they were not deemed particularly profitable. In the 1930s, these 'specialised markets' for the Poverty Row companies included primarily the markets for western films and for serials.[33]

Besides providing a neat distinction, Gomery's approach allows for the great flexibility that is essential for understanding the often-murky terrain of the US film industry. First, the categorisation of United Artists as a specialised company does not negate its status as one of the eight corporations that exerted an oligopolistic control over the American film industry in the studio era. It is both a member of the Little Three (alongside Columbia and Universal) and therefore operates within the industry, and a specialised entity that released a particular type of product. On the other hand, Monogram and Republic share a number of organisational and structural similarities with the major studios (especially being producer–distributors) but that does not mean that they are in the same league as them because the films they produced and distributed were decisively different from studio films. In other words, Monogram and Republic not only operate outside the majors but also are specialised outfits. The one common element linking these specialised companies is that they command modest profits, which puts them in a separate category from the major players.

The application of the concept of specialised (or specialty) companies and films to the field of contemporary American independent cinema removes the ideological and political implications and meanings that have been attached by various institutions to the label 'independent' and its derivatives over the years. More importantly, it enables the examination of a small number of companies that have had a corporate relationship with the major Hollywood studios but which became key participants in a relatively distinct body of work in post-1980 American cinema; this body of work commenced outside the studios' orbit but almost immediately found its way into it, and has consistently been discussed as 'independent'.

In becoming yet another book dedicated to the study of American independent cinema, then, *Hollywood's Indies* tells the story of 'US specialised film' as this was shaped by a particular group of studio 'specialty' film divisions from the early 1980s to date. Divided into three sections, the book proposes that there were three distinct waves, which broadly coincide with the emergence of each of the three dominant expressions of specialty filmmaking in the US: the independent, the indie and indiewood. More specifically, Section I (Chapters 1 to 3) looks at the five classics divisions of the 1980s (United Artists Classics, Triumph Films, Twentieth Century Fox International Classics, Universal Classics and Orion Classics), all of which were formed within a period of three years and played a relatively small, but still significant, role in supporting independent cinema. Section II (Chapters 4 to 5) looks at the two divisions that were formed in the early 1990s (Fine Line Features and Sony Pictures Classics) and the way they participated in and helped shape the vastly modified terrain of American 'indie' cinema during the boom years of the 1990s; it also explores how they evolved in later years when specialty filmmaking started converging with the mainstream in more obvious ways. Finally, Section III (Chapters 6 to 9) examines the specialty labels in the age of indiewod (Fox Searchlight, Paramount Classics [Vantage], Focus Features, Warner Independent Pictures and Picturehouse), a time when 'independence' had become almost impossible to defend – partly because of practices adopted by these divisions – and labels such as 'specialty' and 'niche' were increasingly becoming fashionable. Of course, the above periodisation is far from absolute, as divisions from different waves demonstrated a number of similarities with each other (Sony Picture Classics with Orion Classics; Paramount Classics with Sony Picture Classics and so on); independent, indie and indiewood titles have co-existed; and low-budget independent films made completely outside the Hollywood industry continued to be made throughout the period from the 1980s to date. However, each of these three expressions of filmmaking did become dominant (or at least more visible than the other two) at particular times, and the book proposes that it was during those times that each of the studio division waves started to take shape.

In examining all these divisions, the book is interested in understanding the conditions and rationale behind the establishment of such companies by the majors; their business practices and the ways in which these differed from the practices of the stand-alone 'independent' companies against which they competed; the often-shifting relationship between parent and subsidiary company, especially during the course of management changes in both outfits; the specialty labels' position within the often-labyrinthine structure of their conglomerate parents and the extent to which they adopted practices associated with the studios themselves; and the reasons behind their growth or stagnation and the factors that contributed both to the solidification of some of these divisions' position in the specialty film marketplace and to the closure of others. Discussion of all of these issues will allow for a better understanding of the films they acquired, produced and distributed, a large number of which found their way into the canon of contemporary American independent cinema. To that end, each chapter carries a brief case study that offers a discussion of a representative US film for each of these divisions, with the exception of the chapter on Sony Pictures Classics, in which I decided, for two reasons, to use a non-US film, *Nueve Reinas* ([*Nine Queens*] F. Bielinsky, 2002) as a case study. First, it is a non-US film that none the less mobilises a number of characteristics that are close to the US indiewood films of the time. Second, it was remade by Warner Independent as *Criminal* (G. Jacobs, 2004), only two years after the original film's US release; this film is also examined as a case study in this book.

As is clear from this brief introduction of the book's content, Miramax Films does not form part of this study, and this is for a number of reasons. First, Miramax is the only specialised studio division that had a long history (fifteen years) as a stand-alone company before becoming Disney's studio division in 1993. As a result, almost half of its history lies beyond the scope of this study. Furthermore, in the second part of its history, and despite often being at the epicentre of developments in indie and indiewood filmmaking, Miramax quickly moved to studio turf when it co-financed, produced and distributed $100 million films such as *Gangs of New York* (M. Scorsese, 2003) and *Cold Mountain* (A. Minghella, 2003), prompting the head of Focus Features to declare that the company was involved in a different market from the other specialty labels.[34] Indeed, even the trade press refused to discuss the division as a specialty producer–distributor, opting instead for labels such as a 'mini major'[35] or 'a production driven quasi studio'.[36] Second, partly because of their ability to transcend the specialty market, Miramax and New Line Cinema have been christened 'major independents' rather than specialty divisions. According to Justin Wyatt, who introduced this label, the takeovers of the two formerly independent companies created 'a curious hybrid' that was far removed from both the classics divisions of the 1980s and the new studio labels of the early 1990s.[37] In this respect, despite the fact that most of the second and third wave of specialty labels tried to compete with Miramax, to all intents and purposes Disney's division was a very important participant in US specialised film but from a markedly different industrial and institutional place. Finally, because of its importance in independent film, Miramax has been the only company to have been examined in great detail in scholarly accounts, including in a book-length study aptly entitled *Indie, Inc*.[38] Given all this work and the extremely large output of the company (over 400 releases in its post-takeover history), I opted not to make it a chapter of the specialty divisions' story, even though I make numerous references to it throughout the book.

## A WORD ON METHOD

In her 2004 essay on the ways in which the popular press constructed *My Big Fat Greek Wedding* (J. Zwick, 2002) as an independent film, Alisa Perren fleshed out the key details of an emerging methodological approach in the study of contemporary media industries. Given that, in the vast majority of cases, the researcher has little or no access to contemporary corporate records, he or she must necessarily depend on a range of secondary sources for the collection of data. In the case of the film industry, the sources include the trade and popular press, specialised periodicals and magazines, more general economics publications, and interviews with industry personnel, which could both verify the validity of the data and reveal details or issues that might have been missed or have not been covered by the written sources. These data, then, can be placed within the long-established body of work on 'the structure, conduct and performance of the entertainment industries', which derives from scholarly accounts of media industries' economics, as well as from trade books and manuals that illuminate dominant industry methods and practices.[39]

Perren's work is situated within in a recent body of methodological, historical and theoretical work that has been labelled 'media industry studies' and which aims to bring together previously disparate (and, arguably, artificially created) theoretical and methodological approaches to the study of media, such as political economy and cultural studies,[40] and even broader disciplines such as humanities and social sciences.[41] Such a convergence of previously distinct subject areas and disciplinary approaches, the argument goes, would dovetail with the well-documented media convergence that has become the dominant characteristic of the contemporary media environment and which is very much driven by the global media conglomerates that control entertainment and the technology via which it is delivered to audiences.

Although the jury is still out on the reception of media industry studies by the broader scholarly community, as the approach is still being shaped and the book-length studies that have adopted it are still few, it nevertheless opens the way to carrying out research on particular media organisations and subjects that, until recently, could have been methodologically questionable. A case in point is the subject of this book, the specialty divisions of the major studios. With corporate records not open to the researcher and with other archival material extremely limited, the options available are, first, not to undertake a study of the subject, in which case one of the most visible and important aspects of contemporary US cinema would remain virtually unexamined; or, second, to undertake research following the kind of process that Perren outlined in her essay on *My Big Fat Greek Wedding* and which she further elaborated in her study of Miramax.[42]

In this respect, *Hollywood's Indies* adopts such an approach to the study of US specialised film by the studio divisions. Specifically, I draw on a large number of articles from trade publications such as *Variety*, *Hollywood Reporter* and *Screen International*; specialty industry publications such as *Indiewire* and *Filmmaker Magazine*; the mainstream press; key economics magazines such as the *Los Angeles Business Journal* and *The Wall Street Journal*; publicity material produced by the companies, such as press releases; and a number of interviews I conducted over a period of time with industry personnel involved with these companies in a variety of capacities, such as Ira Deutchman, former executive at United Artists Classics and former President of Fine Line Features. These data have been situated within a considerable body of scholarly work on American independent cinema, which has been a 'hot' topic in film studies since the 1990s and especially in the 2000s, as well as within a framework of studies on media economics which allows me to carry out what Thomas Schatz calls analysis on a 'micro-industrial level'. Unlike work on the macro-industrial level which examines (in this case) 'the film industry at large', analysis on a micro-industrial level shifts the focus to individual production companies and to distinct market sectors and 'classes' of producers – in this case, the studio divisions and the US specialised film market – and concerns primarily 'the *authority* over production rather than the filmmaking process per se'.[43] My discussion examines in detail the ways in which specialised film evolved as a result of these companies' practices, with their entry into production marking a major turning point in their history (and a major theme in my examination of the sector). Finally, given that the object of study operates within larger organisations and structures and is influenced by certain 'macro-industrial dimensions', such as the role of adjacent industries and new technologies, I often bring these into my examination of these companies.

## NOTES

1. Tzioumakis, Yannis, *American Independent Cinema: An Introduction* (Edinburgh: Edinburgh University Press, 2006), 10–11.
2. For instance, for 'independence within the industry' see David E. James, *Allegories of*

*Cinema: American Film in the Sixties* (Princeton: Princeton University Press, 1989), 281; for 'true independence' see Greg Merritt, *Celluloid Mavericks: A History of American Independent Film* (New York: Thunder's Mouth, 2000), 51; and for 'semi-independence' see Matthew Bernstein, 'Hollywood's Semi-Independent Production', *Cinema Journal* 32.3 (Spring 1993), 41–54.
3. King, Geoff, *American Independent Cinema* (London: I. B. Tauris, 2005), 2.
4. Ryan, Michael and Douglas Kellner, *Camera Politica: The Politics and Ideology of Contemporary Hollywood Film* (Bloomington: Indiana University Press, 1990), 1.
5. See, for instance, the Christian apocalyptic film *The Omega Code* (R. Marcarelli, 1999). There was also a number of filmmakers who turned to low budget independent production not because they were motivated by political or aesthetic concerns but simply because they were not successful in convincing any of the majors to finance the films they were interested in making or because they wanted to retain control of their films and of the potential profits. I would like to thank Ira Deutchman for pointing out this aspect of independent filmmaking.
6. See, in particular, Ted Kulczycky, 'By Any Meanings Necessary: Conflict and Resolution in *Do the Right Thing*', *Cineaction!* 40 (1996), 48–56.
7. Collective Editorial, 'The Independent Feature Movement: Changing the Rules of the Game', *American Film* 6.10 (September 1981), 57.
8. Lamont, Austin, 'Independents' Day', *Film Comment* (November / December 1981), 76.
9. Insdorf, Annette, 'Ordinary People, European Style: How to Spot an Independent Feature', *American Film* 6.10 (September 1981), 57–60.
10. Insdorf, 'Ordinary People', 58.
11. Goldman, Debra, 'Business for Art's Sake', *American Film* 12.3 (April 1987), 44.
12. Biskind, Peter, *Down and Dirty Pictures: Miramax, Sundance and the Rise of Independent Film* (London: Simon & Schuster, 2005), 16.
13. 'UA Classics' Coup: Truffaut, "Marleen", Celentano for U.S.', *Weekly Variety* (27 May 1981), n/a.
14. Deutchman, Ira (former executive at United Artists Classics and former President of Fine Line Features), phone interview with the author, 2 June 2011, 1 hour and 15 minutes.
15. Studio divisions were much more active in the financing of non-US films in exchange for North American theatrical distribution rights (see Chapter 3, in particular).
16. For more on Orion Pictures see Yannis Tzioumakis, 'Major Status – Independent Spirit: The History of Orion Pictures (1978–1992)', *New Review of Film and Television Studies* 2.1 (2004), 87–135.
17. Rosen, David with Peter Hamilton, *Off-Hollywood: The Making and Marketing of Independent Films* (New York: Grove-Weidenfeld, 1990 [1987]).
18. For instance, King dedicates only one paragraph to these divisions in the 'Industry' chapter of his book, *American Independent Cinema* (King, *American Independent Cinema*, 21).
19. See, for instance, Michael Z. Newman, *Indie: An American Film Culture* (New York: Columbia University Press, 2011), 3.
20. See, for instance, Jim Hillier, 'Introduction', in *American Independent Cinema: A Sight and Sound Reader*, ed. Jim Hillier (London: BFI, 2001), xvi.
21. Ira Deutchman, President of Fine Line Features, 1990–4, was quoted in Justin Wyatt, 'The Formation of the "Major Independent": Miramax, New Line and the New Hollywood', in *Contemporary Hollywood Cinema*, ed. Steve Neale and Murray Smith (London: Routledge, 1998), 78.

22. Deutchman, interview, 2 June 2011.
23. Perren, Alisa, 'Sex, Lies and Marketing: Miramax and the Development of the Quality Indie Blockbuster', *Film Quarterly* 55.2 (Winter 2002), 37.
24. Perren, Alisa, *Indie, Inc.: Miramax and the Transformation of Hollywood in the 1990s* (Austin: University of Texas Press, 2012), 101.
25. Hillier, Jim, 'American Independent Cinema since the 1980s', in *Contemporary American Cinema*, ed. Linda Ruth Williams and Michael Hammond (Maidenhead: McGraw-Hill, 2006), 255.
26. King, Geoff, *Indiewood USA . . . Where Hollywood Meets Independent Cinema* (London: I. B. Tauris, 2009), 191-234.
27. King, *Indiewood USA*, 2.
28. Trowbridge, Hayley, 'Talking about Independence: IMDb.com and the Discourse of American Independent Cinema', Paper presented at the annual Postgraduate Research Student conference, Department of Communication and Media, University of Liverpool, Liverpool, UK, 20 May 2011.
29. For a detailed history of scholarly work on American independent cinema see Yannis Tzioumakis, 'Academic Discourses and American Independent Cinema: In Search of a Field of Studies. Part 1: From the Beginnings to the 1980s', *New Review of Film and Television Studies* 9.2 (June 2011), 105–31; and Yannis Tzioumakis, 'Academic Discourses and American Independent Cinema: In Search of a Field of Studies. Part 2: From the 1990s to Date', *New Review of Film and Television Studies* 9.3 (September 2011), 311–40.
30. Ryan and Kellner, *Camera Politica*, 12-13.
31. Biskind, *Down and Dirty Pictures*, 19.
32. Tzioumakis, Yannis, *The Spanish Prisoner* (Edinburgh: Edinburgh University Press, 2009), 59.
33. See, in particular, Gomery's distinction between the studios and the specialised studios in Douglas Gomery, *The Hollywood Studio System* (New York: St Martin's, 1986), 173–88.
34. James Schamus, President of Focus Features, was quoted in Tom Roston, 'Life After Miramax', *Premiere* (March 2005), 51.
35. Oppelaar, Justin, 'Pangs of New York: Harvey Beefs Up, Slims Down', *Weekly Variety* (11 November 2002), 62.
36. Rooney, David, 'The Brothers Grim: Weinsteins Bridle at Disney Dictates', *Weekly Variety* (14 June 2004), 57.
37. Wyatt, 'The Formation of the "Major Independent"', 86, 84.
38. Perren, *Indie, Inc.*
39. Perren, Alisa, 'A Big Fat Indie Success Story? Press Discourses Surrounding the Making and Marketing of a "Hollywood" Movie', *Journal of Film and Video* 54.2 (Summer 2004), 19.
40. Kellner, Douglas, 'Media Industries, Political Economy and Media / Cultural Studies: An Articulation', in *Media Industries: History, Theory, and Method*, ed. Jennifer Holt and Alisa Perren (Chichester: Wiley-Blackwell, 2009), 102.
41. Holt, Jennifer and Alisa Perren, 'Introduction: Does the World Really Need One More Field of Study?', in *Media Industries: History, Theory, and Method*, ed. Jennifer Holt and Alisa Perren (Chichester: Wiley-Blackwell, 2009), 11.
42. Perren, *Indie, Inc.*
43. Schatz, Thomas, 'Film Industry Studies and Hollywood History', in *Media Industries: History, Theory, and Method*, ed. Jennifer Holt and Alisa Perren (Chichester: Wiley-Blackwell, 2009), 48 (original italics).

SECTION I

# Independent

CHAPTER 1

# United Artists Classics (1980 to 1986)

## NICHE DISTRIBUTION

In the summer of 1975, United Artists, in collaboration with Metro Goldwyn Mayer, organised the first MGM Festival in a well-known Upper West Side Manhattan theatre. At that point, the former company was one of the most successful major distributors in American cinema, having benefited from a remarkably stable management team since 1951; from the development and cultivation of successful franchises such as the James Bond and the Pink Panther series; and, since 1968, from the additional security that its conglomerate parent, Transamerica, provided. MGM, on the other hand, had fared much worse after becoming a victim of corporate manœuvring on the part of its latest owner, the Las Vegas-based financier and hotelier Kirk Kerkorian. Following his purchase of MGM in 1969, Kerkorian proceeded with a series of moves that turned the most successful studio of the 1930s and 1940s into a small-scale producer, the films of which United Artists agreed to release in the US for a ten-year period (1973 to 1983).[1]

Given these developments, it is not surprising that the festival was not a showcase for new films that were sponsored or produced by the former major, as is normally the case with such events. Instead, it was a vehicle for a limited rerelease of a number of well-known films from MGM's rich archives, including the Vincente Minnelli double-bill *An American in Paris* (1951) and *Father of the Bride* (1950), and a number of other 'classic' titles such as *National Velvet* (C. Brown, 1944) and *Julius Caesar* (J. Mankiewicz, 1953).[2] This move towards reissuing the company's old titles took place as MGM and United Artists rushed to capitalise on the recent success of MGM's *That's Entertainment!* (J. Haley Jr, 1974), a film compiled from clips of old MGM films introduced by a host of stars who had worked for the studio in its halcyon days, including Gene Kelly, James Stewart and Elizabeth Taylor. With virtually no production costs and amidst the sharp decline of the studio's fortunes, the film brought in rentals of over $12 million, becoming one of the surprise hits of 1974.[3]

This unexpected success was noted by a generic division of United Artists that had existed since the early 1970s and which specialised in non-theatrical releases, especially for film societies in college towns.[4] As United Artists had just acquired access to MGM's large library of titles, it made perfect sense for the division to exploit the climate of nostalgia into which *That's Entertainment!* had suddenly tapped. It was at this point that the division was renamed United Artists Classics and devised the MGM Festival as a concrete plan for capitalising on the recent demand for 'classic' Hollywood fare. Furthermore, United Artists was already in possession of a vast library of old Hollywood titles, including ones the company had distributed itself, as well as the pre-1948 Warner Bros. films and all those distributed by RKO, defunct since 1957;[5] United Artists Classics was thus perfectly positioned to become the dominant force, in the likely case that this trend would continue.

The MGM Festival lived up to the financial expectations of the division's executives, with reports of full houses for a number of double-bills that changed twice weekly and with box-office grosses averaging over $10,000 per week,[6] a massive figure for a sole engagement in the mid-1970s. Not surprisingly, then, the festival became a recurrent fixture in the following years and was supplemented by other similar events organised by the division, such as the Warner Bros. Festival. According to reports in the *Village Voice*, the success of these events solidified the division's position within United Artists, as Classics was responsible for revenue of over $3.5 million in 1977, compared to just $0.6 million in 1972.[7]

However, despite mirroring United Artists' overall achievement when the company broke the all-time record in 1977 with global rentals totalling $318 million,[8] this success was cut short. In an unprecedented move, the five senior executives at United Artists, two of whom had been involved with running the company since 1951, resigned *en masse* in January 1978 after a number of clashes with the executives of the company's conglomerate parent. Following their departure from UA, this executive team quickly established Orion Pictures as their new film venture and signed a distribution contract with Warner. Although the exact reasons for resigning from the company are still subject to debate,[9] sources tend to agree that they revolved mainly around Transamerica's effort to impose on its subsidiary business models and practices that were incompatible with the nature of the film business and which stifled the creativity of the longest-standing and most successful management team in Hollywood's history, especially during a period when the company was experiencing unprecedented commercial success. With United Artists in transition and amidst the turmoil of a radical restructuring, it is not surprising that any plans associated with the further expansion of UA Classics had to be put on hold. This was also because two executives from the division also left the company around the same time, with one of them, Don Krim, purchasing Kino International, a recently established distributor of acclaimed world cinema films for the US market in 1978.[10]

Krim's move to foreign film theatrical distribution signalled another trend that had shown signs of growth in the late 1970s after a sustained period of inertia in the early and mid-1970s. Non-US 'arthouse' film theatrical distribution had been a staple of the film business in the North American market since the late 1950s; *Variety* had proclaimed the 'arrival' of foreign films in the early months of 1957,[11] and the Independent Film Importers and Distributors of America was established around the same time to represent a number of New York-based companies that traded in this increasingly vibrant market. In the 1960s, a number of such films, including *Never on Sunday* (J. Dassin, 1960) and *La Dolce Vita* (F. Fellini, 1962), recorded grosses of over $3 million at the US box office, a figure comparable with the box-office takings of successful US productions. However, the majority of these imported films grossed below the $1 million mark, despite ample publicity and accolades such as Academy Awards for Best Foreign Picture and distinctions at major European film festivals.[12]

By the late 1960s, however, the trend started showing signs of decline. According to Wilinsky, foreign films faced increased competition from US films, which, after the abandonment of the Production Code in 1968, started including 'adult themes and sexual elements of art films', blurring the 'demarcation between Hollywood film and art film' that had been quite clear up until then.[13] With the arrival of the 1970s and in a climate of economic downturn that lasted until the end of 1971, the arthouse film market was in sharp decline, with the number of non-US film releases in first-run New York City theatres dropping to 18 in 1973 from close to 40 in 1960.[14] Even United Artists, which had been a significant player through one of its subsidiaries, Lopert Pictures, had to withdraw from this market after more than a decade of critical and sometimes commercial successes with films such as *La Notte* (M. Antonioni, 1962), *Persona* (I. Bergman, 1967) and the afore-mentioned *Never on Sunday*.

With many smaller foreign film distributors not affiliated with the majors having already vacated the market in the late 1960s, the vastly scaled-down distribution of arthouse films in the 1970s took off in a number of directions, blurring the line between art and mainstream cinema still further. First, the major studios themselves distributed – often in dubbed versions – films from celebrated world auteurs like Bergman and Bertolucci; second, smaller and newly established 'boutique' distributors such as Cinema 5 Distributing emerged in the early 1970s in the hope of securing part of the business left behind; finally, and rather surprisingly, some of the key arthouse films of the 1970s by filmmakers like Kurosawa, Fellini and Bergman were distributed by

Roger Corman's exploitation outfit, New World Pictures. In an effort to rid himself of the 'king of schlock' label as his company was making headway into the mainstream, Corman decided to branch out into arthouse film distribution by investing only in well-known filmmakers whose films were bound to find an audience and might even push for a small profit.[15]

In the late 1970s, however, the business of arthouse film distribution started showing signs of revival. With Hollywood cinema gradually leaving the so-called Hollywood Renaissance of the late 1960s to mid-1970s behind and embracing increasingly commercial modes of filmmaking, some audiences started turning once again to arthouse films for thought-provoking and intelligent cinema. It was also at this time that a new body of independently produced, low-budget US 'art' films emerged, inviting direct comparison with their foreign counterparts. Under the telling title 'Ordinary People, European Style: How to Spot an Independent Feature', Annette Insdorf compared recent US productions such as *Northern Lights*, *Heartland*, *Gal Young 'Un* (V. Nunez, 1979) and *Return of the Secaucus Seven* to such arthouse film staples as *La Maman et la putain* [*The Mother and the Whore*] (J. Eustache, 1973), *Les Quatre cents coups* [*The 400 Blows*] (F. Truffaut, 1959) and *Jules et Jim* (F. Truffaut, 1961).[16] Given these conditions, it is no coincidence that new distributors like Kino International and the Samuel Goldwyn Company entered the market in the late 1970s, in the hope of meeting what seemed like an increasing demand for all forms of film that were markedly different from the majors' product.

In this climate, the restructured United Artists quickly realised that its dormant Classics division had still a *raison d'être*. By 1980, the new UA management had reconceived of the division as part of its 'Television, Video and Special Markets structure'.[17] Under the leadership of Nathaniel Kwit, who was also in charge of the larger Television, Video and Special Markets unit, and with a small team of young executives that included Tom Bernard, Michael Barker and Ira Deutchman, who would later be involved with Orion Classics and Sony Pictures Classics (Bernard and Barker) and Fine Line Features (Deutchman), United Artists Classics entered the specialty film marketplace with the release of Brian De Palma's *Home Movies* in May 1980.

## MARGINAL REVENUE THEORY

Unlike De Palma's earlier (*Carrie*, 1976; *The Fury*, 1978) and later (*Dressed to Kill*, 1980; *Blow Out*, 1981) glossy Hollywood productions, *Home Movies* represents an experimental project that the filmmaker pursued in 1979 with a number of film students at the Sarah Lawrence College in Bronxville, New York, where De Palma had accepted an invitation to teach an independent filmmaking class.[18] As such the film has very few points of contact with De Palma's body of work, especially his notable visual style, although it features a number of actors that have appeared in several of his films, including Kirk Douglas, Keith Gordon and Nancy Allen. Given this peculiar mix of elements (student production overseen by a Hollywood maverick filmmaker and with professional actors, including a seasoned Hollywood star), it comes as no surprise that the film did not attract the attention of the major distributors. However, for a new company like UA Classics, it was exactly this peculiar mix of elements that was perceived as attractive, especially as the star power of the film provided the company with a product considerably different from the rest of the wave of American independent films that were bursting on to the scene in 1980. The film, however, did very little business at the US box office.[19]

Despite this inauspicious start, the company fared much better with its second release, François Truffaut's *Le Dernier Metro* [*The Last Metro*], which opened in New York in February 1981. The film, which starred leading French actors Gérard Depardieu and Catherine Deneuve, had enjoyed remarkable critical and commercial success in France, having won a record ten César Awards. Truffaut, who had been widely considered as one of the most important art cinema filmmakers since the success of his 1959 film *The 400 Blows*, had previously had a brief association with UA Classics' parent company when United Artists had financed and distributed four of his films between 1968 and 1970, with varied success. Following the folding of Lopert Pictures in 1970 and signs that the arthouse film market was stagnating, United Artists did not continue to bankroll or distribute Truffaut's films. However, the French filmmaker's pictures consistently found distributing organisations ready to market and release them in the North American market. All Truffaut's films of the 1970s were picked up for distribution in the US, either by major studios such as Columbia and Warner Bros., New York-based boutique operations such as Janus Films and Cinema 5 Distributing, or Roger Corman, whose New World Pictures distributed four of the French director's films.

*The Last Metro* was acquired by UA Classics in the face of great competition and on the basis of a novel business model that the division introduced and which convinced Truffaut to sign a distribution contract with them. Under established business practice, film distributors in the US who were interested in acquiring the rights of independently produced films would normally agree to pay the film's producers an advance (normally was used to cover part of the loans taken out by a film's producers to finance the picture). Once the film was released, the distributor would then deduct the marketing and print costs from the collected rentals, retain a distribution fee (which ranged between 30 and 40 per cent of rental income) and, in the unlikely case that the film performed exceptionally well at the box office, then split the remaining rental income with the producer. However, given the limited box-office success of most of these films in the US, in the majority of cases the advance was the only money the producers of a film would receive. Not surprisingly, then, producers would seek to sell the rights of their films to the distributor offering the highest advance.[20] As most companies interested in distributing foreign and US independent films were normally small outfits that could afford to bid for and distribute only a handful of such films a year, these advances tended to be saved for the most commercially promising films; even then, they remained in the lower hundreds of US dollars, given that the US box office of these films tended to remain below the $1 million mark in most cases, as mentioned earlier.

UA Classics proposed a deal that was structured in a different way. Instead of a model based on an advance, deduction of marketing costs from rentals, distribution fee and a split of the remaining rentals, it offered (some) filmmakers the following:

- no (or a very small) advance upon closure of the deal
- no marketing costs deducted from the rentals
- no distribution fee charged to the rentals
- a fifty / fifty split of the rentals
- marketing and advertising costs deducted from the distributor's 50 per cent share after the split.[21]

This deal allowed UA Classics to take minimum risks while enabling the maximum payoff for both itself and the producer if the film did good box-office business. More specifically, by not offering an advance, the company immediately had more funds at its disposal for a marketing campaign, should the film perform well, and posed little risk if the film did not open well; and, by not retaining a distribution fee, it made more of a film's rentals available to the producer. Once again, if the film did not perform well, it stood to lose very little. However, the most radical element of this model was the deduction of the print and marketing costs after the fifty / fifty split from the distributor's rather than the producer's share.[22] Indeed, such costs were customarily the first ones to be deducted 'off the top' and before any other aspects of the deal kicked in. UA Classics' move to eliminate them from the producer's share was accompanied by the necessary condition that marketing costs would remain extremely low, as would the print-cutting costs, given that most of films would play in a limited number of theatres (sometimes only in one) but for a substantial period of time.

More specifically, UA Classics branded itself as a distributing organisation operating under what its senior management labelled 'marginal revenue theory'.[23] According to this approach, the division was to be extremely frugal in its spending, especially in terms of marketing costs. As its Chief Operating Officer remarked, their average marketing campaign in 1981, their first full year of operation as a theatrical distributor, 'cost under $2000 to create', with the campaign for their celebrated reissue of *Cutter's Way* (I. Passer, 1981) reportedly costing just $150.[24] Even if these figures have been exaggerated for publicity purposes and might have been higher in reality, they are nevertheless a far cry from the average marketing and print costs in Hollywood in the early 1980s, which were close to $4 million for the average studio production.[25]

Such prudence in the marketing spend precluded the company from advertising its films on television, which, since the 1970s, had been deemed the most effective form of advertising to a wide audience and was by far the most expensive one.[26] However, as arthouse films targeted niche audiences, exposure on national television was not a priority. This was because the film-goers UA Classics were specifically aiming for constituted 'a discriminating slice of the "baby boomers"'; for the division's executives, this comprised 'people who are moving up in age, are more serious and who want to see intelligent, sophisticated films'.[27] Given the constitution of this discriminating niche audience and, of course, the division's small operating remit, it is not surprising that it would steer clear of network television and instead seek alternative forms of advertising (especially coverage in influential newspapers), as well as inexpensive methods of publicity and promotion such as bringing a renowned filmmaker or foreign star to the US for the opening of the film.

Despite this marketing austerity, UA Classics was also part of a large corporate branch that also traded in television, video and other special markets. This meant that it was in a position to exploit synergies among the several arms of the key unit to which it belonged, even at this 'low' corporate level. One could argue, then, that, unlike its competitors, UA Classics was a mirror image of an entertainment conglomerate but operating on a much smaller scale and with much lower revenues than its parent company and the other major players. In this respect, besides carrying the clout of its conglomerate parent, UA Classics also enjoyed a hybrid status that equipped it with considerable flexibility in the synergy-driven film business of the 1980s.

When it came to *The Last Metro*, UA Classics beat off its rivals with its novel distribution model. Despite competitors offering advances ranging between $400,000 and $500,000 in a conventional distribution deal, the studio division acquired the film rights for the North American market by offering a much smaller advance (estimated at between $100,000 and $125,000) and the opportunity to split the film's rentals fifty-fifty.[28] The spending on the marketing campaign was originally limited to just $22,000 for the first week of the film's release in New York City.[29] This was mainly because the film was opening to considerable buzz following its great box-office performance in France, where it had been released in late 1980; early rave reviews in newspapers like the *New York Times* and by influential critics like Vincent Canby;[30] and especially its success at the César Awards only two weeks prior to its release in the US. UA

Classics' decision to spend little was justified when the film brought in $87,000 in just one engagement in Manhattan.[31] In the following weeks, UA Classics opened the film in a small number of metropolitan areas that have traditionally worked as arthouse film markets, including Montreal, Los Angeles and Boston, with similar results.[32] In the end, UA Classics spent approximately $250,000 in advertising and print costs in total and the film brought in approximately ten times this in rentals.[33] With the fifty-fifty split, Truffaut stood to receive close to $1.3 million, while the distributor would net around $900,000 (following deduction of marketing costs). Should Truffaut have opted for a conventional distribution deal, he would have received approximately $200,000 less, using the figures above.

With this early success under its belt and, equally importantly, a distribution system that allowed the company to bid for a number of films at the same time as it did not have to pay (a lot of) money upfront, UA Classics went on to dominate the newly revived arthouse sector while, at the same time, claiming a stake in the emerging US independent film market. In this respect, the designation 'classics', which was originally inspired by the company's involvement in the rerelease of classic Hollywood films, and which would be used to describe other such subsidiaries of Hollywood majors that would provide competition for UA Classics in the following years, became something of a misnomer. Still, during the first full year of trading, UA Classics attracted substantial attention after the successful reissue, not of a classic Hollywood film, but of a number of contemporary films that had failed to find an audience on their original release by United Artists; Ivan Passer's *Cutter and Bone* became a prime example of what critics were starting to call 'rescued' films.[34]

The film was produced and distributed by United Artists during the transitional period following the departure of its senior executives in 1978. It cost $6 million to make and featured Jeff Bridges (Bone) and John Heard (Cutter) in the lead roles, playing two friends who believe that an 'untouchable' industrialist is the culprit in a young cheerleader's murder. Despite its premise stemming from the detective genre, the film was much more interested in charting the two men's friendship, their relationship to Cutter's alcoholic wife, and Cutter's problematic rehabilitation following serious wounds in the Vietnam War. Given these emphases and the largely peripheral attention it paid to generic questions, *Cutter and Bone* did not receive the appropriate marketing support and failed to register with cinema-goers.[35] It was pulled from the screens after taking a week's box-office gross of only $13,500.[36]

After its quick closure, however, the film received a number of favourable reviews in influential newspapers and magazines, prompting United Artists to pass the film to its subsidiary with a view to rereleasing it for a more specialised audience. During this assignment, the classics division changed the title of the film to *Cutter's Way* (so that it would not suggest 'surgeons and meat cleavers', as one of its executives put it) and took a different marketing stand by completely removing the inaccurate action-adventure advertising of the previous campaign and emphasising instead the film's 'noir-ish, special quality'.[37] Treating it as an arthouse film and spending only $8,000 on the film's second opening, UA Classics released *Cutter's Way* in Seattle in June 1981 and, following a successful run, in several other big markets such as San Francisco, Washington, DC, and New York, where the film found significant box-office success.[38] The success led United Artists to assign to its classics division the reissue of other recent box-office 'flops', such as Martin Scorsese's *New York, New York* (1977) and Carl Reiner's *Where's Poppa?* (1979), which UA Classics rereleased to very positive financial results.[39]

In the remainder of 1981, the company distributed six other features. Predictably, the majority were art films from Europe, some of which by auteur filmmakers as well known and established as Truffaut; they included Rainer Werner Fassbinder (*Lili Marleen*) and Claude Lelouch, whose 1976 *Si c'était à refaire* [*Second Chance*] had not been released in the US until Deneuve's success in *The Last Metro* gave Lelouch's film a new marketing hook. It also distributed Truffaut's follow-up to *The Last Metro*, *La Femme d'à côté* [*The Woman Next Door*], when *The Last Metro* was still playing in New York, seven months after its initial release.[40] Interestingly, Fassbinder's films prior to *Lili Marleen* had been distributed in the US by New Yorker Films, one of the most established arthouse independent 'boutique' companies that had been in the business since the 1950s.[41] However, the potential for profit that UA Classics' model represented convinced the German filmmaker to sign with the new distributor, who also handled the next two of his final four films, *Lola* (1982) and *Die Sehnsucht der Veronika Voss* [*Veronika Voss*] (1982), before his death in 1982.

However, the company did also venture outside the non-US arthouse circuit, showing that it was also going to become a player in the developing US independent film market and to profit from the outburst of creativity that the 'quality' independent sector experienced in the late 1970s and early 1980s. Indeed, besides the earlier-mentioned *Northern Lights*, *Heartland*, *Gal Young 'Un* and *Return of the Secaucus Seven*, there were many other narrative feature-length films that secured commercial distribution and found some success, including: *The Kirlian Witness* (J. Samo, 1979), *Tuck Everlasting* (F. King Keller, 1981), *The Dozens* (R. Conrad and C. Dall, 1981), *Hito Hata: Raise the Banner* (R. A. Nakamura, 1981), *Union City* (M. Reichert, 1980) and *Alambrista!* (R. M. Young, 1979 [1977]). Add to these an increasing number of feature-length documentaries such as *Joe and Maxi* (M. Cohen and J. Gold, 1978), *The War at Home* (G. Silber and G. A. Brown, 1979) and *The Life and Times of Rosie the Riveter* (C. Field, 1980), and it is clear that the period in question represented a very significant phase in the history of independent filmmaking in the US. In this respect, while film critics like Insdorf were commenting on the kinship of this wave of films to art cinema, other critics of the time saw this activity as a 'movement' and as a sustainable 'alternative' to Hollywood studio filmmaking, in the same way that a group of film practitioners had managed to curb the monopoly of the once-major Motion Picture Patents Company in the first years of the twentieth century.[42] With substantial institutional infrastructure already in place after the success of initiatives such as the Young Filmmakers group in New York City (1968), the Association of Independent Video and Filmmakers (AIVF) since 1974, an increasing number of regional film bureaus, and the launch of the Independent Feature Project in 1979, independent film was perceived as having the potential to break the chains with Hollywood and offer a real alternative to it. And indeed, for a number of more recent film scholars and critics, that moment did mark the beginning of 'contemporary American independent cinema'.[43]

As part of this wave of North American independent film activity, UA Classics took its first tentative steps with the distribution of Murray Lerner's documentary *From Mao to Mozart: Isaac Stern in China* (1981) and with Canadian production *Ticket to Heaven* (R. L. Thomas, 1981). However, for the first full year of its operation, no other film attained the commercial success of *The Last Metro*.

## BOOM AND BUST

Equipped with the positive results of 1981, the company switched gears in 1982 with its decision to distribute eleven films, a number that put it on a par with some of the major Hollywood distributors, including its parent company, which also distributed eleven films that year.[44] Not surprisingly, the lion's share went again to European art films by renowned auteurs who, after witnessing the remarkable commercial success of *The Last Metro*, opted to sign distribution contracts with the new division. The list of these filmmakers included Volker Schlöndorff, whose previous film, *The Tin Drum* (1979), had been distributed by Corman's New World Pictures and had been an international critical and commercial success, and who decided to go with UA Classics with his follow-up, *Die Fälschung* [*Circle of Deceit*] (1981); Paolo and Vittorio Taviani, whose previous films had been distributed in the US by boutique independent companies such as New Yorker Films and Cinema 5 Distributing, but whose latest, *La Notte di San Lorenzo* [*The Night of the Thousand Stars*], was entrusted to UA Classics; Eric Rohmer, whose previous two films had been distributed by New Yorker Films, but who chose UA Classics for *Le Beau Mariage* [*A Good Marriage*] (1982); Fassbinder collaborator Wolf Gremm, whose film *Fabian* (1980) was nominated for an Academy

Award for Best Foreign Picture; and, of course, the two Fassbinder films mentioned earlier, *Veronika Voss* and *Lola*.

This move of international arthouse film talent *en masse* to UA Classics did not go unnoticed by critics and independent distributors alike, who felt that the studio subsidiary was not only changing the rules of the game, but also squeezing the competition in the process. Losing Fassbinder, Rohmer and the Taviani brothers to UA Classics, New Yorker Films in particular felt the pinch and criticised the studio arm for unfair competition, claiming that the rest of the players in the market were entrepreneurs who risked their own capital while UA Classics were essentially studio employees with nothing to lose.[45] Equally, the owner of Libra Films, which had found success with *Return of the Secaucus Seven*, accused UA Classics and the rest of the newly formed divisions of 'hik[ing] up the prices on films to the point where they're not economical to distribute'.[46] In this respect, the pool of small, specialised distributors that existed in the market prior to UA Classics started finding it increasingly difficult to compete.

Despite the criticisms, UA Classics did not just play a 'safe' game; nor did it only lure established auteurs with the promise of increased profits. It also demonstrated great acumen in recognising new talent, as the spectacular commercial success of *Diva*, Jean-Jacques Beineix's debut feature film, suggests. Another film distinguished at the César Awards, *Diva* was acquired by UA Classics following the formula established by *The Last Metro*, but with a considerably lower advance than Truffaut's film: just $25,000. Although the distribution deal was reached in October 1981, UA Classics did not release the film until well into 1982 (April), to avoid competition with other foreign films that are normally distributed in the early months of the year following their pick-up from the New York Film Festival, which finishes in early October.[47] The results clearly justified this strategy; with a total advertising and print budget of $300,000, the film became UA Classics' biggest commercial success, playing for a full calendar year and recording a box-office gross of $7 million. This figure yielded approximately $3 million in rentals and a huge profit for filmmaker and distributor.[48] Equally importantly, the film returned an additional $250,000 in rentals from its licensing to cable television and video, clearly demonstrating the significance of ancillary markets and synergies, even for specialised product that was not deemed commercial by the majors.[49]

The remarkable success of *Diva* and *The Last Metro* in the ancillary markets proved a moot point and reversed the division's philosophy during the uncertain times the industry experienced in the early 1980s.[50] This is because UA Classics had deemed the increasing trend in home entertainment as 'pre-empting standard theatrical product',[51] and therefore not the specialised fare in which the division and the numerous small independent distributors were trading. Indeed, as former United Artists executive Mike Medavoy admitted in an interview, these kinds of film rarely attracted interest from ancillary markets, where the main revenues were coming from, and for that reason their distributors 'had to live frugally'.[52] However, the exponential growth of ancillary markets, and especially of video and cable, from the beginning of the decade onwards made all the players in the sector sit up and take notice and even modify their business plans. This became particularly evident when new cable distributors such as HBO and Showtime went in search of product for their movie channels and for a period of time looked at every single market, including the non-US arthouse and US independent ones. As a result, the early years of the 1980s became a golden period for specialised film as distribution opportunities were expanding in several directions, before a number of mergers that involved the major studios and the representatives of these new home delivery technologies geared the system towards 'films with the largest broad appeal'.[53]

The success of the company's 1982 slate, which also included another film 'rescue' against the odds – this time, celebrated independent filmmaker Joan Micklin Silver's *Head over Heels* (1979), revamped as *Chilly Scenes of Winter* (1982)[54] – brought with it expansion, as well as the opening of a subsidiary, United Artists Classics of Canada. However, halfway through the year, the division became the victim of corporate manœuvring when MGM's owner, Kirk Kerkorian, decided to refocus the ailing studio's business by aggressively entering into the production and distribution of expensive films with the potential for profits from the ancillary markets.[55] As the distribution agreement between MGM and United Artists was due to expire in 1983, MGM decided that the best way to reconfigure its business was to acquire an existing distribution network, United Artists being the main target. Despite its unprecedented success in the late 1970s, United Artists had found itself in a precarious position in the early 1980s following the exit of its management team in 1978 and the massive failure of *Heaven's Gate* (M. Cimino, 1980), which represented the write-off of a $44 million investment.[56] In this respect, MGM executives had little trouble convincing United Artists' parent company, Transamerica, to sell them its subsidiary. This was especially so, as the agreed price of $380 million was perceived by Transamerica as massively over the net value of United Artists' assets and therefore an excellent deal for them.[57]

Following the takeover, the management of the new MGM / UA Entertainment Company had already started restructuring the corporation's distribution and marketing apparatus, which, at first sight, seemed to leave UA Classics not only unscathed but with the potential to develop into a 'more important unit' than in its first two years of operation.[58] At the same time, though, UA Classics' executives attempted to convince MGM / UA to spin off the division and allow it to stand on its own in the market.[59] Not surprisingly, given the success of UA Classics, the new parent company refused and moved to change its subsidiary's management regime, with a view to making it 'an even more aggressive and innovative division of [their] organization', given its increasing recognition as 'the foremost distributor of foreign and speciality films and as the country's largest distributor of repertory films'.[60] Importantly, this was also one of the first times that a classics division acknowledged the potential of American independent film, with the company's new senior executive, Bill Stuart, stating that UA Classics would be committed to 'take one or two independent U.S. and Canadian features, where available every year', even though their 'lifeblood [was] in foreign films'.[61]

Indeed, the 1983 slate looked promising, with the company aiming to release fourteen films. The line-up included, yet again, work from celebrated auteurs such as Andrej Wajda's *Czlowiek z Zelaza [Man of Iron]* and Jean-Luc Godard's *Passion*. Also featured were lesser-known directors from world cinema, whose films were nevertheless commercially promising, such as Pierre Granier-Deferre's *L'Étoile du nord [The North Star]*, with international star Simone Signoret, and Dutch filmmaker Ben Verbong's *Het Meisje met het Rode Haar [The Girl with the Red Hair]*; the latter came along at a time when cinema in the Netherlands had been experiencing substantial international success with films by directors like Paul Verhoeven and Theo Van Gogh. The line-up also included English-language arthouse films, such as Peter Greenaway's *The Draughtsman's Contract* and Lindsay Anderson's *Britannia Hospital*; low-budget genre films from Canada, such as *The Grey Fox* (P. Borsos); documentaries such as the Holocaust-themed *Genocide* (A. Schwartzman) and the exploration of gospel singing, *Say Amen, Somebody* (G. T. Nierenberg); and most importantly, for the purposes of this study, two key low-budget American films firmly associated with the emerging independent sector, John Sayles's third feature, *Lianna* (see Case Study), and maverick New Hollywood director Robert Altman's *Streamers*.

By 1983, the UA Classics 'experiment' had already been emulated by four other divisions of large film companies (see Chapters 2 and 3), clearly demonstrating that the studios were 'moving in'. However, by this time, UA Classics had reached the point of becoming 'too big' and was therefore attracting increasing scrutiny from the top echelon of its parent company. After yet another change of management in the division in early 1983, UA Classics, which, up to that time, had been enjoying administrative autonomy from MGM / UA, was given a directive to collapse its operations into the parent company's accounting and administrative functions. Although such a move was justified by MGM / UA as necessary because of UA Classics' 'rapid growth', industry analysts believed that this was a strike against the subsidiary's relative autonomy on the part of the parent company, arguing that 'one of the things that set UA Classics apart was that it did everything on its own'.[62] Indeed, this interference from the top sparked a second mass exodus of key employees; in a move that mirrored the 1978 departure of United Artists' senior executives, several members of UA Classics' management team left to join Orion Classics, the company established by the former group.

UA Classics' new management made it clear that the division would now be looking equally to independent films (in the US but also in other English-language markets) and to 'major foreign-language films', as the new mandate from the parent company was to aim for 'crossover films that bridge the gap between the "art" and commercial houses'.[63] The Canadian production, *The Grey Fox*, proved to be exactly the type of film that fit the new bill. After a successful release, the film attained crossover status by playing in 500 theatres in the North American market and becoming the company's box-office champion for 1983.[64] On the basis of this and a number of other successes, UA Classics recorded yet another extremely profitable year with approximately $9.5 million in film rentals.[65] These remarkable figures convinced MGM / UA that UA Classics was ready for further expansion, which none the less would be part and parcel of the subsidiary's further integration into the parent company. Indeed, in March 1984 and following yet another change in management (the third one), UA Classics was relocated from New York to Los Angeles, leading analysts to comment 'that superiors in those areas [marketing and distribution] will be keeping closer tabs on the subsidiary's activities', and questioning further the degree of autonomy that the division would enjoy.[66] Perhaps more importantly, the division's relocation to Los Angeles raised questions because of the general assumption in specialised distribution circles that most of the arthouse and independent film business emanates from and is intricately linked to the city of New York. Despite this disadvantage, efficiency of operation was deemed by the parent company to be a more desirable feature. To complement this new version of its subsidiary, MGM / UA renamed the division MGM / UA Classics.[67]

The incessant restructuring, however, was starting to have an effect on the division. After distributing over ten films in the previous two years, the company released only five features in 1984. One of these, Bertrand Tavernier's *Un Dimanche à la campagne* [*A Sunday in the Country*] was a solid hit and, together with Diane Kurys's *Coup de foudre / Entre nous* [*At First Sight*], which was released late in 1983 and did most of its box-office business in 1984, grossed over $6 million combined. The rest, which included Bruno Baretto's Brazilian film *Gabriela, Cravo e Canela* [*Gabriela*] and Nicholas Roeg's star-studded *Eureka* (which MGM / UA originally intended to distribute itself before deciding to pass it to its subsidiary), failed to find an audience.[68] Equally, the distribution of the low-budget, English-language films, *Nothing Lasts Forever* (T. Schiller) and *Kipperbang* (M. Apted), proved unsuccessful, despite the fact that the latter was directed by the well-known British filmmaker Michael Apted.

MGM / UA Classics' uneven performance in 1984 can be partly explained by the fact that its other classics competitors, especially Orion Classics, had quickly caught up with it. As we will see in Chapter 3, Orion Classics found success immediately while also starting to revolutionise the rules of the game by making forays into film finance for specific titles. Furthermore, according to *Variety*, approximately 25 per cent of all releases by major companies in 1984 were 'classics', creating a particularly crowded marketplace that could sustain only a small number of box-office successes.[69] However, increased competition was only one side of the coin. Corporate politics, especially in the parent company for which the early to mid-1980s was a particularly striking period of instability and restructuring,[70] and the overall inability of the MGM / UA executives to understand the rules of the game when it came to specialised distribution, were certainly other important factors. For the increasingly diversified entertainment conglomerates of the 1980s, a classics division such as UA Classics represented little investment and relatively little return. As long as the specialised arm operated profitably and without problems, the parent company was happy to let it retain some autonomy. But if the subsidiary lost its profitability, expanded too far or presented operational problems (even if those were created by the parent company itself), the parent company could close the division quickly and without too much impact on the bottom line.

All three of these reasons, in addition to the increased competition, seemed to have signalled the demise of MGM / UA Classics. In 1985 the company released only two films, the British production *Wetherby* (D. Hare) and the New Zealand film *Sylvia* (M. Firth), neither of which proved a significant success. A third picture, Paolo and Vittorio Taviani's *Kaos* [*Chaos*], was pushed back to early 1986, and proved to be the division's last theatrical release. By that time, all the classics divisions created by the other majors had already folded, with the exception of Orion Classics; the latter had been created, not by a major, but by a hybrid company that many film critics referred to as a mini-major (see Chapter 3).

## CONCLUSION

Despite its forced exit from the niche distribution market in the mid-1980s, UA Classics and its later MGM / UA Classics incarnation managed to make its presence felt in a significant way. By utilising the security its parent company provided, the subsidiary was able to introduce a film distribution model that could bring higher profits for a film's producer if the film was successful at the box office, despite taking away the coveted distribution advance that tended to be the highest determinant in conventional distribution practice. This gave the company the ability to distribute a substantial number of films, especially in the successful three-year period between 1981 and 1983. In the process, UA Classics not only convinced the other majors to create their own classics divisions, but also significantly shaped niche distribution at a point when both world arthouse filmmaking and US independent production were flourishing. In this respect, the division became a particularly important addition to the emerging institutional infrastructure that supported American independent film and which would continue to grow in the 1980s and 1990s.

### Case Study: *Lianna* (John Sayles, 1983)

Following the success of his seminal independent film *Return of the Secaucus Seven*, John Sayles signed a contract for a studio picture (*Baby, It's You* [1983] for Paramount) and started raising finance for the independent picture *Lianna*.

The latter tells the story of a woman that married her college professor when she was very young but who, after several years of marriage and two children, has reached an impasse, especially as she discovers her husband's infidelities with younger female students. As she embarks on a self-developing psychology evening class, Lianna starts a romantic affair with her female professor. Realising that she is attracted to women, she ends her marriage and ventures out on her own, after the affair quickly ends. Despite the difficulties she faces, Lianna learns to deal with the harsh realities of life and develops a strong sense of identity.

Despite the success of *Secaucus Seven*, it took Sayles approximately eighteen months to raise the $340,000 that *Lianna* cost to make and only through organising a limited partnership with no fewer than twenty-four individuals, whose small investments (ranging from just $1,500 to $50,000) covered the film's negative costs.[71] This allowed Sayles complete creative control and the opportunity to make the film according to his own vision. In terms of narrative, this vision often translated into the construction of stories that broadly follow the rules of classical storytelling (cause-effect logic, psychological motivation, character transformation by the end of the film) but which deviate from them on several occasions, allowing for much stronger characterisation to emerge. For instance, while her husband's extramarital activities and overall treatment of her give Lianna ample motivation to leave him, the narrative refuses to take this 'easy' route. Instead, it opts for the more difficult (and arguably less convincing) suggestion that Lianna decided to leave him because, at some indefinite point in the story, her psychology professor awakened her interest. Equally, the often-criticised 'ease' with which Lianna changes her sexual orientation, representing a 'detour' for some critics rather than a new identity,[72] is another manifestation of Sayles's very specific approach to narrative construction. For the filmmaker, the fact that Lianna's new lover is a woman is simply another complication in a life characterised by complications, rather than a politically motivated decision. The psychology professor could have easily been a man and this would not have changed Lianna's story, prompting Ryan, in his study of Sayles's cinema, to note correctly that *Lianna* is a film about 'the life of someone who happens to be gay'.[73]

Just like his narrative choices, Sayles's stylistic choices also bridge mainstream conventions with an unusual approach to visual style. For example, he uses a large number of short scenes which tend to fragment an otherwise linear narrative and invite the spectator to experience the gaps and the unanswered questions the story creates. This approach was developed primarily as a response to the logistics of shooting on a very low budget that does not allow for elaborate camera movement or complex shots. To counter this absence, the many short scenes create pace artificially; just as in *Secaucus Seven*, Sayles also uses very fast editing in a couple of scenes, increasing the pace yet again and standing in contrast to the single-take scenes with no editing that constitute almost a third of the film.

Such a personal independent film was never going to attract a big distributor. UA Classics had bid for *Secaucus Seven* in 1980 but Sayles preferred to arrange distribution with two stand-alone distributors.[74] With the classics division flying high in late 1982 / early 1983, Sayles followed other filmmakers' example by switching to them. At the same time, though, UA Classics also wanted Sayles's second feature film as they thought that they knew how to market it, while the insurance that their parent company provided meant for Sayles that all the people involved in his film would receive some payment.[75]

Sayles received a $40,000 advance with which he paid all the deferred salaries and agreed to travel to promote the film in the key markets to which UA Classics released it.[76] Although the distributor's advertising campaign did not shy away from the film's controversial topic, neither did it opt to make it particularly explicit, the poster showing the two women in close proximity and insinuating a romantic relationship rather than depicting it explicitly. However, given the rare representations of lesbian women in American film, word of mouth circulated quickly; the film attracted groups of lesbian women who, at the end of several screenings, engaged in conversation with the filmmaker and his partner and the film's producer, Maggie Renzi.[77]

The film was received warmly by the public and received mostly positive reviews, despite attracting considerable criticism for the way it treated Lianna's transformation from a heterosexual to a homosexual woman. However, its opening weeks in January 1983 coincided with one of the major restructuring operations at UA Classics, which saw the departure of key executives to Orion Classics and the instalment of new management. In this climate of transition, *Lianna* did not receive the marketing push that Sayles anticipated and did not benefit from the distribution acumen that distinguished the division's young executives who had just left the company. This prompted Sayles's complaint that he was left 'high and dry with *Lianna*' and that his film 'was not well taken care of'.[78] Furthermore, the unfortunate timing of *Lianna*'s release meant that the film did not benefit from any ancillary markets. Specifically, in terms of video, UA Classics did not manage to make a deal, while the big cable players such as HBO and Showtime considered the film 'unprogrammable'.[79] Still, *Lianna* recorded a respectable theatrical box-office gross of $1.5 million, with particularly strong business in New York City[80] – enough to generate a very small profit for the cooperative of investors who financed it.

Despite the bad experience with UA Classics, and after having his films

> distributed by various boutique independent companies, Sayles returned to a classics division in the mid-1990s, when Sony Pictures Classics agreed to release *Lone Star* (1996). By that time, the distributor was run by the same people that Sayles had made the *Lianna* deal with at United Artists Classics and, following the success of *Lone Star*, it released several of the filmmaker's other pictures.

## NOTES

1. Bart, Peter, *Fade Out: The Calamitous Final Days of MGM* (London: Simon & Schuster, 1999), 58.
2. Jacobson, Harlan, 'How the Classics Kids Snatched Foreign Film', *Village Voice* (22 November 1983), 74.
3. This figure was obtained from the Internet Movie Database (IMDb), available at http://www.imdb.com/title/tt0072272/business; accessed on 7 April 2010.
4. Jacobson, 'How the Classics Kids Snatched Foreign Film', 74.
5. Balio, Tino, *United Artists: The Company that Changed the Film Industry* (Madison: University of Wisconsin Press, 1987), 106-7.
6. Jacobson, 'How the Classics Kids Snatched Foreign Film', 74.
7. Ibid.
8. Cook, David A., *Lost Illusions: American Cinema in the Shadow of Watergate and Vietnam 1970-1979* (Berkeley: University of California Press, 2000), 318.
9. See, for instance, Mike Medavoy with Josh Young, *You're Only As Good As Your Next One: 100 Great Films, 100 Good Films, and 100 for Which I Should Be Shot* (Toronto: Pocket Books, 2002); Steven Bach, *Final Cut: Dreams and Disasters in the Making of Heaven's Gate* (London: Faber & Faber, 1986); and Balio, *United Artists*, 333-9.
10. See Eugene Hernandez, 'Positioned for the Digital Future, Krim & Lorber Still Favor the Big Screen', *Indiewire* (9 December 2009), http://www.indiewire.com/article/positioned_for_the_digital_future_krim_lorber_still_favor_the_big_screen/; accessed on 8 April 2011.
11. Hift, Fred, 'Foreign Films "Arrive" in US', *Variety* (30 January 1957), 1.
12. Balio, *United Artists*, 229-31.
13. Wilinsky, Barbara, *Sure Seaters: The Emergence of Art House Cinema* (Minneapolis: University of Minnesota Press, 2001), 132-3.
14. Wilinsky, *Sure Seaters*, 133.
15. Hillier, Jim, 'The Economics of Independence: Roger Corman and New World Pictures', *Movie* 31 / 32 (Winter 1986), 47-50.
16. Insdorf, 'Ordinary People', 58-9.
17. 'UA Classics' Coup', 7.
18. Peary, Gerald, 'Brian De Palma', *Gerald Peary*, 2004 [1979], http://www.geraldpeary.com/interviews/def/depalma.html; accessed on 8 August 2010.
19. According to IMDb, the film grossed a little less than $90,000 (http://www.imdb.com/title/tt0079302/business) on a budget that, according to De Palma, was just below the $1 million mark (quoted in Peary, 'Brian De Palma').
20. Harmetz, Aljean, 'Reporter's Notebook', *New York Times* (26 May 1981), C8; Grover, Steven, 'Film Duds Get Second Chance at UA Classics', *The Wall Street Journal* (14 July 1981), n/a.

21. Harmetz, 'Reporter's Notebook', C8.
22. In a recent interview, Ira Deutchman disputed the part of the deal that stipulated that print and advertising costs should be deducted from the distributor's share. Furthermore, he noted that the distribution model proposed for *The Last Metro* was used only on rare occasions and was not the template for deals at UA Classics (Deutchman, interview, 2 June 2011).
23. Robbins, Jim, 'Restore Hope for Hard-to-Sell Themes: UA Classics as Playoff Doctor', *Weekly Variety* (10 June 1981), 28.
24. Kwit, quoted in Harmetz, 'Reporter's Notebook', C8. For the celebrated reissue of *Cutter's Way* see Grover, 'Film Duds'.
25. This figure is specifically for 1980. See Steven Prince, *A New Pot of Gold: Hollywood under the Electronic Rainbow, 1980-1989* (Berkeley: University of California Press, 2002), 20.
26. Cook, *Lost Illusions*, 16.
27. Quoted in Mary Reinholz, 'UA Classics' Kitt Carrying the Torch, Going for Sophisticates', *Hollywood Reporter* (20 September 1983), 59.
28. *Weekly Variety* carries a quote from Kwit stating that he paid $100,000 upfront ('UA Classics' Coup', 35), while Jacobson estimates the advance as being in the $125,000 region (Jacobson, 'How the Classics Kids Snatched Foreign Film', 75).
29. Kwit, quoted in Deborah Caulfield, 'Studios and Art Films – The Heyday is Over', *Los Angeles Times* (22 April 1984), 16.
30. Canby, Vincent, '*The Last Metro*', *New York Times* (12 October 1980), http://movies.nytimes.com/movie/review?res=EE05E7DF1730BA2CA1494CC0B7799C836896; accessed on 8 August 2010.
31. Kwit, quoted in Caulfield, 'Studios and Art Films', 16.
32. De Baecque, Antoine and Serge Toubiana, *Truffaut: A Biography* (Berkeley: University of California Press, 2000), 360.
33. Jacobson, 'How the Classics Kids Snatched Foreign Film', 75.
34. Atlas, James, 'How "Chilly Scenes" Was Rescued', *New York Times* (10 October 1982), http://www.nytimes.com/books/98/06/28/specials/beattie-chilly.html; accessed on 6 August 2010.
35. Hinson, Hal, 'The Rx for "Cutter's Way"? UA Classics', *LA Herald-Examiner* (22 September 1981), D4.
36. Grover, 'Film Duds'; Hinson, 'The Rx for "Cutter's Way"?', D4.
37. Grover, 'Film Duds'.
38. Robbins, 'Restore Hope', 28.
39. Ibid.
40. Hinson, 'The Rx for "Cutter's Way"?', D4.
41. Grover, 'Film Duds'.
42. Lamont, 'Independents' Day', 15.
43. See Rosen with Hamilton, *Off-Hollywood*; Donald Lyons, *Independent Visions: A Critical Introduction to Recent Independent American Film* (New York: Ballantine, 1994); Richard K. Ferncase, *Outsider Features: American Independent Films of the 1980s* (New Haven: Greenwood, 1996); Geoff Andrew, *Stranger than Paradise: Maverick Film-makers in Recent American Cinema* (London: Prion, 1998); and Biskind, *Down and Dirty Pictures*.
44. Finler, Joel W., *The Hollywood Story*, 3rd edn (London: Wallflower, 2003), 366.
45. Talbot, quoted in Jacobson, 'How the Classics Kids Snatched Foreign Film', 76 (original italics).
46. Berenholz, quoted in ibid.

47. 'UA Classics Has Distrib'n Deal for "Diva" Pic', *Daily Variety* (28 October 1981), n/a.
48. Sutherland, Alex, '"Country" Continues Orion Classics' Art-house Success', *Screen International* (6 October 1984), 6.
49. Jacobson, 'How the Classics Kids Snatched Foreign Film', 76.
50. According to *Variety*, *The Last Metro* brought in the even larger sum of $450,000 from the sale of its pay TV rights. See Steven Klain, 'Prods Over-value US Art Mart: Classics Eye Upfront Stakes as Terms Stiffen', *Weekly Variety* (4 May 1983), 532.
51. Robbins, 'Restore Hope', 28.
52. Medavoy, Mike (former head of worldwide production at United Artists [1973 to 1978] and Orion Pictures [1978 to 1990]), interview with the author, 15 June 2004, Frankovich Building, Los Angeles, USA, 1 hour.
53. Steve Sheffer, HBO executive, was quoted in Caulfield, 'Studios and Art Films', 17.
54. For an account of UA Classics' rescue of the film see Atlas, 'How "Chilly Scenes" Was Rescued'.
55. Balio, *United Artists*, 342.
56. Bart, *Fade Out*, 180.
57. Prince, *A New Pot of Gold*, 15.
58. 'MGM-UA Pondering New Role for Kwit Back Classics?', *Weekly Variety* (21 April 1982), 26.
59. Caulfield, 'Studios and Art Films', 17.
60. United Artists Press Release, 1 July 1982 (obtained from UA Classics Folder, Margaret Herrick Library, Los Angeles, USA).
61. 'UA Classics' Stuart Talks Canadian Pix', *Weekly Variety* (15 September 1982), 3.
62. 'UA Classics Losing Some Autonomy Via MGM / UA "Support"', *Weekly Variety* (16 November 1983), 27.
63. Reinholz, 'UA Classics' Kitt Carrying the Torch', 59.
64. Loynd, Ray, 'UA Classics Changes Name Along with H.Q.', *Weekly Variety* (23 February 1984), 27.
65. 'Kitt Exits Niche at UA Classics', *Daily Variety* (16 January 1984), n/a.
66. Ritzer, Teri and Gerry Putzer, 'UA Classics Moving: New York Staff Pink-Slipped LA Div. will Debut in March', *Hollywood Reporter* (3 February 1984), 25.
67. 'UA Classics Heads West, Alters Logo', *Weekly Variety* (22 February 1984), 26.
68. 'MGM / UA Classics Arm Scouting Pics at Cannes; Five Ready for Release', *Weekly Variety* (1 May 1985), 16.
69. Jacobson, 'How the Classics Kids Snatched Foreign Film', 74.
70. For more on MGM / UA corporate politics see Bart, *Fade Out*, 167–250.
71. Molyneaux, Gerry, *John Sayles: An Unauthorised Biography of the Pioneering Indie Filmmaker* (Los Angeles: Renaissance, 2000), 197; Stone, Judy, 'A Male Director's Look at a Lesbian Relationship', in *John Sayles: Interviews*, ed. Diane Carson (Jackson: University Press of Mississippi, 1999), 44. Originally published in the *San Francisco Chronicle* (20 March 1983).
72. Richard Corliss, quoted in Emanuel Levy, *Cinema of Outsiders: The Rise of American Independent Film* (New York: New York University Press, 1999), 87.
73. Ryan, Jack, *John Sayles: Filmmaker* (Jefferson: McFarland, 1999), 79.
74. Tzioumakis, *American Independent Cinema*, 217.
75. Molyneaux, *John Sayles: An Unauthorised Biography*, 109.
76. 'Interview with John Sayles', in *John Sayles: Interviews*, ed. Diane Carson (Jackson: University Press of Mississippi, 1999), 54. Originally published in *American Cinematographer* (April 1983).

77. Molyneaux, *John Sayles: An Unauthorised Biography*, 110.
78. Quoted in Gavin Smith, '*Lianna* and *Baby, It's You*', in *Sayles on Sayles*, ed. Gavin Smith (London: Faber & Faber, 1998), 78.
79. Ibid.
80. Stone, 'A Male Director's Look', 44.

CHAPTER 2

# Triumph Films (1982 to 1985), Universal Classics (1982 to 1984) and Twentieth Century Fox International Classics (1982 to 1985)

## INTRODUCTION

The almost immediate success of United Artists Classics in early 1981 with the release of *The Last Metro* made an instant impact on the industry. By 1982, Columbia, Twentieth Century Fox and Universal had all created their own subsidiaries to trade in the same three markets UA Classics had successfully targeted: rereleases from the companies' libraries; arthouse fare originating outside the US; and low-budget pictures from the booming US independent sector. Despite the fact that none of these companies lasted for more than three years, as they experienced similar problems as UA Classics with their respective parent companies, they none the less contributed some of the most significant early contemporary independent films, such as *Purple Haze* (D. Burton Morris, 1982, Triumph), *Eating Raoul* (P. Bartel, 1982, Twentieth Century Fox International Classics) and *Repo Man* (A. Cox, 1985, Universal Classics). And, like UA Classics, they also successfully released some very well-known arthouse films, such as *Danton* (A. Wajda, 1983, Triumph), *Piaf* [*Piaf: The Early Years*] (G. Casaril, 1974, Twentieth Century Fox International Classics) and *La Traviata* (F. Zeffirelli, 1982, Universal Classics). The short lifespan of these companies has led film critics to disregard them in the writing of the history of contemporary American independent cinema, with most studies ignoring them or, at best, making only passing references. In this respect, this chapter represents a first effort towards a thorough examination of their business practices and their exact position in the American film industry.

## TRIUMPH FILMS

Chronologically, Triumph Films was the second 'classics' arm to be established in the early 1980s. However, unlike United Artists Classics and the rest of its contemporaries, Triumph was not exactly a subsidiary of a major – in this case, Columbia. Rather, it represented a joint venture between Columbia and French major film producer, distributor and exhibitor Gaumont, which means that it was established primarily to serve the interests of a strategic alliance between two international diversified entertainment conglomerates. The foundation for this alliance was the development of a platform for the commercial exploitation in the North American market of European arthouse films, which, following the success of *The Last Metro* and *Diva*, had convinced distribution companies anew that the market in question had a potential for substantial profits. In this respect, and at that particular time, the collaboration between Columbia and Gaumont made perfect sense, with the French partner providing the 'right' films for the American market, and the US partner providing the infrastructure and resources to push them in the market. As Charles Schreger, Columbia executive and head of the new venture put it on the company's formation in February 1982, 'it's always been thought that the mainstay of the foreign-filmgoing population [in the US] is French film, and the industry there is in very good shape'.[1]

Such a collaboration, then, would stand to put Triumph Films in pole position in the art film distribution market, given that it could count on a steady supply of films from Gaumont, whose earlier films, such as *Cousin cousine* (J. C. Tacchella, 1975), had become commercial successes in the US. Furthermore, and very importantly, the Gaumont–Columbia alliance would not preclude Triumph Films from looking for negative pick-ups (films financed and produced by independent companies without prior distribution arrangements, which are acquired for distribution by a releasing organisation) outside Gaumont (or France for that matter), therefore giving the new distributor the necessary flexibility to determine its own roster of titles.[2] Finally, and equally importantly, despite the early emphasis on non-US product and the absence of rereleases from Columbia's library of titles, Triumph's mission statement as a company formed to 'distribute and produce motion pictures for specialised markets in the US, as well as for all other media, including pay TV and the home video markets', clearly placed it alongside companies such as UA Classics and made the distribution of US-originated films a matter of time.[3]

Even more than UA Classics and *The Last Metro*, Triumph Films enjoyed an extraordinarily successful start with the release of the German film *Das Boot*, by Wolfgang Petersen. The most expensive film ever to be shot in West Germany at the time and telling the story of life in a German submarine at the peak of World War Two,[4] *Das Boot*, seemingly, had few points of contact with the intellectual arthouse films of renowned European auteurs like Truffaut, Wajda and Bertolucci. However, its emphasis on the meticulous details of life in the submarine, complete with long sections when no action takes place and the overall deglorifying of heroism in war, made this otherwise genre film look far removed from the extremely popular action-war films that had a similar subject and were associated with Hollywood, such as *Run Silent, Run Deep* (R. Wise, 1958).

Given these features, its long running time (150 minutes) and the fact that the dialogue was in German, the producers of the film decided that it should open in platform release in the specialised foreign language film market, in the hope of generating positive word of mouth that would allow it to expand in the rest of the country and potentially become a crossover success. In this respect, it was decided that Triumph Films, rather than Columbia, was the right vehicle for the release of the film in the North American market. With a marketing campaign that focused on the film's 'must see' status (given its huge success in West Germany), its evident generic attractions, and its historical value as a document of life on 'the other side of World War II' (as the film's tagline pronounced), Triumph opened the film under its original title *Das Boot* in two theatres in New York City with very positive results.[5] Following this, the film opened in other metropolitan areas in the US and Canada, shattering records and becoming, by the end of its run, the most commercially successful foreign film in the history of the North American market, taking approximately $11 million gross. The film's box-office success was accompanied by rave reviews and a number of accolades, including six Academy Award nominations.

This auspicious start was further supplemented by good results for the other Triumph releases in 1982 that included more 'conventional' European arthouse films, such as the rerelease of Jean-Pierre Melville's *Bob le flambeur* [*Bob the Gambler*] (originally released in 1956), Jean-Claude Tramont's *Le Point de mire* [*The Photographer*] and Moshe Misrahi's *La Vie continue* [*Life Goes On*]. However, the company's other most important early release was Turkish filmmaker Yilmaz Güney's *Yol* [*The Road*] (co-directed with Serif Gören). Based on Güney's escape from prison in Turkey and his flight from that country, the film received a large number of festival awards, including the Palme d'Or in Cannes (tied with Costa Gavras's *Missing*). Although the film did not become a box-office success, the acquisition of such a celebrated arthouse film by Triumph confirmed, in the eyes of the major arthouse producers and filmmakers, the new company's status as a key player in the specialised market. Furthermore, the overall financial performance of the venture in its first year was also enough to convince Columbia and Gaumont to bankroll its 'continued expansion' throughout late 1982 and early 1983, which was part and parcel of an extremely ambitious distribution line-up of twelve films for 1983.[6]

Indeed, these plans – ambitious for such a newly established company – were realised with the release of ten features during 1983. Once again, French films from Gaumont and other arthouse producers dominated the release schedule, the most prominent being Andrzej Wajda's epic *Danton* and Jean-Jacques Beineix's *La Lune dans le caniveau* [*The Moon in the Gutter*], both starring Gérard Depardieu. Interestingly, both Wajda and Beineix signed with Triumph Films, despite the fact that their respective previous films had been successfully released by UA Classics, which clearly suggests the level of competition Triumph provided for United Artists' classics division as well as for the other independent outfits that saw a second studio subsidiary competing for the same product.

Despite the dominance of international film titles, Triumph and its US parent had been 'anxious' to add 'American independent films' to their release schedule, and its staff had been actively examining the sector 'for the right film in the right quality by a film maker in nascent form'.[7] Finally, over a year after its formation, Triumph announced in April 1983 that it would distribute *Purple Haze* by David Burton Morris, a film that had won the Grand Jury Prize at the US Film Festival in January of the same year (see Case Study). Triumph's involvement with Morris, who had been an active player in the establishment of the Independent Feature Project in the late 1970s and early 1980s,[8] also meant close contact with the booming independent film sector for future releases.[9]

However, despite this impressive level of activity, the first problems did not take long to appear. In September 1983, eighteen months after the division was established, it was revealed that Triumph Films had been operating at a loss of $3 million.[10] Arguably more importantly, there seemed to be great dissatisfaction on behalf of the French parent over the way the division operated, especially in terms of its marketing policy, which, for Gaumont, was the main reason behind the deficit. At the epicentre of Gaumont's discontent was Triumph's (and Columbia's) inability to market the French films effectively in the North American market, despite having at its disposal substantial budgets for its marketing campaigns.[11] With Columbia having just its relatively small distribution investment to lose – therefore much less than Gaumont, who also invested in film production – the French partner's position in the Triumph venture did not make economic sense, unless there was greater penetration of its films into the American market. To this end, and along with a demand for Columbia to utilise their resources more effectively, Gaumont arranged to participate in all marketing decisions and asked for a 'major shift' in its partner's practices 'from hard-sell marketing to European-oriented low profile distribution' models.[12] The latter would entail more nuanced and product-specific marketing campaigns, which would allow non-US films time to assert themselves in the specialty film marketplace and therefore not to be abandoned if their results in the opening weekend were not as anticipated.

Despite this major problem, the two sides reached a compromise and the division was allowed to continue with yet another ambitious programme of releases for 1984 that included films by some of the best-known European auteurs, such as Ingmar Bergman (*After the Rehearsal*) and Federico Fellini (*And the Ship Sails On*), as well as new European filmmakers who would go on to forge an extremely successful career in later years, such as Neil Jordan (*Angel*) and Luc Besson (*The Last Battle*).[13] However, reports of more problems between Gaumont and Columbia over the financial performance of Triumph Films resurfaced towards the end of 1984, causing the first restructuring at the top level of the division, with the removal of Schreger from the presidency of the company.[14]

From that point on, Triumph's history had more to do with its parent companies' corporate battles than with cinema, as the subsidiary would release only four more films in 1985. Indeed, as early as February 1985, the trade press was reporting that the 'specialty film division ha[d] been phased out', despite Columbia's reassurance that it was 'alive and well' but still undergoing restructuring.[15] It would not be until early summer 1985 that the company announced the distribution of new product, which included two French films (one of which was a Gaumont production), two Italian films (including Lina Wertmuller's *Sotto . . . Sotto*) and, last but not least, Jean-Luc Godard's controversial update of the Virgin Mary story *Je vous, salue, Marie* [*Hail, Mary*].[16] However, only the first four releases materialised, as Triumph was forced to offload Godard's picture after reported pressure from Catholic groups on Columbia.[17]

In July of the same year and following the news that both Universal and Twentieth Century Fox had decided to close their respective classics arms, Columbia finally admitted the possibility of phasing out Triumph Films, despite decreasing competition for the subsidiary.[18] Part of the reason for the potential closure was the increasing realisation that foreign films, predominantly the company's forte, were still finding it difficult to break into the US market, despite occasional box-office successes.[19] This was especially important as, at the same time, English-language 'arthouse' films – including, of course, homegrown independent features like *Choose Me* (A. Rudolph, 1984, Island), *The Kiss of the Spider Woman* (H. Babenco, 1985, Island / Alive) and *The Gods Must Be Crazy* (J. Uys, 1984, Twentieth Century Fox International Classics) – had started to find increasing success at the box office. In this respect, and amidst the uncertainty surrounding its future, Triumph Films changed its mission statement by announcing 'a shift of emphasis in which "intelligent and thoughtful" English language pick-ups [would] receive priority'.[20]

This change of emphasis clearly confirms how far independent film had come in terms of visibility since the initial outburst of activity in the late 1970s / early 1980s, an achievement that the classics divisions' executives could not fail to see. However, despite the re-adjustment of its plans, Triumph signed no new deals. Shortly after the announcement of its new policy, and approximately three years since its establishment, Gaumont decided to pull out of the venture. Given Triumph's scaling-back on foreign film distribution, Gaumont's move was hardly surprising, especially as, for them, Triumph had been a 'loss making venture', despite the release of fifteen of the most commercial films Gaumont had ever produced.[21] With the French partner out of the picture by October 1985, Columbia's response was immediate. On 1 November, the major announced that Triumph Films would be absorbed by Columbia's classics division, a generic division that co-existed with Triumph Films at Columbia but which had focused exclusively on 'revival and retrospective programs'.[22] By that time, the Columbia–Gaumont venture had distributed twenty-six feature films in total, with *Purple Haze* remaining the only US independent film it released.

The preponderance of non-US films in Triumph's release schedules can partly explain why this particular division has been ignored in histories of American independent cinema. On the other hand, though, like UA Classics and the other three classics divisions of the 1980s, Triumph Films found itself operating at a time that trends in film distribution were shifting and therefore attempted to jump on to the emergent American independent cinema bandwagon, as its late 'shift in emphasis' clearly demonstrates. Irrespective of the fact that it released just one independent feature, it also contributed to the creation of an infrastructure for independent films.

## UNIVERSAL CLASSICS

Three months after the establishment of Triumph Films, in May 1982, Universal became the latest major to unveil its own classics arm, Universal Classics. Like its two principal competitors, Universal's subsidiary would also focus on the restoration and rerelease of classic films from Universal's library of titles (as well as from pre-1948 Paramount films, the rights of which were also owned by Universal and its parent company MCA) and on the 'acquisition of films for art, repertory, and revival houses'.[23] Despite its efforts to compete in all the main markets that characterised niche distribution in the early to mid-1980s, Universal Classics lived up to its name, arguably more than any other classics arm, by focusing on often extremely successful rereleases of old film titles, including five films by legendary Hollywood director Alfred Hitchcock. In this respect, its contribution to the development of American independent cinema was minimal, especially as the company turned out to have the shortest lifespan of all early specialty labels, lasting a little over two-and-a-half years.

Despite Universal Classics' substantial focus on rereleases, the division was originally conceived with a view to target 'cinema far and wide'. In the words of its first senior executive, Ben Cammack, 'we're not just interested in a backlog of Universal product but films that require a personal sort of attention and which we can treat individually.'[24] The reason for the establishment of the division was the realisation that there were numerous niche markets that had not been served to capacity and would therefore welcome additional product, if that product was 'right' and was marketed in the 'appropriate' way for the markets in question. Again, in the words of the division's senior executive, 'we're not going Broadway with this program but hitting markets on a localized basis, trying to find the right theatres and the exhibitor commitment.'[25]

The first of the niche markets that Universal Classics successfully targeted was the rock music film, through the rerelease of the Beatles' *A Hard Day's Night* (R. Lester, 1964). Originally distributed by United Artists at the peak of the band's global success, the rights for the film (and for the next Beatles film, *Help!* [R. Lester, 1965]) had reverted to producer Walter Shenson, whose production company had coproduced both titles. Given the continuing popularity of the Beatles' music over a decade since the band's split and, especially, after John Lennon's murder in December 1980, Shenson decided that this was a good time for the films to be rereleased in search of new audiences. Equally importantly, he decided to rerelease the films with remixed sound, taking advantage of the Dolby Stereo Sound System that had been introduced in American cinema in the mid-1970s and had been popularised with George Lucas's *Star Wars* (1977). Such new, enhanced prints would appeal not only to the fans of the band, who would stand to enjoy the vastly improved sound of many classic Beatles songs, but also, arguably more importantly, to 'a whole new audience that ha[d] never been exposed to the Beatles'.[26] In this respect, it made sense for Shenson to seek specialised distribution for the two titles (only *A Hard Day's Night* was eventually rereleased) to ensure that they would be marketed in such a way as to appeal to both of these very different demographics.

After a second successful reissue, this time of the meticulously restored version of Abel Gance's silent film *Napoleon* (1927), Universal Classics completed its first six months of operation with the release of its first contemporary title, Polish filmmaker Jerzy Skolimowski's partly English-language film, *Moonlighting* (1982). The film, which tells the story of four Polish men stranded in London when the military regime declares martial law in Poland and having to work in difficult conditions, had fared well at the 1982 Cannes Film Festival, where it had won an award for Best Screenplay. To enhance the possibility of commercial success, Universal Classics readily borrowed marketing techniques associated with arthouse filmmaking, including inviting Skolimowski and the film's star, Jeremy Irons, to a press conference in New York City; in addition, the poster for the film focused readily on Irons, whose arthouse star status was on the rise following his participation in the celebrated BBC series *Brideshead Revisited*, as well as on the film's success at Cannes.

The success of *Moonlighting* in arthouse film circles convinced Universal to support its classics arm further. In February 1983, Universal Classics was awarded 'divisional status' by its parent company in what became the first of a series of restructuring efforts to position the company best in the specialised film marketplace.[27] Although this move saw Universal Classics vying to establish a distinct identity within the Universal Motion Picture Group, several areas of business, especially marketing and distribution, remained with big sister Universal. According to the division's new head, James L. Katz, Universal Classics would be 'set up almost like a separate branch', which would none the less be controlled by the same computer system that was utilised by the major. (This was different from the situation at UA Classics, originally established complete with its own computer system before internal restructuring brought the subsidiary more into line with its parent company in the final two years of its history – see Chapter 1.)[28]

Under its new senior executive, Universal Classics attempted to create a more dynamic presence in the three key sectors in which it traded. A core strategy for the division was to establish its status more firmly with exhibitors as a modern 'classics' arm, and not just as a company that tended to specialise in rereleases. Thus, despite the fact that, for the early months of 1983, the company's focus was yet again on the reissuing of classic Hollywood films (this time a package of films by writer–director–producer Preston Sturges),[29] Katz embarked on a mission to make Universal Classics known as a 'funnel for material that normally would not come into the company at all'.[30] However, unlike UA Classics and Triumph Films, Universal Classics took the approach of avoiding the film festival circuit, and therefore potentially expensive bidding wars, privileging instead an 'open door' policy whereby filmmakers could bring both scripts and finished films to the company for consideration.[31] Furthermore, and in order to continue being able to count on the support of Universal and MCA, the newly structured Universal Classics had to keep costs tight and to seek the most efficient ways of taking its niche films in the marketplace. One way to achieve this objective was to convince independent and arthouse exhibitors that, despite the support of its sister company and the financial breadth of its parent company, Universal Classics' distribution budget was on a par with the other companies operating in the arthouse market. In this respect, exhibitors would have to share some of the advertising costs (also known as co-op ad costs), as was the practice with independent distributors and the other classics divisions. In Katz's words:

We'll impress (upon exhibitors) that we are not Universal as they know it. We're not selling 'E.T.' and we're not overspending. The economics are not the same. Because we're MCA, people might take advantage and think we'll spend more than we would.[32]

It is clear, then, that Universal Classics shared a number of features with the rest of the classics divisions but was also playing the niche film distribution game in slightly different ways from its competitors.

The new Universal Classics regime started business with significant success, releasing the film adaptation of Verdi's *La Traviata*. Directed by renowned Italian auteur Franco Zeffirelli and starring Plácido Domingo, the film attracted sustained business, spending twenty-six weeks in the box-office charts and grossing $3.6 million.[33] This level of success, however, was not maintained by the rest of the company's releases for the year, with the Australian *Puberty Blues* (B. Beresford) and Costa-Gavras's *Hanna K.* grossing less than $250,000 each and Merchant–Ivory's production, *Heat and Dust*, also failing to attract significant arthouse audiences.[34]

Despite these failures, which took place throughout 1983, Universal Classics did manage to attract a number of projects that, on paper at least, had much more potential for profit than the aforementioned titles. In a policy-breaking move, the division bought two promising properties from the 1983 Cannes Film Festival: Jean Becker's *L'Été meurtrier* [*One Deadly Summer*], starring top French star Isabel Adjani, and Nagisa Ôshima's *Merry Christmas Mr Lawrence*, with David Bowie in the lead. Both films had attracted considerable attention when they were nominated for the Palme d'Or and had won several awards in their respective countries of production, France and Japan. Ôshima's film, in particular, was perceived as a property possessing several characteristics that would allow for crossover success,[35] including the presence of a well-known auteur, a rock superstar playing against type (David Bowie), a music score from Ryûichi Sakamoto that received rave reviews, and the type of subject matter – the cultural differences between West and East – that could attract a large audience. However, despite a strong marketing campaign that focused firmly on Bowie's starring role in the film and on the clash of cultures, and notwithstanding good results in platform release, the film did not attract the expected business when it expanded wide; just nine weeks after its release, it disappeared from the theatres, with a disappointing box-office gross totalling just $2.3 million.

However, before the box-office flop that was *Merry Christmas*, Universal Classics had announced arguably its most commercially promising property, the adaptation of Malcolm Lowry's celebrated novel *Under the Volcano* by legendary Hollywood filmmaker John Huston and with the participation of such stars as Albert Finney and Jacqueline Bisset. The film signalled the entry of

Universal Classics – and of any of the early classics divisions, for that matter – into the business of US independent film finance, the division agreeing to provide the majority of the film's $5 million budget in exchange for North American distribution rights. *Under the Volcano* was considered by Universal Classics' executives as 'the crowning touch to [their] division' and as a project that the company had to 'get involved in early', especially as the Mexican government was lining up effectively as co-producer, providing substantial funds and resources for the film.[36]

Besides flagging up yet another difference from the other early classics divisions, Universal Classics' involvement with a film at such an early stage heralded a particularly important moment in the history of independent filmmaking in the US. Independent film had generally been understood as a mode of filmmaking that sought finance from sources outside the Hollywood majors (and their subsidiaries) and / or other entertainment conglomerates like the television networks and cable stations. In this respect, Universal Classics' entry into film finance (with the support of Universal) represents a major shift in terms of what can be considered 'independent' filmmaking, and therefore can be been as largely responsible for the problems film critics have encountered in their efforts to provide a definition for it within the US cinema context. As the next two sections of this book will demonstrate, companies involved in the other two waves that we can discern in relation to studio divisions from the 1990s onwards took this model of 'independent' filmmaking to the next level, ushering American independent cinema into the 'indie' era.

Although Universal Classics' involvement with film finance signalled a particularly significant moment for the company and for independent filmmaking in general, it was also another move that militated against the company's efforts to build up an identity that was distinct from Universal. Furthermore, in an interview with the British trade publication *Screen International*, Katz identified himself, first and foremost, as a Universal executive and then as the head of its classics arm, stating:

> [W]e're trying to develop a talent pool – trying to get people to come to the studio who normally would not come here because they maybe think we just deal in mass marketing and exploitation product ... We've got a lot of really talented people in here, not just coming to us with the $20 million and $30 million movies (although we have them and we do very well with them). But we're also getting involved with the million-dollar movies.[37]

Claiming that he would be avoiding the festivals but buying two 1983 Golden Palm nominees; seeking to keep costs down but financing a $5 million project; expressing an interest in $30 million projects but also in $1 million pictures – it is not difficult to see that Universal Classics suffered from lack of a coherent strategy under Katz's managerial regime. Add to this the disappointing box-office receipts of *Merry Christmas Mr Lawrence* and it is not surprising to learn that the division's next move was to return to reissues of classic films, the one area in which it had recorded sustained success. This time, the classics were five 'lost' Hitchcock films, *Rear Window* (1954), *Vertigo* (1958), *Rope* (1948), *The Man Who Knew Too Much* (1956) and *The Trouble With Harry* (1955), some of which had been out of circulation since their original release.[38] By the time the first of these films, *Rear Window*, was rereleased, Universal Classics was in the process of changing its management team for the second time. In this respect, it was Kelly Neal who oversaw the distribution of these titles at the end of 1983 and the beginning of the following year. By April 1984, the five pictures had grossed over $12 million, *Rear Window* and *Vertigo* claiming the lion's share with box-office receipts of more than $10 million between them.[39]

The success of the Hitchcock films, however, turned out to be an exceptional case in the financial performance of the division, renamed Universal Special Projects in May 1984. The name change, intended to remove 'the classics tag'[40] (a trend initiated by Twentieth Century Fox International Classics – see below) and reposition the division anew in the contemporary niche film market, represented yet another contradictory decision, especially as, at the same time, Universal Classics was enjoying the huge success of the 'classic' Hitchcock reissues. Furthermore, the newly named division saw big sister Universal taking over the distribution of *Under the Volcano*, which was to become another box-office failure, taking only $2.5 million from its theatrical release.[41] Universal Special Projects did some good box-office business with Alex Cox's *Repo Man*, which Universal had distributed with disappointing results and which the division relaunched a few months later, rather as UA Classics had rescued *Cutter's Way* (see Chapter 1).[42] On the other hand, the delayed release of *One Deadly Summer* (finally released over a year after the signing of the distribution deal) failed to produce positive results.

Given the problematic financial performance of the division, it is not surprising that in November 1984 Universal decided to close it. As it was reported in the trade press, there was considerable friction between Universal and its classics arm, especially as the major seemed to interfere in the operations of the smaller division. In this respect, Universal's distribution takeover of *Under the Volcano*; its decision to opt for a mainstream release for films that were originally deemed more suitable for specialised distribution, such as *Comfort and Joy* (B. Forsyth, 1984); and its move to revoke Universal Special Projects' bookings without notifying the division, all created tension between the management of the two organisations.[43]

Following the decision that the division would fold, Universal announced that the distribution of both specialised films and classic Hollywood pictures would be handled by the major's main distribution operations arm. Despite its 'diametrically opposed' approach to distribution, Universal claimed that its marketing team would be in a position to handle specialised projects equally well as their failed division. However, the handful of such pictures in 1985, including *James Joyce's Women* (M. Pearce) and *Dreamchild* (G. Millar), failed to reach an audience, the former grossing just over $8,000 in a sole engagement.[44] In this respect, Universal Classics turned out to be the least influential classics division, not only in the field of US independent filmmaking, but in the specialised film market in general, despite initiating the practice of financing 'independent' pictures.

## TWENTIETH CENTURY FOX INTERNATIONAL FILM CLASSICS

The final Hollywood major to establish a classics arm was Twentieth Century Fox, under the long name Twentieth Century Fox International Classics (TCFIC). Formed at more or less the same time as Universal Classics in May 1982, the division's primary focus was the arthouse market. However, unlike the rest of the classics discussed so far, TCFIC concentrated on English-language films, primarily ones originating outside the US from countries like the UK, South Africa and Australia. As a matter of fact, the division distributed the most commercially successful film of all the classics of the 1980s, the South African comedy *The Gods Must Be Crazy* (J. Uys, 1980 [1984]), which grossed an astonishing $30 million from its theatrical release.[45] It also contributed one of the most successful US independent films of the early 1980s, Paul Bartel's *Eating Raoul*.[46]

Like Triumph Films, TCFIC entered the marketplace in mid-1982 with a number of films ready for release. These included *The Chosen* (J. Kagan), a film with significant star power in the form of Rod Steiger and Maximilian Schell, distributed by Fox in the major markets; a Bill Cosby 'special', written, produced and directed by Cosby himself; *Gospel* (D. Leivick and F. Ritzenberg), a live-concert film distributed in collaboration with the recently formed independent company, Miramax Films; Australian film *The Man from the Snowy River* (G. Miller), featuring, among others, Hollywood star Kirk Douglas;[47] *Piaf* (G. Casaril) from France, unreleased in the US since it had appeared in France in 1974 but reconsidered as a commercially promising property at a time when French films were doing good business; and finally, two films from the US independent sector, the aforementioned *Eating Raoul* and *Threshold*, Richard Pearce's follow-up to *Heartland*, a film widely considered to be one of the key works that kick-started the independent film 'movement' of the early 1980s.[48]

Given this eclectic mix of titles, it was clear from the beginning that Fox's division was targeting the specialised film distribution market by placing particular emphasis on English-language pictures that would be easier to market than the subtitled fare that often met with resistance from audiences. As an executive at Fox put it, the division was established:

> to 'diversify' the Fox release schedule with features from independent and Canadian producers and films from abroad that are designed for selective audiences. International Classics will also include release of films from Fox archives in both retrospective and regular commercial houses.[49]

Although none of the division's early films proved a commercial success (with the exception of *The Man from Snowy River*, which was none the less eventually handled by Fox),[50] TCFIC made enough noise in the marketplace to attract the attention of independent film producers. Besides attracting young filmmakers and their low-budget films, like Bartel and Pearce, TCFIC also attracted 'top-rank independent producers' who traded in prestige films that, more often than not, were also accompanied by high budgets.[51] One such producer was Sam Spiegel, who had contributed some of the best-known, top-rank independent films in the US cinema of the 1950s and 1960s, including *The African Queen* (J. Huston, 1951) and *The Bridge on the River Kwai* (D. Lean, 1957). Spiegel, whose last big production was *Nicholas and Alexandra* (F. J. Schaffner, 1971), had produced an adaptation of Harold Pinter's play *Betrayal*, with rising stars Jeremy Irons and Ben Kingsley, and with Pinter himself having written the screenplay. However, lacking the blockbusting qualities of the above titles, *Betrayal* came much closer to an arthouse aesthetic and featured a narrative that unfolded in reverse order, with the opening scene being the last one in the chronology of the story and with each subsequent scene going further and further back in the protagonists' past. In this respect, the film was potentially a difficult sell outside the arthouse theatre circuit in 1983, despite the fact that it attracted rave reviews from critics.[52]

By the summer of 1983, the early performance of TCFIC was deemed satisfactory enough for Twentieth Century Fox Entertainment to merit lending further support to the division. In August of that year, it was reported that the company would 'expand its scope', both in terms of acquisition of completed films and in terms of film financing, following the lead of its competitor Universal Classics, which had announced its financing of *Under the Volcano* only a few weeks earlier. However, unlike Universal Classics, which focused primarily on a single prestige production, the Fox division entered into partnerships on a number of projects, acting mainly as co-financer in exchange for distribution rights. By the end of 1983, TCFIC was backing at least four properties, including *Stone Boy* (C. Cain, 1984), with Hollywood stars Robert Duvall and Glenn Close; *The Secret Diary of Sigmund Freud* (D. B. Greene, 1984), with Bud Cort, Carol Kane and Klaus Kinski; *Joshua, Then and Now* (T. Kotcheff, 1985), with James Woods; and *Death of an Angel* (P. Popesku, 1986), developed at the Sundance Film Institute.[53] Add two negative pick-ups with a number of commercial elements – *Ziggy Stardust and the Spiders from Mars*, D. A Pennebaker's concert-film capturing David Bowie's last performance in his Ziggy Stardust persona in 1973, and *Marvin and Tige* (E. Weston), featuring John Cassavetes and Billy Dee Williams in the main roles – and it is clear that Fox's division was concentrating on the specialised English-language film market and doing so with some panache.

In this respect, one could argue that TCFIC functioned as the prototype for the companies that became part of the next two specialty film division waves, and especially the third wave from the mid- to late 1990s onwards (see Section III). These were companies that focused as much on production as on the acquisition of completed US or English-speaking films with clear commercial elements and selling points, especially star power, that could propel them (arguably) more effectively to crossover success and from there into profitability.

Given the division's decision to focus on this particular sector of the specialised film market, and despite the fact that its release schedule also featured a small number of reissues of films from its archives, including the celebrated restoration and rerelease of Lucchino Visconti's *The Leopard* (1963 [1983]),[54] Fox took the decision to change the division's name to Twentieth Century Fox Specialized Film Division (TCFSFD). For Fox, the classics label seemed primarily to have signified the company's activity in the reissues market, which, of course, was a secondary consideration, given the direction the division had been following from the mid-1983 onwards.[55] Indeed, the company's management unveiled plans for further investment in no fewer than ten properties, primarily from the US and Australia, covering the period from September 1983 to February 1985.[56]

Under its new name, the division started to implement its business plan with a strong push to turn the film *Reuben Reuben* (R. E. Miller) into a crossover hit. The film had opened to great success in December 1983 but when it was nominated for two Academy Awards early in 1984 for Best Actor (Tom Conti) and Best Screenplay (veteran Hollywood screenwriter Julius Epstein), TCFSFD decided to test it in two key markets to see whether its success could be sustained on wider release. Despite a strong performance in both these markets, the advertising costs for a nationwide campaign proved prohibitive and the film therefore continued to play on a small number of screens only. Still, it turned out to be the division's most commercially successful film up until that time.[57]

In March of the same year, the division changed its name yet again, this time to the shorter and catchier Tender Loving Care Films (or TLC Films), and continued its policy of looking for English-language films from around the world. These included two Australian productions, *Man of Flowers* (P. Cox, 1984) and *Careful, He Might Hear You* (K. Schultz, 1984). Interestingly, though, TLC made an exception when it secured the distribution rights to *Nankyoku Monogatari [Antarctica]* (K. Kurahara), a Japanese family movie that had recorded an extraordinary $50 million at the box office in Japan but which did not succeed in finding an audience in the US. However, the division was fortunate enough to offset all its losses with the release of the South African film *The Gods Must Be Crazy*, which chronicles the adventures of a Bushman who, in his efforts to return a coke bottle to the gods, finds himself encountering 'civilisation' for the first time, with all the comic consequences that come from this interaction. Having been a resounding success in a number of countries, the film opened in a sole engagement in New York in July 1984. Good reviews and strong word of mouth created sustained business for the film, which eventually played for over a year and a half and in no more than 185 theatres. It eventually became the most successful non-US film to be released in the country, with a final box-office gross of a little under $30 million.[58]

While *The Gods Must Be Crazy* had started to demonstrate its potential and durability in US theatres in early 1985, TLC Films, like many of its competitors, had found itself in the middle of a series of corporate manœuvres that, with hindsight, signalled the beginning of the demise of the division. The starting point was a change of ownership at the parent company of Twentieth Century Fox and TLC Films – Fox, Inc. – when new owner Rupert Murdoch placed former Paramount senior executive Barry Diller in charge of the company's Film Entertainment Group (which included both the major and the specialty label) in October 1984. Diller's plans for the group did not include TLC Films, despite the fact that, according to the President of Distribution at Fox, it was 'a profit-making division'.[59] In light of Diller's decision to dispose of TLC Films, the classics' senior executive Peter Myers tried to spin the division off, not as a stand-alone independent but as a Fox 'satellite' that would be responsible for its own finance and production but would have a distribution tie to the parent company. Despite intense negotiations,[60] the spinoff of TLC Films did not take place. In April 1985, almost three years after its establishment, Fox announced that TLC Films would cease operations, with all its properties passing to the major for distribution. However, releases of specialised films, such as *Key Exchange* (Kellman, 1985) and especially Kotcheff's *Joshua, Then and Now*, which took place after the dismantling of the division, failed miserably at the box office.

## FAILED EXPERIMENTS OR VICTIMS OF CORPORATE POLITICS?

As is clear from the above accounts, none of these three divisions enjoyed the sustained support of their parent companies or big sister distributors. This begs the question of whether these classics arms were really failed experiments or whether they were victims of corporate politics and of the uncertainty and reluctance with which the major studios approached specialty film. If we judge the financial performance of these companies, none of them performed spectacularly well. Triumph had been a money-losing enterprise from the start, given its propensity to spend handsomely on marketing. However, Triumph was not a true classics arm, as it had the support of a major film company outside Hollywood and therefore took a different approach to the distribution business. The Universal and Fox divisions, on the other hand, performed reasonably well, the former's Hitchcock rereleases offsetting a number of box office failures, and the latter's *The Gods Must Be Crazy* breaking all box-office records for specialised film and also possibly covering the substantial losses that the division's other releases might have incurred. In this respect, the last two divisions at least cannot be seen to have failed.

What is strikingly obvious from the accounts of these divisions, however, is the fact that all three of them had to face a large degree of interference from the top management of the corporations to which they belonged, and especially from their major sister companies. With the divisions' executives removed and replaced on a regular basis, the sister companies taking credit for crossover hits (Fox for *The Man from the Snowy River*) or claiming playdates originally allocated to the classics arms as their own (Universal and the removal of *Repo Man* from the theatres), with changes of corporate regime at the very top automatically initiating a review of the company's assets, including the classics arms, it is clear that these divisions never enjoyed the support of the higher echelons of the entertainment conglomerates under whose umbrella they had been operating. This is especially true because the Hollywood majors' distribution and marketing methods were very different from the practices of the independents and the classics arms. In this respect, unless these divisions were spectacular performers financially, they were deemed to be liabilities rather more than assets and were the first to go, especially when new ownership or management structures were introduced. The lack of support and constant interference from the top also meant that it was extremely difficult for these companies to find their place in the market and to develop a distinct corporate identity. Triumph and Universal Classics, in particular, changed focus midway, opting to distance themselves from non-US film distribution and concentrate instead on English-language film, with little success.

Given their short lifespan and the few American independent releases they handled, the impact of these divisions on the incipient contemporary independent film sector has been relatively minor. However, it was they who initiated a number of key practices that later became the cornerstone of the more successful studio divisions in the 1990s and 2000s, especially the decision to finance 'independent' film production; as we shall see in Sections II and III, this changed the name of the game and ushered in a new phase in independent cinema. In this sense, their importance cannot be overstated.

### Case Study: *Purple Haze* (David Burton Morris, 1983, Triumph Films)

*Purple Haze* was the only contribution to the field of American independent film made by Triumph Films. Despite a number of candidates being examined after the inception of the subsidiary in February 1982, it was not until a year later that Triumph found 'the right film of the right quality' to take this step.[61] Only a month earlier, the film had won the Grand Prize at the USA Film and Video Festival in Park City, Utah, and 'had generated quite a buzz' among studio executives, including Columbia's President of Marketing and Research, who thought that the film was not 'just another one of those films about the '60s'.[62] With its parent company anxious to 'release some American independent films', Triumph's senior executive Charles Schreger decided to make the distribution deal.

The film differs from a number of others released in the late 1970s and early 1980s, which either looked back to the 1960s with nostalgia (*Grease 2* [P. Birch, 1982], *More American Graffiti* [B. L. Norton, 1979]) or used the period as little more than background for the unfolding of a coming-of-age narrative (*Four Friends* [A. Penn, 1981]). Indeed, *Purple Haze* reverses these trends by avoiding both sentimentality and nostalgia, while its own coming-of-age narrative – a college student is thrown out for smoking marijuana, goes back to his small-town home where he does not fit in, is drafted for Vietnam but at the last moment changes his mind and hijacks the bus that was supposed to take him to the barracks, the end of the film leaving his fate unclear – is as much a focal point as are the time and place in which it unfolds.

Morris manages to achieve this effect through a combination of techniques that include a number of shots of the hippy communities of the 1960s, which the filmmaker has processed to achieve a grainy, semi-documentary aesthetic,[63] and which could easily be perceived as archival footage, giving the film a quality that is missing from other, 'cleaner' films about the era; a number of tracking shots of considerable duration, which take place to the accompaniment of classic songs of the era ('A Whiter Side of Pale', 'Are you Experienced?') and which allow the combination of music and image to express ideas, feelings and issues in a way that dialogue can rarely pull off; and whole sequences of narrative events where the music of the time becomes so prominent that takes over the role of narration, becoming the primary agent through which the story world is communicated to the spectator. As the filmmaker admitted, he knew in advance which songs he wanted to use and therefore 'designed the shots to let the music carry the scene'.[64] These techniques, alongside the filmmaker's celebrated stylistic choices for the film's climax – an extremely long shot and take in which the hero tries to avoid being sent to Vietnam and 'gets lost' in the immense fields of Minnesota to the sound of Hendrix's 'Star-Spangled Banner', give the film a very particular energy and feel. These effects are not entirely dissimilar to the ones evoked by one of the most celebrated American independent films of the 1960s, *Easy Rider*: another film in which the rock soundtrack plays an immense part in the picture's critical, commercial and cultural success.

Although *Purple Haze* contains a number of classic rock songs by iconic bands of the 1960s, such as Jefferson Airplane, Cream, Steppenwolf, The Animals and many others, the film was made for just $225,000, a figure that did not cover the cost of the rights to use any of these classic songs. Following its participation in Deauville and London film festivals, Morris and his co-screenwriter Victoria Wozniak raised an additional $250,000 to pay for these rights,[65] ensuring that the film would stand a chance of being distributed commercially. Morris had already mixed the songs with the film, which means that, if he had not been granted the rights, he would either have had to change the music (making for a different picture) or not been able to release the film at all.

Its success at the USA Film Festival gave *Purple Haze* much greater visibility in the film community. Morris wanted his film to be released by a major or by a major's subsidiary, hoping to achieve as wide a distribution as possible, and this is why he agreed to sign with Triumph Films. The distributor predictably focused its marketing on the film's music, making the names of the featured bands prominent on the film poster, as well as playing on the evocative qualities of the phrase 'purple haze' with reference to drugs, peace and the counter-culture. According to Morris, the filmmakers were not involved in the marketing process at all and the distributor refused to release an accompanying soundtrack with ten songs from the movie, as was often the case with mainstream films that featured a large number of songs, even though the costs would have been a fraction of those normally associated with a film soundtrack. With such a lack of support from Triumph, the film did lacklustre business in limited theatrical release, and neither did box-office rentals improve dramatically after Morris managed to convince the classics division to embark on a new campaign mid-release that involved a new poster design and radio advertising.[66] Following this theatrical performance, Triumph and Columbia did not proceed to release the film on video, and the film is still commercially unavailable in digital format today.

If nothing else, the case of *Purple Haze* clearly suggests the limitations of Triumph Films, and of the rest of the short-lived classics arms, in terms of handling specialty film. Having a mandate from the parent company to release American independent pictures, Triumph chose a film that had achieved some visibility following its success in the as yet little-known USA Festival and which contained some commercial elements (the songs) that could be exploited in the marketing process. However, unlike companies such as UA Classics and Orion Classics, which often favoured grassroots approaches to distribution similar to those practised by small independent distribution houses, the case of *Purple Haze* suggests that Triumph possessed neither the experience nor the acumen to place the film correctly in the market; its decision not to release a soundtrack of classic songs to support the theatrical release of Morris's film is certainly questionable, especially as, at the same time as *Purple Haze*, parent company Columbia was using the same formula to great success for one of its key 1983 releases, *The Big Chill*. In the end, Triumph Films remained a company whose purpose was to serve the objectives of the Columbia–Gaumont alliance, and its contribution to American independent film therefore remained minimal.

## NOTES

1. 'Col's Arty Triumph Has French Accent', *Weekly Variety* (3 February 1982), 32.
2. 'New Triumph Veep, Chief of Operations is Mario Anniballi', *Weekly Variety* (8 September 1982), 124.
3. 'McMillan Appointed VP at Triumph', *Hollywood Reporter* (14 March 1983), 3.
4. See the *Das Boot* website, http://www.dasboot.com/original.htm; accessed on 3 October 2010.
5. According to IMDb, the film grossed $27,000 during its opening weekend (http://www.imdb.com/title/tt0082096/business; accessed on 3 October 2010). Later in its run, when it was clear that the film was a success, Triumph released a number of dubbed prints under the English title *The Boat*.
6. 'Juliana Maio Joins Triumph in Veepost', *Daily Variety* (19 January 1983), n/a.
7. Caulfield, Deborah, 'A Domestic Effort Woos Distributor', *Los Angeles Times* (25 April 1983), Section IV: Arts, 1 and 2.
8. Morris, David Burton, independent filmmaker, email interview with the author, 14 September 2010.
9. Franklin, B. J., 'Triumph Team on World-Wide Search for Product', *Screen International* (27 August 1983), 28.
10. 'Col & Gaumont at Odds on Lido; Overcoming U.S. Tastes Not Easy', *Weekly Variety* (7 September 1983), 5.
11. Caulfield, 'Studios and Art Films', 17.
12. 'Col & Gaumont at Odds on Lido', 32.
13. 'Long Distance Partners', *L.A. Herald-Examiner* (13 September 1983), n/a; '12 Films Prepped, Triumph at Venice Looking for More', *Weekly Variety* (31 August 1983), 40.
14. Tusher, Will, 'Schreger Steps Down as Prexy of Triumph Pix', *Daily Variety* (7 November 1984), 1 and 14.
15. '(Contrary to a Remark …)', *Daily Variety* (5 February 1985), n/a.
16. 'Triumph Readying US Release of "Secrets" Comedy', *Daily Variety* (21 June 1985), n/a.
17. Gold, Richard, 'Triumph Drops "Mary" Distrib'n', *Daily Variety* (30 August 1985), 1 and 6.
18. 'Triumph Fate Under Scrutiny Again by Columbia Pictures', *Weekly Variety* (17 July 1985), 4.
19. Tusher, Will, 'Triumph Shifting its Lingo Gears', *Daily Variety* (20 September 1985), 1 and 34.
20. Ibid.
21. Clark, Ted, 'Gaumont Pulling Out of Triumph; Byuse to Be Stateside Rep', *Weekly Variety* (9 October 1985), 41.
22. Desowitz, Bill, 'Triumph Absorbed by Col Classics Div.', *Hollywood Reporter* (1 November 1985), 1.
23. Loynd, Ray, 'New Uni Classics Wing', *Hollywood Reporter* (4 May 1982), 1.

24. Ibid., 18.
25. Ibid.
26. Cammack, quoted in ibid.
27. 'U Classics Gets Divisional Status, Katz Named V.P.', *Weekly Variety* (9 February 1983), 3.
28. Robbins, Jim, 'Universal Classics Finding Place within Parent Firm', *Daily Variety* (2 March 1983), 6.
29. Ibid.
30. Ibid.
31. Ibid.
32. Katz, quoted in ibid., 6.
33. The figures were taken from *The Numbers*, http://www.the-numbers.com/movies/1983/0LTRV.php; accessed on 17 October 2010.
34. The figures were taken from *The Numbers*, http://www.the-numbers.com/movies/index1983.php; accessed on 17 October 2010.
35. Franklin, B. J., 'Universal Classics Aims to Develop "Talent Pool"', *Screen International* (27 August 1983), 8.
36. McCarthy, Todd, 'U Classics into Prod'n with "Volcano"', *Daily Variety* (8 June 1983), 1 and 10.
37. Katz, quoted in Franklin, 'Universal Classics Aims to Develop "Talent Pool"', 8.
38. Greenberg, James, 'Out of Circulation Hitchcock Pix to be Released by U Classics', *Daily Variety* (29 August 1983), n/a.
39. Desowitz, Bill, 'Uni Classics' Hitchcock Coup Ushering in New Library Picks', *Hollywood Reporter* (16 April 1984), 28.
40. 'U Classics Renamed U Special Projects', *Weekly Variety* (2 May 1984), 7.
41. The figure was taken from IMDb, http://www.imdb.com/title/tt0088322/business; accessed on 17 October 2010.
42. 'Deadly Summer Release Set by U Spec Projects', *Daily Variety* (25 June 1984), n/a.
43. Rothman, Cliff, 'Universal Studios Abolishing its Problem-Plagued Classics Div.', *Hollywood Reporter* (30 November 1984), 41.
44. The figure was taken from *The Numbers*, http://www.the-numbers.com/movies/1985/0JJWO.php; accessed on 20 October 2010.
45. The figure was taken from *The Numbers*, http://www.the-numbers.com/movies/index1984.php; accessed on 18 October 2010.
46. The film was released in collaboration with stand-alone distributor Quartet Films.
47. Although TCFIC was the original distributor of the film, Twentieth Century Fox took over the distribution of the title when it found out that it had a gap in its release schedule.
48. Fox, David, 'Seven Pickups on Initial Release Schedule of Fox' Classics Distribution Div.', *Daily Variety* (2 June 1982), n/a.
49. Quoted in 'Fox Establishes International Classics; Jones as Sales mgr.', *Hollywood Reporter* (2 June 1982), 1.
50. Loynd, Ray, 'TLC Packs Up; Fox to Handle Feature Lineup', *Daily Variety* (8 May 1985), 31.
51. For a discussion of top-rank independent producers in US cinema, see Tzioumakis, *American Independent Cinema*, 30–55.
52. Cohn, Lawrence, 'Fox Classics Expanding its Distrib'n Slate', *Daily Variety* (26 September 1983), 23.
53. Franklin, B. J., '20th Fox Classics Expands its Scope', *Screen International* (27 August 1983), 26; Cohn, 'Fox Classics Expanding its Distrib'n Slate', 23.

54. Franklin, B. J., '20th Fox Classics Expands its Scope', 26.
55. 'Fox Classics, Now "Specialized", into Territorial', *Weekly Variety* (11 January 1984), 9.
56. 'Fox Classics, Now "Specialized"', 9; '20th-Fox Classics Set to Acquire Two Completed Pix, Develop Pair', *Weekly Variety* (28 September 1983), 5 and 26.
57. Loynd, Ray, 'Fox Classics is Renamed as TLC, Sets Six Films', *Daily Variety* (12 March 1984), 42.
58. The figures for *The Gods Must Be Crazy* were taken from *The Numbers*, http://www.the-numbers.com/movies/1984/0GMBC.php; accessed on 19 October 2010.
59. Loynd, 'TLC Packs Up', 31.
60. Loynd, Ray, 'Pete Myers Aims to Purchase TLC Films from Fox', *Daily Variety* (1 February 1985), 8.
61. Caulfield, 'A Domestic Effort', 1.
62. Ibid.
63. Morris, interview.
64. Morris, interview.
65. Morris, interview.
66. Morris, interview.

CHAPTER 3

# Orion Classics (1983 to 1997)

## INTRODUCTION

The last classics division to be established in the early 1980s was Orion Classics. As its lifespan suggests, this was not a short-lived enterprise, even though its most active years came to a close in 1992, the remaining five years of its life being associated with just a handful of titles. Still, Orion Classics enjoyed a decade of remarkable success, dominating the specialised film market from the mid-1980s (by which time all the other classics arms had folded) until the early 1990s, when a new wave of specialty labels was established by companies such as New Line Cinema and Sony (Columbia), and aggressively expanding independent firms, like Miramax, started to transform the arthouse and US independent film markets irrevocably.

The longevity of the division and its consistent success over almost ten years are not the only elements that separate Orion Classics from the other early studio specialty labels. Orion Classics was also a specialty film division established, not by a Hollywood major like Universal or Columbia, but by a company whose status in the American film industry has been open to debate. Orion Classics' parent, Orion Pictures, was a production company that was created in 1978 when the five senior executives of United Artists left the company after a rift with the management of United Artists' parent company, Transamerica. Four years later and with the support of a consortium of investors, the Orion team took over large stand-alone producer–distributor Filmways (which had taken over the well-known exploitation film company, American International Pictures, a few years earlier), in effect becoming a new production–distribution entity with a view to competing with the majors rather than with arthouse, US independent and specialty film companies. This created an identity problem for Orion as, strictly speaking, it was a stand-alone producer–distributor, one that shared similarities with the major established powers, as well as with smaller outfits such as New Line Cinema. In this respect, Orion Pictures has rarely been considered in histories of independent film in the USA,[1] while critics have tended to utilise various labels to account for its position in the industry, most notably 'mini-major' and 'neo-indie', with some critics labelling it as a 'major' and other scholars locating it within the independent sector.[2]

The problems with Orion's hybrid identity were exacerbated after the establishment of its classics subsidiary, as Orion Classics was clearly formed to compete with the rest of the classics divisions in the early 1980s (albeit without their emphasis on reissues). This potentially suggests that the parent company was moving closer to the majors in terms of competition and therefore needed a subsidiary that could contribute whatever small profits the arthouse and US independent film market had to offer. In this sense, irrespective of the fact that Orion Pictures avoided corporate takeovers and mergers and remained staunchly independent at a time when all major distributors had become parts of vast diversified conglomerates, Orion Classics has always been perceived as the one closest to the US independent sector. This is despite the fact that the parent company has distributed many films by celebrated independent filmmakers, such as *Desperately Seeking Susan* (S. Seidelman, 1985), *House of Games* (D. Mamet, 1987) and *Eight Men Out* (J. Sayles, 1988). For that reason, it is necessary to remember that Orion Classics was the only specialty label of a non-studio in the 1980s. Furthermore, a number of its practices differed substantially from those of the four divisions I have discussed so far, mainly because, unlike the other classics arms, Orion Classics was conceived of by its parent company as an autonomous subsidiary, having no affiliations with Orion's domestic sales operations, no specific acquisition budget and no minimum or maximum limits for title pick-ups.[3] In this respect, it was 'allowed' to instigate whatever practices and models its executives wished, so long as it remained a profitable operation.

## A NEW UNITED ARTISTS (CLASSICS)?

As soon as Orion Pictures became a stand-alone producer–distributor in 1982, the company initiated plans for the creation of a classics subsidiary. One of the key reasons for this was that, as a new company in the American film industry, Orion lacked established contacts with Hollywood talent and was therefore ready to look for product outside the US, especially from arthouse filmmakers who were enjoying significant success in the early 1980s. Such a move would stand to create links with well-known filmmakers, provide product for the company's empty distribution pipelines, and buy them time to build relationships with homegrown talent – a matter of time, given the reputation of Orion's management team from their United Artists days.

Less than a year later, in April 1983, Orion Classics was created as an 'autonomous division' of the main company,[4] and its establishment became the platform for a second mass departure of executives from United Artists, this time from its own classics division, which was experiencing problems with its parent company (see Chapter 1). Specifically, young executives Tom Bernard, Michael Barker and Donna Gigliotti left their posts at UA Classics for similar ones at Orion Classics. This gave the latter division an already experienced management team that not only knew the arthouse market extremely well but also had established a number of contacts with auteurs across the world during their UA Classics years. In this sense, both parent company and subsidiary were run by former United Artists executives, causing industry analysts and critics to view Orion as a new United Artists, especially in terms of its relationship to creative producers and its well-documented 'hands-off' approach to filmmaking.[5]

One particularly celebrated characteristic of Orion Classics was the division of labour implemented by the management team. Despite each executive having a different job title and remit, the job description was in effect the same for each person, with the team deciding through voting among them whether they would distribute a film or not and taking decisions on all aspects of a film's release.[6] With this unusual managerial style and with a parent company ready to provide them with the necessary space to implement it, Orion Classics entered the market with a mandate to 'acquire and release foreign and high-quality, out-of-the-mainstream features'.[7]

The division was fortunate enough to record a box-office hit with its first release in July 1983, *Pauline à la plage* [*Pauline at the Beach*] by renowned French filmmaker Eric Rohmer. Having released Rohmer's previous film, *Le Beau Mariage* [*A Good Marriage*], while at UA Classics, the Orion Classics trio immediately demonstrated the value of contacts with filmmakers outside the US as they convinced Rohmer to switch to the new company, despite the fact that *A Good Marriage* was a commercial success for UA Classics in 1982. *Pauline*, however, proved an even bigger hit, taking $2.5 million at the US box office (compared to the $1 million of *Marriage*).[8] This was the beginning of a long relationship between the division and the filmmaker, as Orion Classics released the next four of the five pictures that Rohmer made in the 1980s and often invested in the production of his films, in exchange for distribution rights in the North American market.[9]

The cultivation of contacts with European filmmakers and producers had started even before Rohmer as the division's management made its first production deals during the incipient phase of its operation. Thus in August 1983, Orion Classics announced finance deals with renowned German filmmaker

Werner Herzog (*Wo die grünen Ameisen träumen* [*Where the Green Ants Dream*]) and also with British newcomer (to feature filmmaking) Marek Kanievska for *Another Country*, a film about the schooldays of notorious future British diplomat and defector to the Soviet Union, Guy Burgess, which was also financed by the successful 1980s British film company Goldcrest Films.[10] Furthermore, and in a move that had no precedent, Orion Classics joined ANICA, the organisation representing Italian film producers, to '"facilitate" the Italians' market-opening efforts' by showcasing eleven recent Italian films that had failed to attract the attention of American distributors during the arthouse boom years of the early 1980s.[11] Should one or more of these films attract the right amount of attention, Orion Classics would be in pole position to undertake their distribution formally.

Even though no such deals materialised, Orion Classics found another important source of product that supplemented straight negative pick-ups;[12] for 1983, this included two films financed and produced by former Beatle George Harrison's company, Handmade Films – *Privates on Parade* (M. Blakemore) and *Scrubbers* (M. Zetterling) – as well as Carlos Saura's *Carmen*, the second film in the flamenco trilogy by the famous Spanish filmmaker. Just as it did with Rohmer, as soon as *Carmen* was successfully released – the film went on to gross over $3 million – Orion Classics agreed with Saura distribution of his next picture, the third flamenco film, *El Amor Brujo* [*A Love Bewitched*] before the start of production.[13]

Having distributed two immediate hits on the arthouse circuit in 1983 (*Pauline at the Beach* and *Carmen*), Orion Classics was confident from the beginning that the division was there for the long run and would, by necessity, have to squeeze small independent distributors out of the market. These distributors, however, were not perceived as direct competitors for Orion Classics; according to the division's executives, these boutique companies had tended to make profits from exploitation product, with 'art films [used] to complement their release schedules as part of package deals with exhibitors.[14] In this respect, an independent distributor like Horizon Films was in the business of distributing films by Europen art filmmakers, like Marco Ferreri and Nino Manfredi, low-budget US features (*Variety* [B. Gordon, 1983]) and also exploitation pictures such as *I Was a Teenage Zombie* (J. E. Michalakis, 1987). On the other hand, while Orion Classics was located firmly in the distribution of quality films, its finance deals took the division to a level that was different not only from the boutique distribution companies but also from the other 1980s classics who – as we saw in previous chapters – ventured into production finance on rare occasions. For those reasons, while its competitors started experiencing problems in early 1984, Orion Classics looked to be in great shape, with a clear identity and the full support of its parent company. In this sense, although certainly ambitious, the division's proposed distribution slate of 15 to 18 films per year seemed to be within its reach.[15]

The final acquisition the company made in 1983 was its first independent US feature, *Strangers Kiss* (M. Chapman), financed by British producer Michael White. White was an experienced producer who had been involved with commercially successful films in the 1970s, including *The Rocky Horror Picture Show* (J. Sharman, 1975), and who had had a recent arthouse success in the early 1980s with Skolimowski's *Moonlighting*, released by Universal Classics. For *Strangers Kiss*, White pulled off the extraordinary feat of bringing the actual budget of the film down from $2 million to $120,000 by arranging fee deferments with virtually all above-the-line talent involved in the picture.[16] As a result, *Strangers Kiss* had better production values than other, less-refined, low-budget US films of the time, while the presence of Peter Coyote, whose performance was praised by the popular press and whose brief appearance in Spielberg's *E.T.* the previous year had transformed him into a familiar face,[17] provided a substantial marketing hook for the independent film.

Even before the release of *Strangers Kiss* in 1984, Orion Classics had demonstrated an interest in US independent filmmaking, following similar trends in the other classics divisions. As early as August 1983, the division's management was quoted as stating that 'their end goal [was] to go into production themselves on small American films', pointing to late 1984 / early 1985 as the right time to embark on their first projects.[18] However, these plans had to be postponed, as 1983 to 1984 did not prove to be a good period for the parent company, which had a number of box-office failures and only a handful of successes (including *Amadeus* [M. Forman] and *Terminator* [J. Cameron]), therefore recording dismal financial results.[19] Yet the division, which had already secured a number of films through its coproduction and acquisition activities in 1983, continued its very successful operation throughout 1984 and participated in the 1984 Cannes Film Festival with no fewer than three pictures.[20] It also announced eight additional titles for distribution in the final months of 1984 and early 1985, forcing industry analysts to distinguish Orion Classics from the rest of the faltering classics and to describe its approach to the business of specialised film as 'gung ho' and aggressive.[21]

As in the early phase of UA Classics, at the cornerstone of Orion Classics' success was a distinct *modus operandi* that was founded on frugal marketing spending, on knowing in advance how to sell a particular picture to the specific demographics associated with arthouse cinema, and on strict adherence to platform releasing practices. Specifically, its approach revolved around releasing its films slowly and with a small number of prints, starting from New York City and moving to other metropolitan areas. Given that the costs of releasing a film in one theatre in New York City in 1985 was approximately $7,500,[22] Orion Classics would spend, on average, between $200,000 and $250,000 to market and release a film in the major arthouse film markets,[23] opting for anything between 10 and 50 prints, depending on the perception of the division's management as to how successful a film might be.[24] This meant that each film had the necessary time to find its position in the marketplace before moving to a different city, to the extent that it could play for a long period of time in a small number of theatres before finishing its run. For example, *Rue cases nègres* [*Sugar Cane Alley*], a film by Euzhan Palcy from the Caribbean island of Martinique, made $1 million with just fourteen prints.[25]

This frugality in terms of release and marketing costs was supplemented by a small number of other elements that characterised distribution practices at Orion Classics and which included the management team's 'gut reaction' to a film and their voting to determine whether they would take it on; the 'director's track record' (even though, in the case of Euzhan Palcy and several cases later in its history, the division backed a number of newcomers);[26] 'second guessing the critics', which means that, quite often, the division backed films that were not reviewed positively by important film critics; and, finally, 'simple marketing strategies'[27] that included the use of 'stereotypical' images in the posters of films such as *Another Country* and *Pauline at the Beach*, intended to appeal to demographics that like particular types of films such as British heritage pictures and understated French romantic comedies, respectively.[28]

By 1985, when all the other classics divisions had either folded or gone into a rapid decline, and despite complaints from specialised film distributors and studios alike that the boom years of non-US arthouse film were over, Orion Classics continued to grow, maintaining its focus primarily on non-US product. According to the *Hollywood Reporter*, the division was able to generate annual revenues of $10 to $12 million, with approximately $2 to $3 million as net profit.[29] However, this figure may have been somewhat exaggerated as, according to Mike Medavoy, Head of Production and senior executive at the parent company, Orion Classics brought in, on average, profits slightly below the $1 million mark.[30] Whatever the truth, though, Orion's subsidiary was, indeed, going from strength to strength, especially when, in May of the same year, it announced another impressive line-up of films for the coming months, including Eric Rohmer's follow-up to *Full Moon in Paris*, *Le Rayon vert* [*The Green Ray*], and Hungarian arthouse film pillar István Szabó's *Oberst Redl* [*Colonel Redl*]. However, by far, Orion Classics' most expensive title and the one with the greatest potential for commercial success was revered Japanese director Akira Kurosawa's $10 million epic take on *King Lear*, *Ran*. Characterised by the trade press as an 'artistic and business coup of enormous proportions',[31] the acquisition of *Ran* convinced the division to up the stakes substantially in terms of its investment in both marketing and print costs.[32] However, the box-office result was lukewarm, with the company reporting rentals of approximately $3.5 million ten months after the release of the film[33]

– satisfactory for Orion's investment but less than expected for the producers of a film that cost $10 million to make.

Despite the fact that the division's spotlight seemed to remain firmly on the non-US arthouse sector, Orion Classics did not neglect homegrown filmmaking and continued its measured activity in the US independent sector through a deal to distribute celebrated independent filmmaker Wayne Wang's second feature, *Dim Sum: A Little Bit of Heart*. Wang's previous film, *Chan is Missing*, became an integral part of the emerging 1980s independent film canon; the Orion Classics executives had tried to buy it when they were working for UA Classics but it was independent distributor New Yorker Films that managed to acquire the picture. *Dim Sum* seemed to present an excellent opportunity for Orion Classics to stake a firmer claim on this type of cinema; in addition to the foreign arthouse film demographic that had also been responding to US independent film, the division would be able to target a potentially very large Chinese community which was dispersed in the same large metropolitan areas that have customarily been the key locations for arthouse film exhibition: San Francisco, Los Angeles, New York, Seattle, Boston and Washington, DC.[34] In this respect, Orion Classics placed particular emphasis on the distribution of Wang's film, which gave them the opportunity to start 'rebranding' the division at a time when American independent cinema was constantly increasing its visibility as an alternative to Hollywood. As one of the division's executives put it, with reference to the release of *Dim Sum*:

> We feel that American independent film is very important to us especially in light of the slowdown in production in Europe. American independents are a mainstay of specialized distribution, and with this film, we wanted to put something back into the (U.S. indie filmmaking) community.[35]

Despite the efforts to attract two distinct demographics into the theatres, the film did not perform well at the box office,[36] at a time when other US independent films, such as *Kiss of the Spider Woman* and *The Trip to Bountiful* (P. Masterson, 1985), did spectacularly well and even reached the Academy Awards, prompting further support for filmmaking away from the major studios. However, Orion Classics continued to show profitability and therefore to receive support from its parent company, which, by mid-1985, had become a significant force in the US film industry. In this climate of euphoria, Orion Classics continued to attract films by well-known filmmakers throughout 1985 and 1986, including Stephen Frears (*My Beautiful Laundrette*), Andrei Tarkovsky (*Offret* [*The Sacrifice*]) and Peter Wang (*A Great Wall*), all of which became commercial successes during a period that was widely perceived as the subsidiary's 'best year ever'.[37] In this respect, it was not surprising that the company yet again set ambitious release targets, aiming to distribute ten films for 1987 and to be 'in the thick of competitive bidding for the most desirable titles' at the major film festivals.[38]

These ambitious distribution targets, however, were once again supplemented by the division's renewed plans to become more heavily involved in the US independent film sector. This time, Orion Classics became one of the principal financial backers in the $3 million production *End of the Line* (J. Russell, 1987), thus taking another step towards their original aim of producing low-budget American films. Their decision to invest heavily in this production in late 1986 was likely to have been influenced by the commercial and critical success of Spike Lee's *She's Gotta Have It* and Jim Jarmusch's *Down by Law*, both of which Orion Classics saw as competition for its own films during that time.[39] For *End of the Line*, which was released in 1987, Orion Classics followed a different model of distribution, which involved producing a slightly larger number of prints (sixty) and concentrating on targeting particular regional audiences with heavy local advertising, before taking the prints to a different region and doing the same.

## TOTAL DOMINATION

Although *End of the Line* became a modest box-office success, the division enjoyed other, often spectacular, results in 1987 that made it the undisputed leader in the specialised film market in the US. Leading the pack was Claude Berri's *Jean de Florette* and *Manon des sources*, the two-part $17 million film adaptation of Marcel Pagnol's novel *L'Eau des collines*, which had proved a huge hit in France with over 15 million admissions for both films.[40] The two instalments represented the highest level of investment in the history of Orion Classics, who outbid competition by paying between $500,000 and $600,000 upfront in exchange for film rights in the North American market.[41] Furthermore, the films represented a big gamble for the company, as they stood to be released within six months of each other, a technique largely untested in the American film market despite the fact that it had proved widely successful in France.[42] Indeed, the first film was released in the US in June 1987 and proved to be a hit, grossing a little less than $5 million and paving the way for the second film, which was released in December of the same year. *Manon des sources* also proved to be a huge commercial hit, recording approximately $4 million at the US box office.[43] Furthermore, Louis Malle's *Au revoir, les enfants* [*Goodbye, Children*] was yet another unmitigated success story, taking over $4.5 million in the US and being nominated for an Academy Award for Best Foreign Film – the division's third nominated film following *Carmen* in 1984 and *Colonel Redl* in 1986.[44] As it turned out, *Goodbye,*

*Children* lost to the division's fourth nomination in the same category, *Babette's Gaestebud* [*Babette's Feast*] (G. Axel, 1987), a film that Orion Classics acquired in 1987 but did not fully release until after its victory at the Oscars, and with equally spectacular financial results.

The extremely strong performance of these films covered the less impressive run of the other pictures from 1987, such as Marco Bellochio's *Diavolo in Corpo* [*Devil in the Flesh*] and Yugoslavian picture *Hey Babu Riba* [*Dancing in Water*] (J. Acin). Finally, Orion Classics also released the British film *Rita, Sue and Bob Too* (A. Clarke), the first film of a new collaboration the division had initiated with Britain's leading production company, Four Films International. Following the success of *My Beautiful Laundrette*, which Orion Classics had released in 1986, the division sought out more British titles and the relationship with Channel Four's film division seemed to provide yet another strong source of product. In the first instance, the agreement was for two films, the second being *A Month in the Country* (Pat O'Connor).[45] Both films performed moderately well at the US box office.

With *Babette's Feast* doing as well as Orion Classics' high-grossing 1987 films, 1988 promised even greater domination of the specialised market by the division. By that time, however, both the world arthouse and the US independent film fields that comprised the specialised film market in the US had started showing clear signs of maturation and the potential for extraordinary profits – as Steven Soderbergh's *sex, lies, and videotape* would clearly demonstrate the following year. During this period, the biggest commercial successes in the specialised market still remained firmly under the $10 million mark in terms of box-office gross as, according to Peter Biskind, in order for a specialised film to improve its box office, it had to 'play the suburban multiplexes', and therefore break away from the 300 to 500 screens that were dedicated to these kinds of picture.[46] In this respect, even the most successful specialised films did not gross more than $10 million, with *Kiss of the Spider Woman* becoming the one film that crossed the $10 million barrier ($17 million), helped along by William Hurt's Oscar for Best Actor.[47]

In the late 1980s, however, an increasing number of films had started doing well at the box office, clearly demonstrating a maturing market, at least in terms of the extent to which it could be considered a viable alternative to Hollywood. Swedish film *Mitt Liv so Hund* [*My Life as a Dog*] (L. Hallstrom, 1987) took over $8.5 million for independent distributor Skouras Pictures; *Mystic Pizza* (D. Petrie, 1988) made $12.3 million for the Samuel Goldwyn Company; while the Merchant–Ivory production *Room with a View* (1986) became a huge hit, grossing over $16 million for Cinecom. In addition, video companies, like Vestron, were branching out into the theatrical production sector, occasionally releasing ultra-successful films such as *Dirty Dancing* (E. Ardolino, 1987) and *Young Guns* (C. Cain, 1988), which grossed approximately $70 and $45 million, respectively.⁴⁸ As a result, an increasing number of distribution companies started trading in the specialised film sector, providing further competition for Orion Classics; these companies included Skouras Pictures, Cineplex, Avenue Pictures and the theatrical film production and distribution branch of Vestron, all entering the market between 1985 and 1988.⁴⁹

In light of this increased competition, Orion Classics' great success in 1987 and early 1988 becomes even more impressive and demonstrates the solid foundations upon which the division was operating, while also justifying its business practices. In a profile of the division in the *Independent Feature Project / West Newsletter* that featured interviews with its management team, the Orion Classics executives tried to differentiate themselves from the majority of their rivals, citing their competitors' increasing embrace of 'mass market commercial production' to balance 'their independent production' in order to survive, especially companies like Atlantic, New World Pictures and New Line Cinema which pre-existed Orion Classics.⁵⁰ In contrast, Orion Classics had remained firmly in the specialised film market and had therefore avoided some of the practices in which its competitors were indulging, such as accepting production finance from video distributors in exchange for video rights to films – a tactic that would have done away with a major ancillary market; or financing films in the $5 to $6 million range that would require a significant box-office gross to recoup the initial production, distribution and marketing investment. In this respect, the division, arguably, had remained more conservative than other companies in terms of the films it handled – which tended primarily to come from established filmmakers and to have some commercial angle that could be exploited in the marketing process.⁵¹

In line with this, Orion Classics continued its 'conservative' selection of films for release in 1988 with two pictures that also proved extremely profitable: Wim Wenders's *Himmel über Berlin* [*Wings of Desire*] and Pedro Almodóvar's *Mujeres al Borde de un Ataque de Nervios* [*Women on the Verge of a Nervous Breakdown*]. The former, which came out in May, was a 'textbook' Orion Classics release: a world-renowned auteur with a serious track record; a film that had attracted mixed reviews and 'love-it-or-hate-it viewer reactions';⁵² and a clear marketing hook in the romantic storyline featuring an angel and a mortal, encapsulated in the tagline 'There are angels in the street of Berlin,' and in a striking poster featuring the hero (played by Bruno Ganz) sitting on the shoulder of a giant statue of an angel and looking down on the female protagonist. Attracting viewers that were much younger than the average audience for arthouse films, the film recorded a satisfactory final gross of approximately $4 million.⁵³ *Women on the Verge of a Nervous Breakdown*, on the other hand, became the most successful film in the division's history, grossing approximately $8 million at the US box office.⁵⁴ Prior to *Women*, all previous Almodóvar films had been released by independent distributor

Cinevista but had had marginal results. Despite this unprecedented success, however, Orion Classics did not succeed in cultivating a relationship with the Spanish director, who, for his next films, opted to work with Miramax, a company that became the undisputed leader in the specialised film sector in the 1990s.

At the time of this remarkable success, Orion Classics' parent company had started experiencing a number of problems which would fast lead to bankruptcy. A long-term debt accrued following the establishment of Orion Home Entertainment in 1987, a number of underperforming films at the theatrical box office and in the video market, and, especially, a war between major stockholders who would use the company as a pawn in a series of elaborate corporate manœuvres, all contributed to the creation of an unstable environment at the parent company and inevitably impacted on the specialty label too.[55] Perhaps it is not surprising that this period also saw the one change in the management of the division since it was established, when one of its three executives, Donna Gigliotti, left her post and was replaced by Marcie Bloom.

Still, the period between 1989 and 1990 saw the classics arm releasing more than a dozen films and doing steady business with a number of homegrown and foreign specialised films that grossed over $1.5 million in the theatres, including: *Mystery Train* (J. Jarmusch, 1989; see Case Study), *Trop belle pour toi* [*Too Beautiful for You*] (B. Blier, 1990), *Jésus de Montréal* [*Jesus of Montreal*] (D. Arcand, 1990), *Monsieur Hire* (P. Leconte, 1990) and *Milou en mai* [*Milou in May*] (L. Malle, 1990). Furthermore, two of its films, *Camille Claudel* (B. Nuytten, 1989) and *Cyrano de Bergerac* (J.-P. Rappenau, 1990), became solid box-office successes, grossing $3.3 and $5.9 million and receiving Academy Award nominations for Best Foreign Film in 1989 and 1990, respectively.[56] Both starring Gérard Depardieu, whose earlier hits (such as the classics-distributed *The Last Metro*, *Danton* and *Jean de Florette*) had made him a recognisable star for the US arthouse film audience, these films consolidated the French actor's reputation in the US still further and *Cyrano*, in particular, became one of the most commercially successful titles in the division's history.

Towards the end of 1990, and as the parent company was experiencing even more severe financial problems, Orion Classics established yet another impressive collaboration with international talent. This time, it announced a deal to co-finance and distribute the next Merchant–Ivory production, *Howards End*. This was the third adaptation by the British production company of an E. M. Forster novel following *Maurice* (1987) and *Room with a View* (1985). With Cinecom (which had successfully distributed the latter titles) on the way out of the distribution business due to financial overexposure,[57] the British production outfit agreed to sign with the division. Given the proven track record of Merchant–Ivory, as well as Orion Classics' intensified efforts to release films in the English language, *Howards End* was a very important film for the division;

so much so that this was the earliest the distributor had ever moved to acquire a film, which clearly suggests that the level of competition among distributors for the right film had reached such a height that the best-capitalised companies were keen to be involved increasingly early in the production process to secure the distribution rights. In previous years, most specialised pictures had to wait for the film festivals to solicit distribution interest, but from the late 1980s onwards this ceased to be the case.[58]

Prior to *Howards End*, which represented an exceptional package for any specialty distributor, Orion Classics had also secured, at a very early stage in the production process, Louis Malle's *Milou in May* and Akira Kurosawa's *Hachi-gatsu no Kyôshikyoku* [*Rhapsody in August*], with the latter benefiting further for distribution purposes from the casting of Hollywood star Richard Gere. However, as it turned out, neither *Milou in May* nor *Rhapsody in August* did particularly well at the US theatrical box office. *Howards End*, on the other hand, became a giant critical and commercial success, grossing $26 million and receiving three Academy Awards out of nine nominations.[59] Yet the film was actually distributed by new classics division Sony Picture Classics (see Chapter 5) as, by the end of the production process, both Orion and its specialty division were in the middle of a lengthy process of litigation following Orion's declaration of bankruptcy in December 1991.

Despite difficult times for the parent company and the underperformance of the above titles, 1991 was another successful year for Orion Classics overall. With only $200,000 in total being spent to secure the rights of *Europa, Europa* (A. Holland), *La Gloire de mon père* [*My Father's Glory*] (Y. Robert), *Le Château de ma mère* [*My Mother's Castle*] (Y. Robert) and *Slacker* (R. Linklater, 1991), and a limited number of prints being produced for each of these titles, by September 1991 these four films had together grossed in excess of $3 million.[60] *Europa, Europa* reached a final gross of over $5.5 million and became one of the most successful films in the division's history, while the micro-budgeted *Slacker* passed the $1 million mark and went on to become one of the most influential films in the American independent cinema canon.[61] This undisputed success, however, contributed very little to the parent company's balance sheet. With plans to restructure its debt failing and its financial position becoming increasingly untenable, on 11 December 1991, Orion invoked the federal bankruptcy code and filed for protection from its creditors.[62]

Orion's bankruptcy had immediate repercussions for its classics arm. Although the latter was allowed to continue operations while the administrators were trying to design a restructuring plan that would satisfy Orion's numerous creditors, its long-serving management team were, in effect, removed from their posts when they were asked to become 'consultants to the division' instead.[63] With reported attempts by various parties (including Canal Plus and Polygram Entertainment) to buy the division failing, Barker,

Bernard and Bloom started negotiating with a number of other majors who were considering establishing a classics arm.[64] After reported discussions with both Paramount and Sony, the team agreed to head Sony's newly established Sony Pictures Classics, with effect from 1 April 1992.[65]

Following their departure, Orion Classics continued to operate for the rest of the year under John Hegeman but without having a clear sense of the future. Although the court had ordered the division and its parent company to return the distribution rights to *Howards End* to Merchant–Ivory (who would sell them immediately to Sony Picture Classics and therefore create the opportunity to have their film released by the former Orion Classics executives), it none the less did not do the same with Yimou Zhang's *Da hong deng long gao gao gua* [*Raise the Red Lantern*] (1991) and Paul Cox's *A Woman's Tale* (1992).[66] The Australian *Woman's Tale* created little stir at the box office but *Raise the Red Lantern* was a major critical success, nominated for an Oscar for Best Foreign Film and recording a gross of over $2.5 million, despite its release during this transitional period for the distributor.[67]

In October 1992, the US Bankruptcy Court approved a restructuring plan for Orion Pictures. Although the court decision did not entirely prevent the company from re-entering the production business, Orion found it extremely difficult to find financial backers for in-house productions.[68] Under new management after the last of the original executives that established the company in 1978 had resigned during the restructuring process, Orion quickly became a marginal player in the American film industry, releasing only a few film titles post-1992 and functioning primarily as a film licensing company. In this radically new environment, Orion Classics 'made the cut' and was allowed to operate as a distributor 'on a fee basis' but not as a (co)-financer.[69] This arrangement allowed the division not only to release the films that had been signed by the previous regime, which, apart from *Raise the Red Lantern* and *A Woman's Tale*, also included Rohmer's *Conte de printemps* [*Tale of Springtime*] and Atom Egoyan's *The Adjuster* (1992), but also to seek new films. Equally importantly, parent company and division were relocated from New York to Los Angeles, a decision that removed Orion Classics from the epicentre of the specialty film market that New York City had historically occupied. Under these new conditions, the division also quickly became a marginal player in the market, managing to attract only a handful of titles in five years. These included *Rain without Thunder* (G. Bennett, 1993); indie star Steve Buscemi's debut film as a director, *Trees Lounge* (1996); *This World, Then the Fireworks* (M. Oblowitz, 1997); and Christopher Ashley's *Jeffrey* (1996), which became the only minor hit during that period, grossing $3.5 million.[70]

In 1996, Orion, Orion Classics and the Samuel Goldwyn Company, a successful independent distributor of the 1980s and 1990s, merged to form the Metromedia Entertainment Group, part of the Metromedia International

Group, a global communications, media and entertainment conglomerate controlled by John Kluge, Orion's majority shareholder. However, despite plans by Metromedia to handle film releases while allowing each of the two companies to remain 'in control of [their] own destiny',[71] a year later Metromedia sold its entertainment holdings to MGM for $578 million.[72] Under MGM, Orion Classics ceased its distribution activities and its library of titles became yet another source of supply for the MGM Home Entertainment unit, which also handled the United Artists Classics titles.

## CONCLUSION

During its ten active years (1983 to 1992), Orion Classics released over seventy films in the US theatrical market, including fifteen of the sixty most commercially successful non-US arthouse and US independent films in the five-year period between 1986 and 1991. Ten of its films were nominated for the Academy Award for Best Foreign Film, while the company received twenty-one Academy Award nominations in total.[73] In this respect, Orion Classics was by far the most successful classics division of the 1980s and, arguably, the most important specialised film distributor of the decade, if one excludes much larger and better-capitalised independents such as New Line Cinema and, of course, Orion Classics' parent company, Orion Pictures.

This history of Orion Classics clearly demonstrates the shortcomings of the 'failed studio experiment' position (irrespective of whether one thinks of the parent company as a studio or an independent). Orion Classics was, arguably, at the peak of its success in the early 1990s, when its parent company entered into administration; *Howards End* was poised to become the elusive $10 million plus hit that would propel the company to the next phase of specialised distribution, when US independent films, in particular, would raise the bar to unprecedented levels in terms of possible commercial success. In this sense, it is rather ironic that *Howards End* was released by the ex-Orion Classics executives and became the first Sony Pictures Classics hit, as is the fact that Michael Barker and Tom Bernard have remained at the helm of Sony's specialty label ever since their departure from Orion Classics in 1992. Orion Classics demonstrates that a well-managed division operating with a high degree of autonomy from the parent company in a well-defined niche market can enjoy long-term success and profitability. As we will see in Chapter 5, under the management of the former United Artists Classics and Orion Classics executives, Sony Pictures Classics has enjoyed almost two decades of consistently profitable specialised film production and distribution.

## Case Study: *Mystery Train* (Jim Jarmusch, 1989)

After the critical and commercial success of *Stranger than Paradise* (1984), widely perceived as a seminal film in contemporary US independent cinema, and the generally warm reception of *Down by Law* (1986), which none the less did not prove to be as commercially successful as *Stranger*, Jim Jarmusch quickly became an emblematic figure on the independent film scene. Equally importantly, the filmmaker had been enjoying significant success outside the US, especially in countries like France and Japan, where he was considered 'a great foreign art film maker',[74] with his films functioning as paradigmatic examples of the burgeoning American independent film movement of the 1980s.

Jarmusch's increasing international visibility opened production finance avenues that enabled him to continue working away from the Hollywood majors and their subsidiaries as sources of funding, at a point when the budget for his films had started to grow. While *Stranger than Paradise* had cost approximately $100,000 to produce and *Down by Law* a little over $1 million,[75] the budget for *Mystery Train* was considerably higher at $2.8 million. With small independent companies, like Island (which had underwritten the production costs of *Down by Law*), reluctant to act as financial backers for a film with that level of budget, Jarmusch exploited his 'international stardom' by managing to secure the complete negative costs for his film from Japanese electronics manufacturing giant, JVC.[76]

This budget enabled Jarmusch to initiate a number of practices for the first time in his filmmaking career, including shooting in colour; spending considerable time in improvisation and rehearsals; hiring a Japanese interpreter to help with the direction of the first segment of the film, which is about a Japanese couple visiting Memphis on a rock'n'roll pilgrimage,[77] and, of course, clearing the rights for legendary songs by Elvis Presley, Roy Orbison and Otis Redding. Despite these novel practices, *Mystery Train* retains a number of distinct characteristics that have been associated with Jarmusch's cinema, including an unflattering view of America that is far removed from the images of success and the ideals of the American Dream, especially as seen through the eyes of migrants or visitors; chance encounters and random events that often displace the idea of firm character motivation that is a central tenet of mainstream Hollywood filmmaking; and formal experimentation – in this case, the presentation of three stories that apparently take place simultaneously but which are presented successively and therefore are linked through repetition of stylistic elements, as well as tenuous character relationships.

However, behind this seemingly loose narrative there exists a precisely orchestrated selection of narrative components that clearly demonstrate the centrality of formalism in Jarmusch's cinema. More specifically, the film seems to be exploring the nature of the relationship between screen time and 'real time' in a way that makes the three stories of the film a secondary concern for the spectator. Certain elements (the passing of a train over a bridge nearby the hotel, the song 'Blue Moon' heard on the radio, the gunshot) that are seen or heard in each of the three segments ('Far from Yokohama', 'A Ghost' and 'Lost in Space') that comprise the narrative make very specific claims about the way images can be and are manipulated by cinema.

In this respect, what seem to be three distinct stories linked, however tenuously, by time and space may, in actual fact, have even fewer points of contact with each other (except for the gunshot, which is heard by the characters in both of the first two segments and caused by the protagonists in the third). Indeed, the passing train might have been three different trains passing over the bridge at three different times in the night; 'Blue Moon' might have been played at different points during the night or even by different stations (the voice of the DJ is not heard in one of the segments); and so on. And yet, we are invited to understand the stories as overlapping and to make connections and links that, arguably, are not there. In this respect, as Andrew puts it, *Mystery Train* is about 'both the fundamental methods of cinematic storytelling and the experience of watching and understanding a film', a film about cinema.[78]

Like the director's two previous films, *Mystery Train* also participated in the Cannes Film Festival (at a time when two other paradigmatic independent films, *Do the Right Thing* [Spike Lee] and *sex, lies, and videotape* [S. Soderbergh], also competed). Although it was Soderbergh's film that received the Palme d'Or, *Mystery Train* received an award for Best Artistic Contribution. It was in Cannes that Orion Classics bought the film's rights. With the division eager not only to increase the number of homegrown specialised films in its line-up but also to remain faithful to its 'conservative' distribution choices, *Mystery Train* seemed to be the perfect film. The director had a good track record and a great reputation on the specialised film circuit, and the film had been reviewed warmly but had also attracted some negative comments,[79] while the title and the narrative lent themselves to some interesting advertising. For Jarmusch, on the other hand, going with Orion Classics was an easy choice, as the division had been enjoying great success in the late 1980s and was therefore the top specialty distributor on any filmmaker's list.

Given Jarmusch's reputation as a paradigmatic independent filmmaker, Orion Classics' approach was to expose the film as much as possible to the festival crowd in order to generate free publicity and build word of mouth. Targeting, in particular, the Telluride, Toronto and New York film festivals – all key events in the independent film scene calendar, all taking place successively within the space of four months and all receiving considerable media coverage – Orion Classics had the specialised film audience ready for a November release, also in time for the Academy Award nominations. For the poster, the distributor chose a design that included a set of two identical images from each of the three segments of the film, sandwiched between the words of the film's title and the filmmaker's name. This concept clearly alluded to the narrative experimentation at the core of the film, with the repetition of particular images in each story, while also strongly emphasising Jarmusch's authorship. Finally, and as in most posters for specialised films, the Orion Classics design carried the endorsement of influential *New York Times* film critic, Vincent Canby.

Despite the well-conceived marketing campaign, the film's box-office performance was not the anticipated one. In the period when specialised films had increasingly started to break the $10 million mark, *Mystery Train*'s US gross of $1.5 million came as a disappointment. And even though the gross was consistent with Jarmusch's previous film, *Down by Law* ($1.4 million), the latter had cost far less than *Mystery Train* to make. In contrast, *Mystery Train*'s fellow Cannes competitors from the independent film sector, *sex, lies, and videotape* and *Do the Right Thing*, grossed over $25 million each for Miramax and Universal, respectively, both becoming seminal works in the popularisation of US independent film. This financial failure, however, did little to hinder Jarmusch's career, as he continued to secure funding for his idiosyncratic and personal films throughout the next twenty years (with JVC continuing to finance his films) and to collaborate with specialty divisions such as Fine Line Features and Focus Features.

## NOTES

1. Indeed, Orion is not even mentioned in passing in the vast majority of studies of the independent film sector, including Lyons, *Independent Visions*; Jim Hillier, ed., *American Independent Cinema: A Sight and Sound Reader* (London: BFI, 2001); E. Deidre Pribram, *Independent Film in the United States, 1980–2001* (New York: Peter Lang, 2003); King, *American Independent Cinema*; and Chris Holmlund and Justin Wyatt, eds, *Contemporary American Independent Film: From the Margins to the Mainstream* (London: Routledge, 2005), even though some of the above do mention Orion Classics (King, *American Independent Cinema*, 38; Pribram, *Independent Film*, 23).
2. Prince labels Orion a 'major' (Prince, *A New Pot of Gold*, 17); Wasser calls the company a mini-major (Frederick Wasser, *Vini, Vidi, Video: The Hollywood Empire and the VCR* [Austin: University of Texas Press, 2001], 125); while Hillier calls Orion both a mini-major and a neo-indie (Jim Hillier, *The New Hollywood* [New York: Continuum, 1994], 21). On the other hand, Insdorf perceives of the company as independent and as part of the independent film scene (Insdorf, 'Ordinary People', 57) and so does McLane (Betsy McLane, 'Domestic Theatrical and Semi-Theatrical Distribution and Exhibition of American Independent Feature Films: A Survey in 1983', *Journal of the University Film and Video Association* 35.2 [1983], 18). Finally, in a series of works, I have also argued in favour of a view that places the company in the independent sector (Tzioumakis, 'Major Status', 87-135; Tzioumakis, *American Independent Cinema*; and Yannis Tzioumakis, 'Entertainment in the Margins: Orion Pictures Presents a Filmhaus Production of a David Mamet Film', in *The Business of Entertainment: Vol. 1 Cinema*, ed. Robert C. Sickels (New Haven: Greenwood, 2008), 153–77.
3. Klain, Stephen, 'Orion Pictures Establishing Classics Arm', *Daily Variety* (1 April 1983), 22.
4. Klain, 'Prods Over-value US Art Mart', 532.
5. Klain, 'Orion Pictures Establishing Classics Arm', 22; Tzioumakis, 'Major Status', 89.
6. Levine, Hedi, 'Democratic Style of Orion Classics', *Screen International* (16 February 1985), 40.
7. Toumarkine, Doris, 'A Giant among Specialty Distributors', *Hollywood Reporter* (9 July 1991), S-34.
8. Levine, 'Democratic Style', 40.
9. Gigliotti, quoted in Sutherland, '"Country" Continues', 6.
10. McCarthy, Todd, 'Orion Classics Acquires Three More Features', *Daily Variety* (24 August 1983), 16; 'Orion Classics to Scout Films at Venice Fest', *Daily Variety* (1 September 1983), n/a.

11. 'Italo Films Get Showcase Courtesy of Orion', *Daily Variety* (21 November 1983), 14.
12. Ibid.
13. McCarthy, Todd, 'Orion Classics Lines Up 6 Pix', *Daily Variety* (14 May 1985), 16; Levine, 'Democratic Style', 40.
14. Putzer, Gerry, 'Orion Classics Trio Running Shop in Venerated Path of UA Classics', *Hollywood Reporter* (24 August 1983), 21.
15. Ibid.
16. 'Orion Classics Nets Three More Films for Domestic Mill', *Weekly Variety* (31 August 1983), 8.
17. See, in particular, Janet Maslin, '*Strangers Kiss* in the Hollywood of 1955', *New York Times* (13 August 1984), http://movies.nytimes.com/movie/review?res=9807E5D9143AF930A2575BC0A962948260; accessed on 1 December 2010.
18. Franklin, B. J., 'Orion Classics Trio Aims Towards Production', *Screen International* (27 August 1983), 28.
19. Tzioumakis, 'Major Status', 94.
20. Ryweck, Charles, 'Orion Heads for Cannes with 3 Films', *Hollywood Reporter* (27 April 1984), 3.
21. McCarthy, Todd, 'Orion Classics Surges with One Film per Month for All of '84', *Weekly Variety* (7 March 1984), 16.
22. Ibid.
23. Sutherland, '"Country" Continues', 6.
24. Ryweck, Charles, 'Kurosawa's "Ran" Latest Coup for Orion Classics Division', *Hollywood Reporter* (11 June 1985), 49.
25. Sutherland, '"Country" Continues', 6; Levine, 'Democratic Style', 40.
26. See, for instance, Peter Wang, whose *A Great Wall* proved a significant success in 1986, and Gary Bennett, whose controversial 1992 film *Rain without Thunder* became the first picture to be released by Orion Classics after the bankruptcy of its parent company and the regime change in the division's management.
27. Ryweck, 'Kurosawa's "Ran"', 49.
28. Sutherland, '"Country" Continues', 6.
29. Ryweck, 'Kurosawa's "Ran"', 49.
30. Medavoy, interview.
31. Ryweck, 'Kurosawa's "Ran"', 49.
32. Ibid.
33. Gold, Richard, 'Orion Classics, Riding Best Year Ever, Firms Fall Marketing Plans', *Weekly Variety* (15 October 1986), 6.
34. Robbins, Jim, 'Orion Classics Seeking Crossover B.O. with Asian "Dim Sum" Dates', *Weekly Variety* (7 August 1985), 6.
35. Bernard, quoted in ibid.
36. Allom, Yoram, Del Cullen and Hannah Patterson, *Contemporary North American Film Directors: A Wallflower Critical Guide* (Harrow: Wallflower, 2002), 556.
37. Gold, 'Orion Classics, Riding Best Year Ever', 6.
38. '3 Orion Classics Execs on the Riviera Prowl', *Weekly Variety* (7 May 1986), 16.
39. Gold, 'Orion Classics, Riding Best Year Ever', 6.
40. Gold, Richard, 'Orion Trying Six-Month Intermission: "Jean" Sequel Due Out at Christmas', *Weekly Variety* (24 June 1987), 34.
41. Ibid.; Gold, Richard, 'Orion Classics Wins Rights to Berri Films', *Daily Variety* (19 February 1987), n/a.
42. Gold, 'Orion Trying Six-Month Intermission', 3.

43. McCarthy, Todd, 'Soaring "Wings" Ready for Long Flight', *Daily Variety* (25 July 1988), n/a.
44. Ibid.
45. Gold, Richard, 'Orion Forges Deal with Film Four', *Daily Variety* (12 February 1987), 1.
46. Biskind, *Down and Dirty Pictures*, 81.
47. According to IMDb, the film grossed $17 million (http://www.imdb.com/title/tt0089424/; accessed on 28 December 2010).
48. All box-office figures were taken from IMDb and were accessed on 28 December 2010.
49. See also Tzioumakis, *American Independent Cinema*, 258.
50. Lanouette, Jennine, 'Distributor Profile: Orion Classics', *Independent Feature Project / West Newsletter* (April 1988), 14.
51. Ibid.
52. McCarthy, 'Soaring "Wings"', n/a.
53. Ibid. The figure for the film's gross was taken from IMDb, http://www.imdb.com/title/tt0093191/business; accessed on 28 December 2010.
54. The figure was taken from Toumarkine, 'A Giant among Specialty Distributors', S-44.
55. Tzioumakis, 'Major Status', 103.
56. The box-office figures for *Mystery Train*, *Cyrano de Bergerac* and *Camille Claudel* were taken from Box Office Mojo (http://www.boxofficemojo.com). The figures for *Too Beautiful for You*, *Jesus of Montreal*, *Monsieur Hire* and *Milou in May* were obtained from IMDb. All figures were accessed on 28 December 2010.
57. Biskind, *Down and Dirty Pictures*, 19.
58. 'Cannes Briefs', *Daily Variety* (14 May 1991), n/a.
59. The film's box-office figure was taken from IMDb, http://www.imdb.com/title/tt0104454/business; accessed on 28 December 2010.
60. Fleming, Michael, 'Artful Grosses for Orion Classics', *Weekly Variety* (9 September 1991), 22.
61. The figures were taken from Box Office Mojo and were accessed on 28 December 2010.
62. For a detailed account of efforts to tackle the company's financial problems see Tzioumakis, 'Major Status', 111-18.
63. Layne, Barry, 'Top Orion Classics Trio Shift to Consulting Roles', *Hollywood Reporter* (3 February 1992), 3.
64. King, Andrea, 'Orion Classics Execs in Talks with Par, SPE', *Hollywood Reporter* (29 January 1992), 1.
65. Hazelton, John and Colin Brown, 'Orion Classics Keeps Lantern as Parent Seeks Guiding Light', *Screen International* (27 March 1992), 5.
66. Ibid.
67. The figure was taken from IMDb, http://www.imdb.com/title/tt0101640/business; accessed on 28 December 2010.
68. Tzioumakis, 'Major Status', 118.
69. Toumarkine, Doris, 'Orion Classics Heads West as Distrib for Hire', *Hollywood Reporter* (22 October 1992), 3.
70. The figure was taken from IMDb, http://www.imdb.com/title/tt0113464/business; accessed on 28 December 2010.
71. Honeycutt, Kirk, 'Metromedia's 17-film Slate a Mixed "Bag"', *Hollywood Reporter* (6 February 1997), 17.
72. Medavoy with Young, *You're Only As Good*, 204.
73. King, Andrea, 'Raised on the Classics: Orion Trio Gets Sony Unit', *Hollywood Reporter* (12 February 1992), 22.

74. Wilmington, Michael, 'Interview', *Los Angeles Times* (27 February 1990), http://www.jim-jarmusch.net/films/mystery_train/read_about_it/interview_in_la_times_1990.html; accessed on 30 December 2010.
75. Levy, *Cinema of Outsiders*, 118.
76. Rosenbaum, Jonathan, 'Strangers in Elvisland: Jonathan Rosenbaum on *Mystery Train*', *The Chicago Reader* (9 February 1990), http://www.jim-jarmusch.net/films/mystery_train/read_about_it/strangers_in_elvisland_-_jo.html; accessed on 30 December 2010; McGuigan, Cathleen, 'Shot by Shot: *Mystery Train*', in *Jim Jarmusch: Interviews*, ed. Ludvig Hertzberg (Jackson: University Press of Mississippi, 2001), 100. Originally published in *Premiere* 3.5 (January 1990).
77. Sante, Luc, 'Mystery Man', in *Jim Jarmusch: Interviews*, ed. Ludvig Hertzberg (Jackson: University Press of Mississippi, 2001), 94. Originally published in *Interview* (April 1989).
78. Andrew, *Stranger than Paradise*, 151.
79. See in particular Rosenbaum, 'Strangers in Elvisland'.

SECTION II

# Indie

CHAPTER 4

# Fine Line Features (1990 to 2005)

INTRODUCTION

The first new classics arm in seven years was established in December 1990 by another well-capitalised, stand-alone producer–distributor, New Line Cinema. By that time, New Line had enjoyed over twenty years in the American film industry, which had seen the company grow from a marginal distributor of 'foreign, sexploitation, gay cinema, rock documentaries and "midnight specials"' to a reputable and consistently successful producer–distributor without any ties to the Hollywood majors.[1] Having managed to build lucrative franchises out of films such as *A Nightmare on Elm Street* (W. Craven, 1984) and having seen a number of their low-budget genre productions (*The Hidden* [J. Sholder, 1987]) and unusual auteur films (*Hairspray* [J. Waters, 1988]) doing good business at the box office, the company had become a significant player in the industry by the end of the 1980s. However, 1990 was the threshold year for New Line, as two of its properties, *House Party* (R. Hudlin) and *Teenage Mutant Ninja Turtles* (S. Barron), found great commercial success (especially the latter) and spawned two sequels each, further solidifying the company's position in Hollywood.

It was exactly at this point that New Line established its specialty film arm as, according to its chairman, Robert Shaye, the company was gradually moving 'at that point in time towards more "commercial" movies'.[2] However, as New Line had also seen its low-budget acquisition, *Metropolitan* (W. Stillman, 1990), become a big critical and commercial success, and with the triumph of *sex, lies, and videotape* still fresh, it made sense for the company to maintain its presence in the US specialty film market. With funds from its successful franchises readily available, New Line Cinema formally established Fine Line Features in December 1990.

Fine Line marks the beginning of a second, mini-wave of specialty film divisions in the wake of the popularisation of American independent cinema – a wave that also includes Sony Pictures Classics (SPC) (1992) and, arguably, Miramax after its takeover by Disney in 1993. Unlike the classics divisions of the 1980s, these companies concentrated much more forcefully on films originating in the US and on imports of films in the English language. And even though SPC and Miramax maintained some form of balance between non-US arthouse films and English-language specialty features, Fine Line concentrated predominantly on US films. Furthermore, and equally importantly, these post-1990 divisions were much more active in terms of providing production finance, even though acquisitions remained the dominant business practice, at least until the mid-1990s, when a new wave of studio specialty labels focused more intensely on production than on acquisitions. In this respect, as Fine Line was an active specialty label until the mid-2000s, its mandate and practices changed substantially after the mid-1990s and, increasingly, it started to resemble divisions such as Fox Searchlight and Focus Features. However, the first part of the company's history is firmly located in practices that became associated with the transition of US independent cinema to its 'indie' years, an era when American independent film ceased to be defined primarily in terms of its lack of ties to the Hollywood majors and became instead a category of filmmaking that could be identified by a number of textual and contextual parameters. This type of cinema could be produced both by companies with no corporate or financial ties to the majors and their subsidiaries and by companies affiliated corporately or financially to the majors (and, in rare cases, by the majors themselves).

The history of Fine Line Features can be divided into three periods, each corresponding to a particular management team and, arguably, to a particular business strategy. The first one extends from the creation of the division in 1990 to the end of 1994. Under the management of Ira Deutchman, Fine Line established itself as a prolific distributor of primarily US independent film acquisitions. The second period is between 1995 and 1997, under the management of Ruth Vitale. During that time, Fine Line remained equally prolific but started to emphasise film production clearly, while its acquisitions programme focused increasingly on more mainstream films in a bid to become 'more commercially viable, like its Manhattan-based competitor Miramax'.[3] Finally, its third phase covers the remaining years (1998 to 2005) when, under Mark Ordesky, the company tried to balance production and acquisitions but gradually found itself with lacking a distinct identity, until it was shut down by its parent company (by then, Time Warner) and effectively replaced by Picturehouse (see Chapter 9). During this final period, the division's releases decreased in number, and there were stretches of time when it was virtually inactive.

## 'NOT A CLASSICS DIVISION': THE EARLY YEARS (1990 TO 1994)

Once New Line decided to establish Fine Line, the parent company's management envisaged a subsidiary that would go beyond the 'conventional classics division' model of the 1980s,[4] which they perceived as an organisation that 'acquire[d] foreign language films with limited potential'.[5] Instead, they were interested in establishing a specialty label that would trade in films with much more crossover potential 'than classics-oriented films',[6] titles that could emulate the kind of box-office success that *sex, lies, and videotape* showed the specialty sector that it was possible to achieve.

Even though New Line executives' perception of the 1980s classics divisions does not entirely do justice to their practices and their own emphasis on films with crossover potential, the trade press of the time was quick to indentify points of contact between the new division and the only remaining classics arm, Orion Classics, by suggesting that Fine Line would be 'enlisting similar specialized marketing and platform-release strategies on films with crossover potential'.[7] However, in terms of the type of product that Fine Line would be handling, Ira Deutchman, the division's first senior executive, was quick to highlight English-language films as the most desirable product for the new specialty label. Specifically, Deutchman was mostly interested in being involved with 'mid-level films', the kind of pictures associated with Orion Pictures,[8] which, by 1990, was in dire financial trouble and whose position in the US film industry had become precarious. Having been involved with two of the biggest commercial successes of specialised films in the 1980s, *sex, lies, and videotape* and *A Room with a View* – both films with clear commercial attractions – and witnessing the home video companies' distinct privileging of films in the English language, Deutchman wanted Fine Line to push specialty filmmaking to 'the next level of slightly more commercially oriented movies',[9] compared to the 'low-budget, low-key' specialty films of the previous decade. On the other hand, Deutchman had also been involved with very low-budget films, which, if successfully distributed, could allow for substantial profit margins, and so Fine Line aimed to trade in these kinds of picture too.[10] In this respect, then, Fine Line's business plan had both strong continuities with and significant departures from the business approach of the classics divisions of the 1980s.

As it turned out, it was Deutchman's involvement with the extremely low-budget *Metropolitan* that signalled the beginning of Fine Line. In his role as producer's representative, he had arranged a distribution deal for the film with New Line, as word about New Line's intention to establish a specialty division that would handle independent films with commercial potential had already reached him. However, by the time the film was released, New Line had yet to produce firm plans about the proposed division. This meant that *Metropolitan*, an $80,000 production, was in danger of being handled by New Line's marketing department, which lacked expertise in the distribution of such films, and could potentially be buried amidst a line-up of films that normally open in saturation release. Deutchman, then, was brought in as a marketing consultant to work on the film's marketing campaign, which became one of the surprise hits of 1990. It was during that period (mid-1990) that serious negotiations about the establishment of the division started to take place, with the birth of the company officially announced in December 1990.[11]

Under the leadership of Deutchman, who came to Fine Line with a wealth of experience in the specialty film sector, having previously worked at United Artists Classics and Cinecom, New Line's division enjoyed an auspicious beginning. First, Fine Line found itself almost immediately with product as, in anticipation of its establishment, New Line had secured a number of low-budget films in the English language, which Fine Line would distribute once it was set up.[12] These included three British films, two by established screenwriters who branched out into directing (Hanif Kureishi's *London Kills Me* and Mark Peploe's *Afraid of the Dark*) and one by established filmmaker Peter Medak (*Let Him Have It*). They also included US independent filmmaker Hal Hartley's second feature, *Trust*, which had attracted a lot of critical attention after its premiere at the Toronto Film Festival in September 1990.[13] Although the latter did not prove a commercial success (and neither did the three British productions),[14] these four pictures immediately telegraphed the division as a significant new arrival in the sector that handled the work of talented filmmakers like Hartley, whose first film, *The Unbelievable Truth* (1989), had been hailed as an important independent picture and who would carve a significant career in the indie film sector in the years to follow.

Besides Hartley's picture, Fine Line also managed to release a few other films by up-and-coming directors who would enjoy considerable success in later years, such as Michael Tolkin, whose film *The Rapture* (another picture inherited from New Line) had received rave reviews from influential critics such as Roger Ebert,[15] and especially New Zealand filmmaker Jane Campion, whose low-budget second feature, *Angel at My Table*, became Fine Line's first release and proved a modest commercial success, with a box-office gross of slightly over $1 million.

However, the division also enjoyed great commercial success in its first year with a film that quickly joined the emerging canon of US indie cinema as this was being shaped following the success of *sex, lies, and videotape*: Gus Van Sant's *My Own Private Idaho*.[16] This film was also inherited from New Line, which had purchased the non-US rights and retained first refusal on domestic rights. For Deutchman, *Idaho* represented the first example of the kind of film he had envisaged for Fine Line Features. The film attracted considerable media attention, as it featured the well-known young stars River Phoenix and Keanu Reeves. Furthermore, Van Sant's previous film, *Drugstore Cowboy*, had won a large number of awards and was a significant commercial success for Avenue, an independent distributor that was being squeezed out of the market just as Fine Line was being established. Based loosely on a number of Shakespeare's plays and featuring a storyline about male prostitutes on the streets of Portland, Oregon, *Idaho* drew a significant audience that could have been initially attracted to it by its stars. Furthermore, the film was released at the same time as a wave of commercially successful films with explicitly homosexual characters and storylines about sexual identity that was later (1992) identified by film critic B. Ruby Rich as the 'New Queer Cinema',[17] and which also made the film appealing to a different demographic. In this respect, Fine Line had a number of different audiences to market the film to, which became a solid success with a US gross of $6.4 million on a budget of $2.5 million.[18]

With the division enjoying an energetic and auspicious start following the release of a mix of negative pick-ups and New Line properties that were deemed more appropriate for its subsidiary, Fine Line went on to increase its release roster for 1992 through more acquisitions and also through financing productions. At that stage, Fine Line followed the Orion Classics example and became co-financer with a number of other investors rather than operating as a sole party. Its first two deals involved the co-financing, with British Zenith Pictures and US public service broadcaster PBS, of Hal Hartley's third feature, *Simple Men*, which was budgeted at $3 million, and its participation in the British film, *Waterland* (S. Gyllenhaal). The latter seemed to be the kind of picture that could be nurtured as a crossover hit, as it carried the substantial budget of $8 million and boasted the presence of an international star (recent Oscar-winner Jeremy Irons) as well as a number of well-known British and American actors.[19] Furthermore, Fine Line immediately followed these two projects with a third co-finance deal, this time of US indie film *Swoon* (T. Kalin). *Swoon*'s director, Tom Kalin, had screened only a five-minute work-in-progress clip at the 1991 Independent Feature Film Market in New York, but on the strength of it he managed to attract both Fine Line and PBS as investors in the film,[20] which also became one of the key films of New Queer Cinema and received a number of awards in 1992. These co-productions were supplemented by a number of straight acquisitions, including Derek Jarman's *Edward II*, Australian filmmaker Jocelyn Moorhouse's *Proof* and Jim Jarmusch's follow-up to *Mystery Train*, *A Night on Earth*. Finally, the division moved to make its first acquisition of a film not in the English language, Italian comedian–director Maurizio Nichetti's *Volere Volare* (*To Want to Fly*).[21]

All this activity made for an impressive fourteen-film line-up for 1992 (even though two of the films were eventually moved to 1993). After only a year of existence, Fine Line was moving increasingly to more commercial fare, targeting 'broader audiences' than originally envisaged and creating 'in-house' facilities to plan the advertising of its releases more effectively.[22] Indeed, despite the presence of some 'small' or 'difficult' films (*Edward II*, *Swoon* and Broomfield's *Monster in a Box*), the division's line-up featured a number of properties that could attract broader audiences, especially its key US indie titles, *A Night on Earth* and *Simple Men*. With many of its non-US films also boasting certain commercial elements (for instance, the international cast of *Waterland*), it became clear that Fine Line was on course to handle the more commercial type of specialised film rather than the low-key, low-budget one.

Even though none of these films became the breakthrough hit the division was hoping for, Fine Line announced the acquisition in February 1992 of Robert Altman's *The Player*. The film was scripted by *The Rapture*'s writer–director, Michael Tolkin, and represented a comeback of sorts for maverick Hollywood filmmaker Robert Altman, mostly associated with the Hollywood Renaissance of the late 1960s and 1970s, and with key films from the period, like *M.A.S.H* (1970) and *Nashville* (1975). Since the late 1970s, however, Altman had been working in low-budget films for various specialty distributors, including UA Classics, which released his film *Streamers* (1983), and in made-for-TV movies such as *Come Back to the Five and Dime, Jimmy Dean, Jimmy Dean* (1982), released by Deutchman's Cinecom. *The Player*, however, was far removed from the films Altman made in the 1980s and represented an $8 million gamble for Avenue Pictures,[23] the film's principal financial backer (and almost distributor, had the company not withdrawn from the theatrical distribution arena when *The Player* was in production).

The film had substantial commercial appeal, boasting a large number of Hollywood stars playing themselves in cameo appearances (including Julia Roberts and Bruce Willis), and so fit New Line's post-1990 remit for more commercial fare. However, Fine Line convinced its parent company that this was a movie for them. Obtaining the rights to distribute it for $5.1 million, Fine Line pre-tested the film to determine whether it had the potential for wider distribution right from the start rather than the customary platform release, but the tests suggested that it would play better as a 'big art film, rather than a small commercial film'.[24] Indeed, Fine Line designed a careful platform release, opening the film slowly in New York and Los Angeles to build further word of mouth before planning to take the picture to as many as 200 screens, the widest release in the division's history at the time. With the marketing campaign focusing on Altman's return to form and his status as an outsider who therefore had the appropriate credentials to critique Hollywood, the film opened on 10 April 1992 to considerable buzz and did great box-office business for a film on limited release. Fine Line took the film wide three weeks later with very strong results and by the end of May it peaked at 452 engagements, finally grossing almost $22 million and becoming the kind of crossover hit the division wanted.[25]

The success of *The Player* gave Fine Line enormous visibility, making it a very attractive option for filmmakers in both the US and the rest of the world. Perhaps more importantly, it allowed New Line's subsidiary to make co-production and distribution deals from a position of power and to attract potential investors more easily for the properties it hoped to develop and eventually distribute. After the successful release of *The Player* and throughout 1992, Fine Line went on to strike a number of deals with companies and producers, sending a very clear message to its rivals in the sector that it was there for the long run. For instance, it made a deal with leading European producer–distributor Polygram to co-finance and distribute the $5 million western *The Ballad of Little Jo* (M. Greenwald) in the US, and another arrangement with Columbia Tristar Home Video to co-finance the $5 million star-studded indie film *Naked in New York* (D. Algrand).[26] Furthermore, and following the success of *My Own Private Idaho*, Fine Line and its parent company co-financed Van Sant's next feature, an adaptation of Tom Robbins's cult novel *Even Cowgirls Get the Blues*, which boasted a number of stars and carried a substantial budget of $9 million.[27] Perhaps most impressively, Fine Line negotiated a $15 million co-production deal with Spelling Entertainment for Altman's much-anticipated follow-up to *The Player*, *Short Cuts*.[28] As will be clear, the division was developing a strong reputation as a filmmaker-friendly organisation, and repeat business with important directors like Altman and Van Sant further enhanced its status as a top specialty distributor. According to an article in *Variety*, by August 1992 and despite its still-brief presence in the industry, 'Fine Line Features ha[d] already risen to the top of its field as a distributor of sophisticated American art-house films.'[29]

All this activity, however, created a new wave of anxiety for and criticism from independent distributors, who felt, yet again, that studio divisions which were nothing more than 'another product line, or marketing arm' for their parent companies (in this case, New Line Cinema), were squeezing them out of the market.[30] As mentioned in the previous chapter, the late 1980s had seen another influx of independent production and distribution companies into the American film industry, making for a particularly crowded specialty film marketplace. Driven by the continuing penetration of home video and cable television into US homes and as an increasing number of specialty films were crossing over, old and new independent distributors were vying for the 'right' film in an even more fiercely competitive environment than the early 1980s. In this respect, small stand-alone distributors had every reason to fear a repeat of what happened in the early / mid-1980s, when the first wave of classics divisions 'stole' significant business from a market that was once safely theirs.

Despite all this activity, many of the division's films continued to underperform at the North American box office. For example, its ten-strong film line-up for 1993 included only two titles that recorded grosses over $1 million

– Altman's *Short Cuts* ($6.1 million) and British filmmaker Mike Leigh's *Naked* ($1.8 million) – while pictures like *The Ballad of Little Jo* and *Amongst Friends* (R. Weiss), expensive for the independent sector, proved to be commercial disappointments, with grosses of approximately $500,000 and $250,000, respectively. Under these circumstances, Fine Line had to look to other sources of income, especially in ancillary markets such as cable television. With the help of its parent company, Fine Line arranged cable distribution for a number of its products with leading cable film broadcaster, Showtime,[31] while in March 1993 Bravo, another major cable channel, created the monthly show *Fine Line Theater*, with the explicit intention of showcasing films from New Line's division. The latter cable deal, in particular, was seen as a 'coup' for both parties, as it would stand to 'enhance Bravo's and Fine Line's roles as key players "in the distinctive world of specialty film"',[32] while also providing valuable income for the division.

The box-office underperformance of Fine Line films in 1993 did not deter independent producers and filmmakers from continuing to perceive the company as a top distributor, especially as, since August 1993, it had become a subsidiary of entertainment conglomerate Turner Broadcasting System (TBS) when the latter took over New Line Cinema for approximately $570 million. Indeed, Fine Line secured yet another impressive line-up of films for release in 1994.[33] These included productions with a large budget for the specialty film sector, such as Gus Van Sant's above-mentioned *Even Cowgirls Get the Blues* and Roman Polanski's star-studded $12 million *Death and the Maiden*; and indie films by key directors, such as Whit Stillman's *Barcelona* (see Case Study), David O. Russell's Sundance success *Spanking the Monkey* and Alan Rudolph's *Miss Parker and the Vicious Circle*; star-studded British film *Widows' Peak* (J. Irvin); and two Italian films by arthouse cinema pillars Paolo and Vittorio Taviani (*Fiorile*) and breakthrough filmmaker Nanni Moretti (*Caro Diario* [*Dear Diary*]). Lastly, the division also decided to release its first documentary, *Hoop Dreams* (S. James), which had received rave reviews and won a number of awards in the documentary category.

However, 1994 turned out to be yet another year of box-office disappointment, despite the fact that, by that time, the division had created in-house facilities to market its films more effectively and therefore had more control over the advertising of its product.[34] Even though films such as *Widows' Peak* and *Barcelona* did strong box-office business (grossing around $7 million each) and *Hoop Dreams* became the highest-grossing documentary ever to that date, taking almost $8 million in US theatres, the division's big-budget films misfired. *Even Cowgirls Get the Blues*, in particular, was panned by critics,[35] and grossed only $1.6 million, proving a major flop. With *Death and the Maiden* also greatly underperforming, with a gross of just $3.1 million, and the rest of the films doing minimal business, Fine Line found itself in a precarious position.

It was around that time that new owners TBS moved to make changes in both the philosophy and the management of the company.

## 'MINING THE COMMERCIALITY OF THE ARTHOUSE MARKET' (1995 TO 1997)

During 1994, when Fine Line's biggest hit was the documentary *Hoop Dreams*, the division's main rival, Miramax Films, could boast successes like *Pulp Fiction*, which grossed over $100 million at the US box office alone, and *Il Postino* [*The Postman*] (M. Radford), which took over $25 million, while films like *The Piano* (J. Campion) and *The Crying Game* (N. Jordan) had also become major crossover hits in 1993 and 1992, respectively. In this sense, Fine Line's inability to cultivate the crossover film, especially after the release of over forty films in four years and at a time when box-office records for specialty film were being shattered every year, became the primary reason for the first major change in management. Furthermore, the level of autonomy with which the division had been operating was deemed problematic in certain circles at the top of the corporate structure, especially as Deutchman had been actively trying to arrange for Fine Line to do the booking of its own films rather than having to rely on New Line's distribution department. This would have given Fine Line even more autonomy, something that senior executives in the parent organisation found difficult to accept.[36] In a bid to make it 'more commercially viable', the parent company removed Ira Deutchman from the presidency of the division and instead brought in Ruth Vitale from New Line Cinema, where she was in charge of acquisitions. The move clearly signalled TBS and New Line's efforts to target more commercial films, which would take Fine Line to the 'next step' and fulfil its 'potential to mine the commerciality of the arthouse market'.[37]

With its mission statement considerably redefined, the division also moved to form a new business plan. While, under Deutchman, Fine Line had primarily been handling acquisitions which were supplemented by a small number of co-finance deals, under the new management Fine Line was to enter film production in a much more forceful way. Specifically, the division was to produce between ten and twelve films per year, with a hefty $12 to $15 million budget each,[38] including up to three pictures produced under the aegis of its former president, Ira Deutchman, who retained a relationship with the division after agreeing a first-look production deal.[39] As for acquisitions, Fine Line would still compete for films with crossover potential, hoping that the much-reduced target number would help the division bid only for the most 'special' of those films.

Fine Line's decision to shift its emphasis to production in the mid-1990s was in line with the business plans of the other key specialty divisions. By this time, these divisions included Miramax and Fox Searchlight (see Chapter 6), and also new distributors with ties to the majors that were oriented towards more commercial films, such as Gramercy Pictures; this left Sony Pictures Classics as the only specialty label associated with a major studio to remain focused on an acquisitions-driven policy. The reasons for this shift of focus will be explained in greater detail in later chapters. However, one of the main factors that should be raised at this point was the increasing popularisation of US independent film, especially after the remarkable commercial success of several films of that designation, and in particular those distributed by Miramax. Given this popularisation, the parent companies of divisions like Miramax were happy to authorise increasingly large budgets for the production of 'independent' films in an effort to ensure the presence of commercial elements, especially stars, and, of course, to receive all the rental income following the success of what Alisa Perren has called the 'quality indie blockbuster' model.[40] It is not coincidental, then, that the newly coined 'indie' cinema label also became popularised from the 1990s onwards; instead of a type of production, it designated a type of film, which could be financed, produced and distributed by both independent companies and the majors' specialty labels.[41]

Despite these ambitious plans for production, the reality proved somewhat different. For the 1995 line-up, the nine films the company was set to distribute were either negative pick-ups (*Once Were Warriors* [L. Tamahori]) or co-financed productions (*Little Odessa* [J. Gray]), arranged by the previous regime or brought to Fine Line by Vitale when she was in charge of acquisitions at New Line. Furthermore, that particular year proved to be the worst in Fine Line's history in terms of box-office performance; the division's own production, *The Incredibly True Adventure of Two Girls in Love* (M. Maggenti), turned out to be the top grosser, making just $2.2 million at the US box office,[42] while pictures like the $7 million-budget *Frankie Starlight* (M. Lindsay-Hogg), expensive for the sector, proved to be major box-office disappointments.[43]

In many ways, these dismal results gave the new regime the rationale it needed to instigate its programme of film production, the first taste of which was provided in 1996. From a roster of another nine films, three were productions financed entirely by Fine Line and boasted the participation of some major Hollywood stars: Trevor Nunn's adaptation of Shakespeare's *Twelfth Night* (the deal for which was actually made by the previous regime), which featured an illustrious cast of British film and theatre stars;[44] Keith Gordon's *Mother Night*, which starred Nick Nolte; and Steven Baigelman's *Feeling Minnesota*, with Keanu Reeves and Cameron Diaz playing the leads.[45] The rest of the films, however, represented the same mixture of negative pick-ups (*The Grass Harp* [C. Matthau]), films in which Fine Line invested at the production stage in exchange for distribution rights, and pictures that were originally developed and produced by New Line but were deemed to be more appropriate for the subsidiary (*Pie in the Sky* [B. Gordon]. This line-up too, though, proved to be unsuccessful at the box office, with the three in-house productions recording a combined gross of just $4 million and representing a major write-off in terms of production investment.

Fine Line's last release for the year, however, turned out to be the elusive crossover hit the division was looking for: Scott Hicks's *Shine*. Ironically, rather than being an in-house production, this was a straight acquisition from the 1996 Sundance Film Festival, where the film had created considerable buzz.[46] After a carefully orchestrated limited release in November and December that also positioned the film for the Academy Award nominations, Fine Line expanded *Shine* slowly, allowing it to maintain its reputation in the early weeks of 1997. On the news that the film had received eight Academy Award nominations, including one for Best Picture, Fine Line took the film wide (approximately 1,000 theatres) and allowed it to play throughout February and March, generating a North American gross of over $35 million; it thus became the division's highest-grossing film, a title it held until Fine Line's closure in 2005.

The commercial and critical success of *Shine* gave Fine Line some much-needed relief in an otherwise commercially disappointing year. Arguably more importantly, it came at a time when both New Line and Fine Line's future was at stake following yet another change of corporate parent. In September 1995, TBS and leading entertainment conglomerate Time Warner agreed a merger worth $7.2 billion, creating the largest media company in the world.[47] Although the deal was not ratified until a year later,[48] it none the less had placed a lot of pressure on New Line and Fine Line, as they would have to co-exist in the same structure as the Hollywood major, Warner Bros. Although the pressure was more for New Line, whose emphasis on franchise pictures and wide-release distribution patterns meant that it would be forced to compete with Warner, Fine Line felt the pinch too, as it would have to prove its commercial viability to its new corporate parent. Indeed, with both New Line and Fine Line reporting significant net losses in 1996, their place in the new structure was precarious, with reports suggesting that New Line was to be put up for sale.[49] And even though, reportedly, Time Warner wanted to retain Fine Line, as it did not have its own classics division prior to the merger, it needed a subsidiary that would be able to arrange for its own finance rather than expecting it to come from the pockets of its parent company.[50] With the stakes set this high, it might not be unfair to suggest that the success of *Shine* gave Fine Line the kiss of life.

With the division still trying to find its place within the new corporate structure, the ambitious programme of in-house productions came to a sudden halt, the trade press reporting that 'two years after Fine Line redefined itself almost exclusively as a production entity under Vitale, the banner [was] shifting back toward an equal number of acquisitions and productions.'[51] Those productions, however, would have a much lower budget than in the previous year, with films like *Gummo* (H. Korine) and *Roseanna's Grave* (P. Weiland) costing far less than the star-studded prestige productions of 1996. On the other hand, acquisitions were much more attention-grabbing, especially as Fine Line secured Woody Allen's *Deconstructing Harry*, despite the fact that his previous three pictures had been handled successfully by Fine Line's rival, Miramax. This rather sudden shift in its business strategy, however, did raise questions about the division's identity in the marketplace, while the end-of-year (1996/7) reports in the trade press characterised the division as 'a company in flux', which was treated with scepticism by the creative community. And there were persistent rumours about a change in the top echelon of the division's management following the takeover by Time Warner.[52]

## IN SEARCH OF AN IDENTITY

Despite a return to the distribution volume of the early 1990s (twelve releases), 1997 turned out to be yet another disappointing year for the division. No fewer than eight Fine Line films grossed below $1 million and five out of these below $200,000, including canonical indie films such as *Gummo* ($117,000) and Greg Araki's *Nowhere* ($195,000). Only Woody Allen's *Deconstructing Harry* seemed to be a solid hit, with a theatrical gross of slightly over $10 million. However, as its production budget was estimated at $20 million, it was also deemed to be an underperforming feature.[53] These results made a change in the top tier of the company an inevitability, and, exactly three years after the first management shakeout in January 1995, Fine Line Features had a third president, Mark Ordesky. Like his predecessor, Ordesky was brought into the division from the New Line ranks.

Under the new management, the division attempted to redefine its role in a marketplace that, by this time, had also witnessed the introduction of an increasing number of specialty labels with ties to the majors, including Paramount Classics (see Chapter 7). One of the main difficulties Fine Line was facing was that it had to compete not only with the new classics established by Fox and Paramount, which traded in a similar type of product to Fine Line, but also with a number of newcomers that specialised primarily in relatively low-budget genre films (Dimension Films, Screen Gems), often generating huge box-office figures. In this newly transformed marketplace, Fine Line seemed to be particularly ill equipped, focusing as it did primarily on quality indie films with only rare ventures into low-budget genre film territory.

One of Ordesky's first moves to improve the bottom line was to create Fine Line International, a sales branch that would be responsible for the distribution of the division's films abroad. While Fine Line pictures were normally handled outside the US either by international agents representing particular territories or by New Line International, representing its subsidiary's films alongside its own roster, Fine Line International was created to cater specifically for the specialised Fine Line product. Given that the division would continue to be involved in film production (irrespective of the lower number of films it would finance), being able to sell its films outside the US created an opportunity for increased revenue for Fine Line. Equally importantly, Fine Line International would also look to develop long-term partnerships with local distributors so that all Fine Line product could be pre-sold, with the advances from these sales going back to the division as funds for its production slate.[54] The new management's most important move in terms of redefining the division's identity, though, was to balance out acquisitions and productions, as it was clear that the company needed both to survive. According to the division's profile in the *Hollywood Reporter* in 1999, the new management was to 'split the annual eight to 12 Fine Line releases 50/50 between acquisitions and production, with budgets ranging from what Ordesky calls "nothing" to $15 million plus'.[55]

The transitional stage at which Fine Line had found itself following the management change can be seen in its 1998 roster of releases, which was down to seven films compared to the twelve of the previous year. All the titles were acquisitions and, yet again, none achieved commercial success. *Hurlyburly* (A. Drazan), in particular, proved to be the biggest disappointment, given its commercial appeal on paper. Based on a well-known play by renowned American playwright David Rabe and featuring an illustrious cast that included Sean Penn, Kevin Spacey and Meg Ryan, the film grossed less than $2 million. Still, this was the division's second-best performer after John Waters's *Pecker*, which did slightly better, recording a gross of $2.3 million. The more balanced slate of acquisitions and productions that comprised the 1999 line-up proved equally disappointing. Despite an enhanced slate of nine films, Fine Line saw four of its films recording less than $200,000. Furthermore, a second prestige adaptation of a play, this time Sam Shepard's *Simpatico*, with the participation of another set of Hollywood stars such as Jeff Bridges, Sharon Stone and Nick Nolte, also failed to find an audience, grossing a little less than $1 million. Yet again, the company's biggest hit grossed slightly over $2 million, and that was the Sundance acquisition *Trick* (J. Fall).

The continued underperformance of the division's films in the face of even greater competition raised more questions about the future of Fine Line.

These questions became more pressing when the division's senior executive was seconded to a long-term assignment in New Zealand, being placed in charge of production for New Line's tentpole *Lord of the Rings* trilogy in October 1999.[56] However, despite a significant reorganisation in the division's staff base in the first months of 2000,[57] Ordesky was not replaced during his four-year secondment (1999 to 2003) but continued to oversee Fine Line's business. During that period, and especially after the 2000 season for which the division had already arranged the distribution of nine films, Fine Line found itself 'almost ground to a halt',[58] a state from which it would never recover, despite some activity in its last two years of operation.

Despite the problems with (the lack of) management, Fine Line enjoyed a marginally better year than the previous two at the US box office. While many of its films continue to underperform, the division saw one of its Sundance acquisitions, the British film *Saving Grace* (N. Cole), grossing over $12 million and its key US indie film release, David Mamet's *State and Main*, reaching $7 million. Finally, despite the rather disappointing theatrical box office of $4 million, Fine Line achieved substantial visibility in the international film community when *Dancer in the Dark* (L. Von Trier), a film it co-produced and distributed, won the Palme d'Or at the Cannes Film Festival in 2000 and received a large number of awards in both the US and the rest of the world. This visibility allowed Fine Line to start cultivating relationships with talent outside the US, at a time when a number of world cinema titles had started finding commercial success anew in the North American market, especially after the remarkable popularity of Roberto Benigni's *La Vita è Bella* [*Life is Beautiful*], which grossed close to $60 million. Indeed, Fine Line made deals with Danish production company Zentropa Films (one of the main producers of *Dancer in the Dark*) for three additional films, and with a number of established Italian filmmakers, including Liliana Cavani and Gabriele Salvatores.[59]

Despite these glimpses of moderate success and the deal-making with arthouse film talent, the division was increasingly being perceived as an organisation in trouble. In *Variety*'s overview of specialty distributors for 2000, Fine Line was described as 'a releasing arm in search of an identity', despite the fact that the existing management had been running the division for almost three years.[60] And while, arguably, its improved performance in 2000 was a sign of better things to come, its roster for 2001 and 2002 was significantly reduced, pointing clearly to an uncertain future. More specifically, in 2001 the division released only three films: *The Invisible Circus* (A. Brooks), *The Anniversary Party* (A. Cumming and J. J. Leigh) and *Hedwig and the Angry Inch* (J. C. Mitchell). Although the extremely low-budget, digitally shot *Anniversary Party* became a success, taking over $4 million at the North American box office, the division's other two 2001 releases fell short. The more disappointing one was the in-house production, *The Invisible Circus*, which grossed a meagre $77,000 in US theatres and represented a major write-off in terms of its production and marketing budget. Similarly, in 2002, the company continued with a low number of releases – four in total. Yet again, none of its films took over $1 million, with Todd Solondz's *Storytelling* becoming Fine Line's top-grossing films at approximately $900,000.

While both box-office figures and number of releases in the early 2000s demonstrated beyond any doubt that Fine Line was in decline, the division announced a significant deal in mid-2003 that could potentially have given it a new lease of life. The deal involved a pact between HBO and Fine Line, with the latter handling theatrical distribution of a number of 'idiosyncratic' films that were produced or acquired by HBO for cable broadcasting in an effort to enhance their market value. HBO had seen an early example of such a practice producing encouraging results in 2002, when its film *Real Women Have Curves* (P. Cardoso) was handled theatrically by independent distributor Newmarket Films and grossed close to $6 million before it was added to the schedules of the HBO channels for further exploitation.[61] Following this, HBO had made an one-off deal with Fine Line to distribute *American Splendor* (S. Springer Berman and R. Pulcini), which HBO had also financed and which had won the top prize at the Sundance Film Festival in 2003. However, before that film was released, the two parties, both under the Time Warner corporate umbrella, agreed to extend the deal to all the films that HBO would release theatrically, and which were estimated to number between two and five titles per year.[62]

The deal seemed to make sense for both parties. As well as providing an example of synergy within Time Warner (which, by that time, was part of AOL), it allowed for HBO, increasingly active in film production and acquisition, to engage the services of an established and experienced specialty distributor for its more 'idiosyncratic' productions. For Fine Line, the deal was nothing less than a lifeline. By the time the deal was announced, Fine Line had gone through a period of approximately a calendar year with no theatrical releases at all, creating increasing speculation about its future.[63] In this respect, the deal with HBO stood to provide the distributor with a steady supply of much-needed quality product.

As it turned out, HBO was the only film supplier for Fine Line in 2003, in which year the distributor released just two films: *American Splendor* and Gus Van Sant's *Elephant*, which had won the Palme d'Or in Cannes in 2003. Two other films that the company had arranged to distribute, Liliana Cavani's *Ripley's Game*, which Fine Line had secured in 2000 during its cultivation of relationships with talent in Italy, and *The Sleeping Dictionary* (G. Jenkin), which the division had bought at script stage in 1998,[64] were not deemed commercially promising and were released in the direct-to-video market in the US. In the end, only *American Splendor* proved a hit, grossing almost $7 million, while *Elephant* joined Fine Line's list of vastly underperforming titles, grossing a little over $1 million, despite gaining closer to $10 million outside the US.

Fine Line's relationship with HBO provided the distributor's final hit film the following year – *Maria, Full of Grace* (J. Marston) – despite a roster of other titles with crossover potential, including John Waters's *A Dirty Shame*, Mike Leigh's *Vera Drake*, Jonathan Glazer's *Birth* and Alejandro Amenábar's *Mar Adentro [The Sea Inside]*. This activity coincided with the return of the division's President, who, by that time, had also become New Line's Chief Operating Officer following the end of the final instalment of the *Lord of the Rings* trilogy. In his expanded remit and with substantial funds from the success of the *Lord of the Rings* films, Ordesky proceeded to sign a number of acquisitions for both New Line and Fine Line, which explains why the specialty division had found itself with such a promising roster. This was also because some of the projects were originally bought for Fine Line, only for their distribution to be 'upgraded' to New Line. For instance, *Birth*, which boasted Hollywood star Nicole Kidman, was released with the help of New Line to over 500 screens. However, as it turned out, the HBO-produced *Maria, Full of Grace* was the division's highest-grossing film for the year, taking $6.5 million.

Ordesky's presence in the top echelons of both New Line and Fine Line quickly became a thorny issue for the future of the latter organisation. According to trade press reports, Ordesky did not want to return to Fine Line after the global success of the *Lord of the Rings* films; neither was he particularly forthcoming in (re)defining Fine Line's identity post-2003. This structural problem, in tandem with a cost-cutting exercise that followed Time Warner's takeover by AOL in 2000, made Fine Line's position untenable. Accordingly, and not surprisingly, Fine Line's status as a 'freestanding division' finally came to an end in September 2004. As part of a general restructuring at both New Line and Fine Line, the former classics division became 'a specialty marketing label' with plans to release six to 10 titles per year by using New Line's resources and with product coming primarily from its relationship with HBO, but also through acquisitions and the financing of production.[65] These plans, however, never did materialise. Following a handful of releases in early 2005, the label ceased to trade in the summer of the same year.

## CONCLUSION

The history of Fine Line Features is intricately linked with the history of US independent film at a time when, as Chris Holmlund and Justin Wyatt have argued, this mode of filmmaking had started moving away from the margins and into the mainstream.[66] The establishment of the division in 1990 was a clear attempt by New Line to capitalise on the increasing commercial success of English-language specialty films, especially as the company was itself moving to wider releases and adopting business practices associated with the major distributors. Under Deutchman's leadership, Fine Line was quick to establish itself as one of the top specialty distributors, primarily through acquisitions, at a time when US independent film production was taking giant strides and a number of films with crossover potential had been available at a relatively low price. With over forty titles in its first four years, many by celebrated indie filmmakers, the division never achieved the crossover hit that became the trademark of its main rival, Miramax Films. However, its high annual distribution volume, in tandem with its many deals in the ancillary markets, generated substantial revenue and helped cushion the losses from theatrical distribution.

From the mid-1990s onwards, however, Fine Line had to change policy. As the Disney-backed Miramax had started investing more and more in production and as the acquisition price for 'indie' films had already reached great heights, it became difficult for a specialty label to trade in both areas of filmmaking unless it had the full support of a diversified parent company. With backing from TBS and later from Time Warner, Fine Line tried to shift its focus to the production of indie films. Although it did not entirely cease its acquisitions, both types of films continued to underperform in what was becoming an increasingly overcrowded marketplace that could support only a handful of crossover hits per year. In this respect, Fine Line saw only one of its films, the acquisition *Shine*, become a huge commercial success.

In its third and final phase, the division desperately tried to find an identity through a balance of production and acquisitions, at a time when the specialty marketplace had yet again changed radically. By the 2000s, all majors had their own specialty divisions, each one operating with a variety of budgets and practices, while many had also established low-budget genre labels which were partly vying for the same specialty audience. Under these circumstances, Fine Line could have been competitive if it had had firm direction and the full support of its giant conglomerate parent. Having neither, the division went quickly into decline, despite a distribution arrangement with HBO that generated the division's last commercial successes.

Although Fine Line ceased to operate in 2005, in the same year New Line and HBO established a new specialty label, Picturehouse, which effectively occupied Fine Line's space, especially as it continued the theatrical release of HBO films (see Chapter 9).

## Case Study: *Barcelona* (Whit Stillman, 1994)

Following the significant critical and commercial success of *Metropolitan*, Stillman was offered a production deal for his second film, *Barcelona*, at well-capitalised neo-indie Castle Rock in 1992. At that time, the company had a distribution deal with Warner Bros, which none the less covered primarily commercial films, the budget of which was $10 million and above. With a number of titles, including Stillman's second film, budgeted well below that threshold, Castle Rock looked for a different distributor, one with expertise in specialty product. Given his relationship with Deutchman dating from the time of *Metropolitan*,[67] the filmmaker convinced Castle Rock to take the picture to Fine Line. Under the terms of the deal, Castle Rock would provide the print and advertising costs, while Fine Line would function primarily as a service distributor, 'supply[ing] marketing and distribution expertise' and receiving a distribution fee for releasing the film in the US.[68]

Like *Metropolitan*, *Barcelona* became an integral part of the US independent cinema canon of the 1990s. The film's narrative revolves around the experiences of two American cousins in the Spanish city of Barcelona in the 1980s, during the last years of the Cold War and a time when anti-American sentiment was at its peak. These experiences are recounted through an endless series of parties, dates and talks with young local women, who provide ample romantic interest for the two protagonists. However, while a substantial part of the narrative deals with the formation, dissolution and re-formation of cross-cultural couplehood and the two protagonists' views on romance, an equally large part of the story looks at the political climate of the time. Specifically, there are several conversations between characters covering – often in some detail – Spanish and US views about US foreign policy and its role in global geopolitics. The central place of politics in the film reaches a crescendo approximately two-thirds into the narrative, when one of the two American protagonists is shot in the head because he is suspected of being a CIA agent.

The unusual mix of geopolitics and cross-cultural romance gives the film a very distinctive feel. Rather than functioning as background for the romantic entanglements among young people and the anxieties these generate, politics and the characters' views about political matters are an integral part of the discourse that characterises the lives of all these people. No matter the time, place or situation, political discussions always manage to creep into the exchanges between the film's characters and, not surprisingly, politics becomes one of the key reasons why Montserat and Marta break up with the two American protagonists. Despite this unusual emphasis on the articulation of arguments about global geopolitics from both sides, what is particularly interesting is that none of the film's characters is represented as a stereotype of the political or politicised young person. No character is seen taking part in protests, belonging to a political organisation or even making political statements through dress code, appearance and personal styling. On the contrary, when we first meet Aurora and Marta, two of the key Spanish characters, they are dressed in elaborate ballroom gowns and are on the way to the disco. This creates no suspicion whatsoever that they might be knowledgeable about political matters. In this respect, the film manages to make political debate part of everyday life without having to resort to conventional political iconography and stereotypes of any kind.

The early scene at the disco provides the key to understanding both the film's perspective and the cinematic techniques upon which this perspective is built. In trying to construct cross-cultural heterosexual couples and comment on the politics of this kind of romance, Stillman opts to alternate the emphasis between gender and sexual politics (the norm in more heavily genre-imbued romantic comedies) and geopolitics and cultural politics. Dates, picnics, dancing, car rides and other courtship rituals that normally form the battleground for the articulation of gender and sexual politics also become the terrain where geo- and cultural politics are played out. This is repeated throughout the film and constitutes its main structural axis. In this respect, Stillman succeeds in making a romantic comedy that is 'political' in the literal meaning of the word.

Not surprisingly, the filmmaker's weapon of choice in the construction of such an unusual film is editing. The use of long scenes and takes where the characters have the space to explore fully ideas on love, romance and politics is rare. Instead, the film consists of a large number of shorter scenes that allow for a quick alternation from one focal point to another. As a result, the characters' perspectives on both romance and politics are presented in a fragmented, but also extremely immediate, way that is not the case in more genre-specific films. Add to this the many shots of beautiful Barcelona dispersed throughout the film when no action takes place, and the number of scenes that constitute the film's narrative looks even larger.

Despite the central place of politics in the narrative, Fine Line opted for a marketing campaign that focuses almost exclusively on the romantic aspect of the narrative. The poster features the two protagonists sitting on the steps of one of the city's monuments, while a large image of Montserat becomes the focal point of the design, suggesting a potential romantic entanglement among the three characters (something that is not exactly the case in the film). In the middle of the poster, the tagline 'Americans, Anti-Americans, in Love' provides the one piece of evidence about the political subtext of the film. The reason behind Fine Line's choice was to avoid branding the picture as being about politics, as such films tend to attract small audiences. Besides highlighting the romantic aspect much more forcefully, the poster also utilises the fame of Stillman's debut film, aiming to attract the same demographic that made *Metropolitan* a hit in the US independent film sector. 'From the makers of *Metropolitan*' is placed at the top of the poster and becomes the first piece of text people would see when looking at the poster, while Whit Stillman's name accompanies the title of the film, giving it a very strong authorial signature.

The division's campaign paid dividends as the film became more successful than *Metropolitan*, grossing $7.2 million. Stillman, on the other hand, famously made only one film after *Barcelona – The Last Days of Disco* (1998) – and in the following years saw his reputation as a cult filmmaker grow considerably. At the time of writing and thirteen years since *Disco*, Stillman is finally making his fourth feature, *Damsels in Distress*.

## NOTES

1. Wyatt, 'The Formation of the "Major Independent"', 76.
2. Shaye, quoted in Andrea King, 'New Line Drawing Fine Line in Bid for Upscale Film Biz', *Hollywood Reporter* (6 December 1990), 2.
3. Cox, Dan, 'Vitale Fine Line Prez', *Daily Variety* (10 January 1995), 42.
4. King, 'New Line Drawing Fine Line', 2.
5. Deutchman, quoted in Claudia Eller, 'New Line Cinema Expands Base: Opens Specialized Feature Division in N.Y.; Deutchman Tapped to Head Subsidiary', *Daily Variety* (6 December 1990), 23.
6. Ibid.
7. Ibid.
8. Deutchman, interview.
9. Deutchman, interview.
10. Brown, Colin, 'Fine Line for "Indies"', *Screen International* (8 December 1990), 11.
11. Deutchman, interview.
12. Deutchman, interview.
13. Voland, John, 'Fine Line Snaps Up Hartley's "Trust"', *Hollywood Reporter* (21 January 1991), 70.
14. *Trust* grossed only $350,000, while the filmmaker has never enjoyed the commercial success proportionate to his influence on the sector.
15. Ebert, Roger, '*The Rapture*', *The Chicago Sun Times* (27 October 1991), http://rogerebert.suntimes.com/apps/pbcs.dll/article?AID=/19911027/REVIEWS/110270301/1023; accessed on 28 December 2010.
16. The film is mentioned as an important indie title in many surveys, including Levy, *Cinema of Outsiders*, 454–5 and Andrew, *Stranger than Paradise*, 348–9; it is discussed in detail in Lyons, *Independent Visions*, 231–45.
17. Rich, B. Ruby, 'New Queer Cinema', *Sight & Sound* (September 1992), 30–5.
18. The figure for the film budget was taken from IMDb, http://www.imdb.com/title/tt0102494/; accessed on 28 December 2010.
19. Eller, Claudia, 'Fine Line Features Enters Coprod'n Arena via 2 Pix', *Daily Variety* (24 October 1991), 1.
20. Brown, Colin, 'Fine Line *Swoon* Swoop', *Screen International* (8 November 1991), 2.
21. Dawes, Amy, 'Fine Line Seals Pick-Up Deals on "Proof", "Volere", "Edward II"', *Weekly Variety* (2 December 1991), 2.
22. 'Fine Line Taps Manne Sr. VP, Caldwell Advertising Director', *Daily Variety* (6 February 1992), n/a.
23. Frook, John Evan, 'Altman's "Player" to be Released via Fine Line', *Weekly Variety* (17 February 1992), 28.
24. Deutchman, interview.
25. Details of the film's box-office performance were taken from Box Office Mojo, http://www.boxofficemojo.com/movies/?page=weekend&id=player.htm; accessed on 28 December 2010.
26. Brown, Colin, 'Manifesto Gives Lift to Little Joe', *Screen International* (17 July 1992), 4; Marx, Andy, 'Fine Line, CTHV Getting "Naked": Comedy Marks Directorial Debut of Scorsese Protégé Algrant', *Daily Variety* (16 October 1992), 3.
27. '"Cowgirls" Gets Distrib Deal at New Line Cinema', *Weekly Variety* (10 August 1992), 13.
28. Dawtrey, Adam, 'Spelling, FLF Take "Short Cuts"', *Daily Variety* (13 May 1992), 3.

29. Stevenson, William, 'Fine Line Finesses Art-House Mainstays', *Weekly Variety* (10 August 1992), 40.
30. Ibid.
31. Quinn, John, John Dempsey and Jennifer Pendleton, 'New Line Inks Showtime Deal', *Weekly Variety* (14 September 1992), 24.
32. Gold, Richard, 'Bravo for "Fine Line Theater"', *Hollywood Reporter* (24 March 1993), 6.
33. Fabrikant, Geraldine, 'Turner Buying New Line and Castle Rock Film Companies', *New York Times* (18 August 1993), http://www.nytimes.com/1993/08/18/business/turner-buying-new-line-and-castle-rock-film-companies.html?src=pm; accessed on 28 December 2010.
34. Toumarkine, Doris, 'Zeidman Takes Fine Line Post', *Hollywood Reporter* (7 March 1994), 67.
35. See in particular Roger Ebert's scathing review, *'Even Cowgirls Get the Blues'*, *The Chicago Sun Times* (20 May 1994), http://rogerebert.suntimes.com/apps/pbcs.dll/article?AID=/19940520/REVIEWS/405200301/1023; accessed on 28 December 2010.
36. Deutchman, interview.
37. Cox, 'Vitale Fine Line Prez', 1.
38. Cox, Dan, 'Fine Line Ups Profile in Market Battle', *Weekly Variety* (13 February 1995), 9.
39. Cox, 'Vitale Fine Line Prez', 1.
40. Perren, 'Sex, Lies and Marketing', 30–9.
41. Tzioumakis, *The Spanish Prisoner*, 21–2.
42. The box-office figure for the film was taken from Wyatt, 'The Formation of the "Major Independent"', 78.
43. Dawtrey, Adam, '"Starlight" Rights to Fine Line', *Daily Variety* (23 September 1994), n/a.
44. Honeycutt, Kirk, 'Nunn Stages New Line Deal', *Hollywood Reporter* (9 December 1994), n/a.
45. Cox, Dan, 'Fine Line Realigns Strategy', *Daily Variety* (6 May 1997), n/a.
46. 'Fine Line Features', *Hollywood Reporter* (1 August 1996), 14.
47. Balio, Tino, '"A Major Presence in All World's Major Markets": The Globalization of Hollywood in the 1990s', in *Contemporary Hollywood Cinema*, ed. Steve Neale and Murray Smith (London: Routledge, 1996), 69.
48. Saporito, Bill, Bernard Baumohl and Stacy Perman, 'Time for Turner', *Time* (21 October 1996), http://www.time.com/time/magazine/article/0,9171,985338,00.html; accessed on 28 December 2010.
49. Wyatt, 'The Formation of the "Major Independent"', 70.
50. Cox, 'Fine Line Realigns Strategy', n/a.
51. Ibid.
52. 'Fine Line Features', 14; 'Fine Line Features', *Hollywood Reporter* (4 September 1997), 19.
53. The figure for the film's budget was taken from IMDb, http://www.imdb.com/title/tt0118954/business); accessed on 28 December 2010.
54. Carver, Benedict, 'Fine Line Grows Int'l Sales Arm', *Weekly Variety* (30 March 1998), 18.
55. Harris, Dana, Thom Geier and Chris Gennusa, 'Fine Line Features', *Hollywood Reporter* (1 August 1999), 12.
56. '"The Lord of the Rings" to Begin Principal Photography in New Zealand; Peter Jackson

Directs International Cast in Production of Unprecedented Scope', *PR Newswire* (7 October 1999), n/a.
57. Lyons, Charles, 'Fine Line Revamps, Refines Goals', *Weekly Variety* (24 January 2000), 18.
58. Maynard, Kevin and Nicole LaPorte, 'Fine Line Divides Ordesky Between Niche, Event Pix', *Weekly Variety*, Showmen of the Year Supplement (23 August 2004), 10.
59. Dawtrey, Adam, 'Fine Line Nabs Rights to 3 Zentropa Pix', *Weekly Variety* (15 May 2000), 11; Rooney, David and Adam Dawtrey, 'Hungry Studios Ciao Down in Italy', *Weekly Variety* (24 July 2000), 8.
60. Cox, Dan and Jonathan Bing, 'Arts Distribs: An Overview', *Weekly Variety* (2 October 2000), 63.
61. Dunkley, Cathy and David Rooney, 'HBO Draws a Fine Line', *Daily Variety* (19 May 2003), 15.
62. Rooney, David and Cathy Dunkley, 'HBO's Theater Ticket: Fine Line to Distrib Pix from Cabler's Film Arm', *Daily Variety* (25 July 2003), 4.
63. Dunkley, Cathy, 'HBO Deal, Prod'n Puts Pics back in the Pipeline', *Daily Variety* (17 August 2003), 12.
64. Dawtrey, Adam, 'New Fine Line Team Nabs Hat Trick Pic', *Weekly Variety* (18 May 1998), 17.
65. Harris, Dana, 'Redrawn Lines Making a Mark: Ordesky Reorienting on Big Pics', *Daily Variety* (16 September 2004), 13.
66. This is the central argument in Holmlund and Wyatt, *Contemporary American Independent Film*.
67. Deutchman, interview.
68. Frook, John Evan, 'Castle Rock Greenlights Stillman's "Barcelona"', *Daily Variety* (20 November 1992), 3.

CHAPTER 5

# Sony Pictures Classics (1992 to date)

## INTRODUCTION

The next film division to be established during the second wave of specialty labels in the early 1990s was Sony Pictures Classics (SPC). Formed in early 1992 as Columbia's sister specialty label, the division started to trade officially on 1 April of the same year, once Sony had secured the former Orion Classics trio of executives, Tom Bernard, Michael Barker and Marcie Bloom, as the new outfit's management. Since then, the division has recorded sufficient commercial success to enjoy a longevity that has been rare in the field of niche film distribution. With Barker and Bernard still at the helm of the company after nineteen years, and over 350 film releases later – the second-largest number of releases for a company in the post-1980 specialty film market after Miramax – SPC has built a track record that is unparalleled 'in terms of continuity and profitability', and has been allowed to 'operate with a unique degree of autonomy'.[1] Indeed, the division's reputation has been so exemplary that it is often perceived as a company without ties to corporate Hollywood, a genuinely independent film finance and distribution firm.[2]

Like Fine Line Features, Sony Pictures Classics embraced business models that promoted a mixture of acquisitions and film production, though its emphasis remained firmly on the former. However, unlike Fine Line, Sony's division adhered strictly to a policy of keeping costs low both in terms of acquisition and marketing budgets and in terms of production finance investment. Opting for a low-risk business strategy that privileged distribution volume, the division focused on releasing a substantial number of films per year, seeking small profits from all of them rather than actively pursuing the big hit, the box-office gross of which could offset losses incurred by other films on its slate. This strategy, which ran counter to the emerging rules of the game in the post-*sex, lies, and videotape* niche distribution market of the early / mid-1990s and, of course, in the hit-driven indiewood sector of the late 1990s and 2000s, attracted criticism from the industry and the trade press, who accused SPC of conservatism and a reluctance to take risks or tap its full potential.[3] On the other hand, though, it has allowed the division to maintain a consistent profitability – no matter how small the profits have been.[4]

Besides its low-risk business strategy, SPC also differed from Fine Line in terms of the kind of product it handled. Given its emphasis on distribution volume, SPC handled approximately twenty pictures per year (almost double the number of Fine Line films), the majority of which were non-US arthouse films from around the world. This focus on 'foreign' film was partly because of the expertise of the division's executives and their success in the arthouse market following their stint at UA Classics and Orion Classics, and partly because of their low-risk philosophy. With an increasing number of specialty labels often getting locked into bidding wars to secure distribution rights of hyped US independent films at festivals like Sundance and Toronto, and with prices reaching often dizzying heights,[5] SPC had to resort to the international market to secure the substantial number of films it needed to fill its slate. In this particular aspect, the company resembled the 1980s classics divisions rather more than Fine Line and Miramax, and invited the widely held perception that it was simply the 1990s reincarnation of Orion Classics, the most successful specialty film distributor of the 1980s.

On the other hand, SPC's lack of involvement with the more expensive indie movies, the 'quality indie blockbusters',[6] which became the holy grail for most specialty distributors in the 1990s and 2000s, did not necessarily mean that the division was not a significant player in the US independent sector. On the contrary, despite its reluctance to commit large sums of money, SPC managed to secure the rights of numerous independent films, with a particular emphasis on titles that were often deemed too risqué for the other studio specialty labels. In the process, it became associated with some of the most celebrated indie films of the last two decades, including *Safe* (T. Haynes, 1995), *Welcome to the Dollhouse* (T. Solondz, 1996), *Lone Star* (J. Sayles, 1996), *In the Company of Men* (N. LaBute, 1997), *The Fog of War* (E. Morris, 2003), *Capote* (B. Miller, 2005), *Baghead* (M. and J. Duplass, 2008), *Please Give* (N. Holofcener, 2010) and many others.

Given the remarkable stability in the higher ranks of the division's management and their strict adherence to a particular set of business practices that changed little in almost two decades, it is difficult to divide SPC's history into clear-cut periods, in the same way that one could do with Fine Line. However, for the purposes of this chapter, the division's history will be split into three parts. The first one is from its establishment in 1992 up until 1997. During that period, SPC successfully established its identity in the niche film market, primarily through acquisitions and with a heavy emphasis on non-US films which it released successfully in the market. From 1997 to 2003, the division had to compete with several new rivals as, during that period, all the other majors introduced their own specialty labels. SPC's response was to continue its frugal policies but to start investing in production in a more substantial way, in partnerships but also as sole financial backer of films such as David Mamet's *The Winslow Boy* (1999).[7] Following another financially and critically successful period, Sony decided to commit more funds to its subsidiary and since then SPC has become an even stronger player in the specialty market, with its annual slate of films often surpassing the twenty title mark on average.[8] With a number of its rivals exiting the market following some closures in 2008 to 2009 (see next section), SPC has managed to consolidate its position as a leading specialty distributor.

## LABOUR-INTENSIVE DISTRIBUTION

Following the takeover of Columbia in November 1989 for $3.4 billion,[9] parent company Sony proceeded to restructure its subsidiary, which became part of Columbia Pictures Entertainment and was renamed Sony Pictures Entertainment (SPE) a year later. SPE consisted of a number of production, finance and distribution organisations, including Columbia Pictures, Tri-Star Pictures, Columbia Home Entertainment and other television-related outfits like Screen Gems (reinvented in the late 1990s as a specialty label distributing genre films). As part of the restructuring, Sony brought in new management regimes for its companies. One such move saw the arrival of Mike Medavoy from Orion Pictures, the parent company of Orion Classics, as the new Chairman of Tri-Star Pictures in March 1990.[10]

At that time, Orion was already experiencing serious financial problems while, as we saw in Chapter 3, Orion Classics was at the top of its game. In December 1990, the division made a co-finance and distribution agreement with Merchant-Ivory Productions for *Howards End*, the company's new adaptation of the E. M. Forster novel, following *Maurice* and *A Room with a View*. However, a year later and as Orion Pictures was filing for bankruptcy, the company's major stockholder, John Kluge, refused to authorise a payment of $1 million that Classics owed to Merchant–Ivory for the rights to distribute the film. With the future of the division uncertain, Medavoy approached Barker, Bernard and Bloom and asked them to come to Sony and lead the new specialty label Sony Pictures Classics.[11] In the early months of 1992 they agreed to follow one of their former bosses to Sony and be involved with their third classics division, and the second in senior executive roles.

With Orion reneging on its agreement with Merchant-Ivory, the distribution rights for the film went back to the production company following a court decision (see Chapter 3). Given that Merchant–Ivory had chosen Orion Classics because of its reputation and its executives' expertise in handling specialty films, it is not surprising that the production company immediately made a deal with SPC for the release of *Howards End*, which became the new division's first release. With a marketing campaign that focused strongly on the stereotypical elements of period film (especially costumes, location and the film's title written in an old-fashioned calligraphic font), and which was strongly anchored by the Merchant-Ivory Production trademark of quality and the E. M. Forster connection, the film was released on a single screen and stayed there for five weeks, building great word of mouth. Gradually, SPC opened it on over a hundred screens and circulated it slowly from one market to the next. This continued for almost a calendar year until, in February 1993, the film received nine Academy Award nominations, including one for Best Picture. By that time, *Howards End* had become a runaway hit in the specialty market, having grossed almost $19 million and surpassing the commercial success of *A Room with a View*. On hearing news of the nominations, SPC immediately expanded the film to over 500 screens to exploit the publicity. Helped by three Academy Awards, including one for Best Actress for Emma Thompson, *Howards End* added an additional $6 million to its box-office gross, finally finishing its theatrical run almost fifteen months after its release with $26 million.[12]

This early success – which would remain unsurpassed for almost a decade – gave the division a most welcome gift that would help justify SPC's conservative distribution practices while also demonstrating to Sony that there was certainly space for a specialty label division within a transnational diversified entertainment corporation in the age of blockbusters and synergies. Indeed, as Fine Line was the specialty label of a stand-alone mini-major that was still a relatively small player in the US film industry, SPC became the first major studio division since the establishment of Twentieth Century Fox International Classics in 1982. In the intervening decade, however, the US film industry had undergone remarkable changes, the most significant of which was, arguably, the majors' accelerated move towards mergers and acquisitions that would pronounce a structure of 'related areas of operation',[13] allowing individual areas (film, television, publishing, music, cable and so on) to work together and exploit particular properties in a variety of ways. It was becoming clear, then, that there was little place for classics divisions, at least in the way that they had been conceptualised in the 1980s. In this respect, a new division that seemed to have some points of contact with that model but which began life with a runaway commercial success was certainly making it easier for the management of the parent company to accept its role in the new transnational media and entertainment order.

However, hits like *Howards End* turned out to be the exception rather than the rule for SPC, with only two other films in the division's history grossing more at the theatrical box office. This was because SPC was founded on a set of principles that flagged it up as a conservative outfit that would be reluctant to gamble on expensive film properties with strong commercial elements that could prove major box-office champions. These principles could be summarised as follows: autonomy from the operations of the parent company; stability; small-scale operations; and adherence to distribution policies that, according to industry practitioners, tend to be 'labor intensive rather than capital intensive'.[14] Indeed, these principles made the division stand out from the rest of the post-1989 studio specialty labels that went aggressively for the 'big hit' and go some way towards explainng why films that grossed over $10 million remained a rare occurrence for SPC.

More specifically, the division's management team negotiated a strong contract with Sony Pictures Entertainment, which gave them 'complete autonomy' over the pictures they selected to finance and distribute, and precluded the much larger sister companies Columbia and Tri-Star from forcing them to take on films that they did not want to release.[15] Furthermore, their contract enabled them to undertake all distribution and marketing work 'in-house', rather than depending on the resources of the other distributors under the SPE umbrella. This has allowed them to 'protect the freedom and the ability to have an independent spirit of the way [they did] business' in all aspects of their work and has given them the opportunity to be solely responsible for their own campaigns.[16]

With the thorny issue of autonomy from parent and sister companies settled contractually, SPC's executives moved immediately to establish a distinct identity for the division. In the words of Tom Bernard, the division's philosophy right from the start was that 'every movie should be bought and worked to try to succeed, and be a financial success.'[17] This suggested an eclectic approach to the choice of films that comprised the division's annual slate, as each title needed to have a clear hook to ensure effective marketing and therefore a chance to succeed in the increasingly crowded specialty marketplace of the 1990s. Part and parcel of this approach was the devising of customised, labour-intensive marketing campaigns, designed to locate core audiences for each title before targeting more general audiences. As long as the company was successful in finding the small core audience for each of its titles, all its films stood a chance of bringing in sufficient revenue to return SPC's investment and might often turn in a small profit. Any other audiences would just add to the bottom line and, on rare occasions, provide the division with a crossover hit.

The division's identity can be seen clearly in its roster of releases in the first year of operation. As well as the upmarket British period costume drama *Howards End*, with its clear marketing hooks and obvious appeal to arthouse audiences, SPC distributed three other films in 1992, including well-known French auteur Maurice Pialat's *Van Gogh*, an expensive French production that examined Vincent Van Gogh's final days, which also targeted an upmarket arthouse audience that tended to respond to prestige European titles. Mexican filmmaker Maria Novarro's *Danzón* is a film about a middle-aged Mexican woman and the journey of self-discovery she embarks upon when her long-term dancing partner suddenly disappears. With its emphasis on *danzón*, a popular Mexican dance, the film targeted both Mexican cinema-goers and the substantial audience for films in the Spanish language that had made a number of films from South American countries and Spain commercial successes in the specialty market (for instance, the Carlos Saura films for Orion Classics). Finally, the division also released *Indochine* (R. Wargnier), an epic production starring Catherine Deneuve and telling a tragic love story that takes place during the war in Indochina. The epic scale of the film and Deneuve's stardom in arthouse circles, helped by two Academy Award nominations for Best Foreign Film (which it won) and Actress in a Leading Role for Deneuve, made *Indochine* a solid success at the US box office, taking almost $6 million and giving SPC a second hit in its first year of operation. SPC's identity, then, revolved primarily around films that targeted the upmarket subsection of the arthouse film audience that favours prestige non-US films which deal with literary, artistic or historical subject matter. From that basis, the division could also branch out to any clearly defined niche market, as was the case with *Danzón*. The division followed a similar approach to film selection in its second year of operation, when it released ten pictures.

As is clear, the division's identity in this early period had nothing to do with US independent film, especially compared to Fine Line, which had released over ten titles of this designation in the first two years of operations. However, in May 1993, SPC made its first deal to distribute such a film when it secured the North American rights to Allison Anders's third feature, *Mi Vida Loca*. Anders, who had been in the vanguard of indie cinema after the critical and commercial success of her low-budget second feature, *Gas Food Lodging* (1992), had secured finance for *Mi Vida Loca* from HBO Showcase,[18] a film production branch of the giant cable broadcaster, and the film was originally intended for a straight-to-cable release. However, in much the same way as HBO agreed to release some of its made-for-TV films theatrically through Fine Line in the early 2000s in order to increase their market value, HBO Showcase made a similar decision in 1993, allowing *Mi Vida Loca* to be released in theatres. The film opened a year later, in July 1994, and proved a modest success, grossing approximately $3.3 million at the US box office. Furthermore, as the Disney-backed Miramax had started acquiring an increasing number of films from around the world, often outbidding SPC in securing the rights for arthouse films with commercial potential, SPC became more active in looking for product in the US independent sector.

Sticking to its plan to release between nine and fourteen films a year, each budgeted between $100,000 and $5 million,[19] SPC had an almost full slate in 1995 and 1996, with almost half of its releases originating from the US. These included *Amateur* (H. Hartley, 1995), *Living in Oblivion* (T. DiCillo, 1995), *Safe*, *Welcome to the Dollhouse*, *Lone Star*, *Waiting for Guffman* (C. Guest, 1996) and *Denise Calls Up* (H. Selwyn, 1996), as well as documentaries such as *Crumb* (T. Zwigoff, 1995) and *The Celluloid Closet* (V. Russo, 1996). Yet despite the critical success of all the above films and their almost immediate acceptance into the US independent cinema canon, only John Sayles's *Lone Star* became a crossover hit, bringing in $12 million at the US box office; the much lower-budgeted *Welcome to the Dollhouse* and *Crumb* came a distant second and third, taking slightly over $4 and $3 million, respectively. With the remaining releases performing modestly, especially in 1995 when SPC recorded a total theatrical box-office gross of slightly over $20 million from fourteen releases, SPC's performance raised concerns, articulated clearly in the *Hollywood Reporter* headline: 'The Big Question: Can [SPC] Find Boxoffice Magic Again?'[20]

Indeed, capturing only 0.39 per cent of the theatrical market not only did not compare favourably with Miramax, which had recorded grosses of over $180 million in 1995 and had claimed 3.41 per cent of the distributors' market share. It was also lower than the share of several stand-alone distributors, although better than Fine Line's, which recorded just $14 million and captured about 0.27 per cent of the US theatrical market in the same year. However, the success of Sayles's *Lone Star* in the following year drove SPC's annual theatrical gross to almost $40 million, in effect doubling the division's market share to 0.72 per cent from eighteen pictures. Even though it still trailed Miramax substantially (4.31 per cent from thirty-eight titles), these results none the less placed the division above key stand-alone specialty distributors such as Samuel Goldwyn Company, October Films and New Yorker, as well as studio arms Fine Line and Fox Searchlight.

Despite the sizable contribution from *Lone Star*, the doubling of SPC's annual box-office gross was largely due to two other films that had little to do with the division's work in the independent and arthouse film markets: *Across the Sea of Time* (S. Low, 1995) and *Wings of Courage* (J.-J. Annaud, 1996). These were 'large-format' films and represented Sony's presence in the large-format (IMAX, SimEx-Iwerks) market, at a time when this type of technology was still in its incipient phase and it therefore was still not clear whether the new format would be adopted more widely. Given the niche status of this market, it made sense for Sony to position its large-format distribution team as part of its classics division and, in this respect, to create Sony Pictures Classics Large Format as a subdivision of SPC in August 1994.[21] With the first two releases of SPC Large Format mentioned above recording a combined gross of over $13.5 million, it is clear that the improvement in the division's financial performance was not as dramatic as comparison of the annual figures would perhaps suggest.

The division's increasing visibility in the US independent film sector, and in particular its presence in showcases for films of that designation, did not go unnoticed, especially as it was awarded the Friend of the Independent Filmmaker title in the Independent Film Project / Spirit Awards of 1996.[22] Becoming increasingly known as an organisation that 'acquires, markets and distributes foreign and American independent films' was certainly important for the division's identity,[23] particularly as its main competitor at the time, Miramax, was also concentrating equally on both these fronts, though on a considerable larger scale than SPC. In this respect, in order to remain competitive, SPC could not have ignored the enormous amount of activity that was taking place in the US indie sector – especially after the extraordinary commercial success of *Pulp Fiction* in 1994. SPC's increasing presence in the period 1995 to 1996 therefore sent a message to the industry that the division was not simply an updated model of the 'old-style' classics arms, but a modern niche film division that was aware of where the specialty film game was being played. Still, at the same time, SPC did not hesitate to venture into the rerelease market, seemingly forgotten by the other existing studio divisions; it restored and rereleased nine films by acclaimed Indian filmmaker Satyajit Ray in 1995, along with Vittorio de Sica's Oscar-winning film *The Garden of the Finzi-Continis*, which originally appeared in 1972.[24]

Interestingly, SPC's minor success in 1996 took place within an environment of economic and organisational instability, following parent company Sony's $3.2 billion loss in November 1994 (incurred primarily because of a five-year period of mismanagement and expensive flops in its Sony Pictures Entertainment group);[25] the retirement of longstanding Sony chairman and co-founder Akio Morita shortly after; his replacement by Nobuyuki Idei in March 1995; and the inevitable reorganisation of the whole Sony structure in the following months. In August 1996, a new management team was installed at SPE, with John Calley taking over from Peter Guber. In the ensuing restructuring, Columbia and TriStar merged into a single entity, Columbia TriStar Pictures, and in January 1997, SPE's new chairman reached a new long-term agreement with SPC. Despite reports in the trade press that Barker, Bernard and Bloom were being courted by Paramount in order to launch the major's new specialty division, Paramount Classics, the three executives decided to stay with Sony.[26]

## PLAYING THE PRODUCTION GAME

Prior to the extension of their contract with Sony, the SPC executives had followed a business model that relied primarily on acquisitions, along with a small number of co-production deals. However, by the mid-1990s and as competition for the best negative pick-ups intensified due to the increasing buying power of Miramax and the entrance of several new niche distributors, SPC had started 'get[ting] involved [with films] at an earlier point of development, frequently at script stage', effectively co-financing films in exchange for distribution rights. Indeed, by 1996, the division was becoming more adventurous and was even acting as sole financial backer of low-budget productions, such as Bart Freundlich's *The Myth of Fingerprints*, which SPC financed for $2 million.[27] With the support of its parent company, SPC was now in a position – on paper, at least – to finance more expensive productions, if it so desired, while also committing larger sums to acquisitions and potentially rivalling Miramax (and the Time Warner-owned Fine Line Features), both in terms of bidding for commercial hits and in terms of the number of titles that it could release annually.

Despite the fact that Sony was certainly as financially powerful as Disney and Time Warner and therefore the new agreement could have entailed the channelling of more substantial funds from parent company to subsidiary, SPC's mandate and conduct in the market post-1997 changed little. More specifically, the division's annual output showed no great variation, with the company still releasing fifteen films on average and with its box-office and market share remaining at similar levels to the pre-1997 era. For instance, according to *Hollywood Reporter*, SPC released thirteen films in the 1997–8 season, with box-office revenues reaching $23 million,[28] which is certainly on a par with the division's fourteen releases in the 1995 calendar year and a total box-office gross of $21 million. Where, perhaps, the division's game plan differed from the pre-1997 era was in the size of its production investments, as SPC was now more prepared to invest at the top bracket of its production budget – $5 million – in one film; it did just that in 1998, when it became sole financial backer of David Mamet's *The Winslow Boy*, which was budgeted at $5 million and therefore represented a more substantial risk than other lower (co-)production investments.[29]

The absence of dramatic change in the division's conduct of business attracted some criticisms,[30] the foundation for which could be located in the recent success of Miramax, which had managed to balance quality and commerce in a series of very successful films in the 1996–8 period; these included *The English Patient* (A. Minghella, 1996), *Good Will Hunting* (G. Van Sant, 1997) and *Shakespeare in Love* (J. Madden, 1998). New specialty labels, like Fox Searchlight, had also distributed the British comedy *The Full Monty*

(P. Cattaneo) in 1997, which went on to become a global hit, grossing over $200 million worldwide. Compare these to SPC's number one hits in the respective years – *Lone Star*, $12 million in 1996; *Waiting for Guffman*, $3 million in 1997; and *The Spanish Prisoner* (D. Mamet), $10 million in 1998 – and it is clear that the former two distributors were operating in a different league from SPC.

Despite the criticisms, it is obvious that the new management of Sony Pictures Entertainment was actively committed to supporting SPC and its low-risk philosophy. This became particularly evident in 1998, when the parent company decided to launch a new specialty film label with the explicit intention of handling films with a more 'commercial sensibility' and a larger budget, in the $4 to $12 million range.[31] In spite of some concerns in its first few years of operation that the new label would undermine SPC, given the fact that it distributed a number of titles that one would have expected to be released by the latter (*Limbo* [J. Sayles, 1999], *Girl Fight* [K. Kusama, 2000] and *Adaptation* [S. Jonze, 2002]), Screen Gems eventually turned its focus almost exclusively on to low-budget genre production; therefore it was mainly competing against a different breed of specialty labels, which included Dimension Films (Disney) and Rogue Pictures (Universal), from the quality film specialty divisions that this book examines.

With the full support of the parent company and notwithstanding the changing conditions of the specialty film market effected by the entry of the third wave of studio specialty divisions, SPC continued with 'business as usual', though with a more substantial emphasis on production. Following the success of *Lone Star*, SPC pre-bought Sayles's next film, *Men with Guns*, after approving the final shooting script, and in May 1997 made a similar deal for *The Governess* (S. Goldbacher) with French production company Pandora Cinema. As Tom Bernard stated after SPC had secured the latter title:

> While we have occasionally acquired such films as *The Myth of Fingerprints* and *Howards End* at the script stage in the past, our deal on *The Governess* and our recent acquisition of John Sayles's *Men with Guns* should be a signal to the community that we are aggressively pursuing more pre-buys. Our goal is to become involved with many more high quality films prior to production on a multi-territory basis.[32]

True to its word, SPC continued to make similar deals in the final years of the 1990s, fully exploiting relationships with filmmakers that its executives had been building since their time at UA Classics in the early 1980s and for the next two decades, including Carlos Saura (*Goya in Bordeaux*, 1999), Agnieska Holland (*The Third Miracle*, 1999) and Terence Davies (*House of Mirth*, 2000). At the same time, however, SPC continued its programme of acquisitions by renewing a longstanding relationship with French production and distribution company Union Générale Cinématographique (UGC) and *Indochine* director Régis Wargnier, whose new epic, *Est ouest* [*East West*], was secured by SPC for approximately $400,000.[33] Finally, it also continued to be active on the US indie scene, though the influx of new specialty distributors from the mid-1990s onwards had limited its involvement substantially; David Mamet's *The Winslow Boy* (1999), Hal Hartley's *Henry Fool* (1998) and Don Roos's *The Opposite of Sex* (1998) were the main indie films distributed by SPC.

Even with all this activity, the division's financial results did not improve drastically. For the calendar year 1999, SPC's box-office revenues remained stagnant at approximately $22 million (excluding large-format releases) and a share of approximately 0.30 per cent of the theatrical market, compared to the $380 million that Miramax recorded at the North American box office, corresponding to a 4.33 per cent market share.[34] The next year, 2000, turned out to be a better one financially, with approximately $39 million (again without including large-format releases) and a corresponding 0.60 per cent share of the theatrical market. However, if one deducts from that total the $12 million made by *Crouching Tiger, Hidden Dragon* (Ang Lee) in the last month of 2000,[35] the division's total annual box office reverts to the figures it has been associated with from its first years of operation.

*Crouching Tiger, Hidden Dragon* was produced by well-known independent film packager, producer and occasional distributor Good Machine, with whom SPC had longstanding ties, having released a number of its past productions, including *Safe* and *The Myth of Fingerprints*. When Good Machine, which had a close relationship with Taiwanese director Ang Lee, having produced all but one of his previous films, put together the package for *Crouching Tiger, Hidden Dragon* and budgeted the film at $15 million, SPC became one of the cofinanciers of the project, in exchange for distribution rights in English-speaking territories and South America.[36] After its premiere at the 2000 Cannes Film Festival, where it was screened out of competition, the film built an incredible word of mouth, helped by rave reviews and participation in key international film festivals. With all this hype and following a number of publicity-building exercises that included private screenings for numerous parties in exchange for coverage in various media outlets,[37] the division released the film in platform in December 2000 in sixteen engagements. For the next five weeks, it gradually started adding prints, reaching 172 engagements by the end of the film's fifth week of release and recording a gross of $18 million. In the face of such an overwhelming response, SPC went to sister company Columbia Pictures (by that time renamed Sony Pictures) and used its resources to take the film wide. By March 2001 and assisted by ten Academy Award nominations, the film was playing in over 2,000 theatres and had grossed over $60 million, surpassing Miramax's *Life is Beautiful* as the most commercially successful non-English-language film at the North American box office. By the time the film was taken off the screens in August of the same year, it had reached a figure of almost $130 million at the theatrical box office.

Although *Crouching Tiger, Hidden Dragon* is certainly an anomaly in terms of box-office success, especially for a company whose greatest commercial success up until then, *Howards End*, had grossed over $100 million less than Lee's film, it none the less did not represent a break in the division's philosophy and approach to distribution. With SPC acquiring the US film rights in exchange for providing a percentage of the $15 million budget and following a marketing campaign that was labour-intensive and aimed at generating as much free publicity for the film as possible, *Dragon* became a 'fortunate accident' for the division. At the same time, however, and as I have argued elsewhere, the incredible financial success of the film came at a time when world cinema had been emerging in the late 1990s and early 2000s as another commercial alternative to Hollywood, taking its place alongside indie cinema.[38] In this respect, a large part of the industrial infrastructure and the resources used to support mainly US indie film in the 1990s had been shifting to support European and Asian commercial cinema, leading to several significant box-office successes; Lee's film proved to be the biggest of them all.

While the remarkable success of *Dragon* was seen by many industry commentators and the trade press as a catalyst for SPC to shift gears and become involved more aggressively with more commercially promising films, the division's executives refused to reconsider their low-risk philosophy.[39] Instead, what the millions in rental income from *Dragon* allowed SPC to do was to continue to target, but with greater aggressiveness and conviction, the types of films they would normally target (such as Argentinian box-office smash *Nine Queens*, which is the Case Study for this chapter);[40] this meant that the division was in a position to become involved in a bidding war for the right film – as in the case of Pedro Almodóvar's *Habla con Ella [Talk to Her]* (2002), which was courted by a number of distributors, following the success of his previous film *Todo sobre mi madre [All about My Mother]* (1999). It also allowed SPC to increase its participation in production finance and therefore continue to invest in finance deals with key indie filmmakers, either as a sole party (John Sayles's *Sunshine State* [2002]) and Paul Schrader's *Auto Focus* [2002]) or in co-finance arrangements such as that for David Gordon Green's *All the Real Girls*, which SPC bankrolled in association with well-known independent producer Jean Doumanian.[41] In terms of box-office revenues, however, the division's performance in 2002 quickly returned to pre-*Crouching Tiger, Hidden Dragon* standards. In stark contrast to the $128 million that Lee's film had grossed in 2001, the top earners in 2002 were *Thirteen Conversations about One Thing* (J. Sprecher) and John Sayles's *Sunshine State*, each grossing a little over $3 million and giving the division a total box-office and market share for that calendar year of approximately $20 million and 0.23 per cent, respectively (down from approximately $136 million and 1.69 per cent in 2001).

Despite the return to its normal market share, SPC's films continued to attract great critical interest and numerous awards, keeping the division in the public eye and helping increase its cultural capital and its reputation as a top destination for niche films. As well as the large number of awards that, among others, *Crouching Tiger, Hidden Dragon*, *Talk to Her* and *Pollock* (E. Harris, 2001) brought in, SPC received a number of other distinctions as a company. For example, in late 2001 it was awarded the prestigious medal of Chevalier of the Order of Arts and Letters 'for promoting independent cinema and cultural diversity',[42] while in June 2002 it became the first distributor to receive a Directors Guild of America Award for its support of filmmaker-driven cinema.[43]

Garnering so much prestige and with its films remaining profitable, despite the very tight margins, SPC had little reason to change its philosophy and business model. An improved financial performance followed in 2003, with nature documentary *Winged Migration* (J. Perrin and J. Cluzaud) and Almodóvar's *Talk to Her* recording grosses of approximately $10 million each, as did further critical success, with *Talk to Her* and Errol Morris's documentary *The Fog of War* receiving Academy Awards for Best Original Screenplay and Best Documentary film, respectively; the SPC trio of executives were ready for a second extension of their contract with Sony. In May 2004, they agreed to stay with Sony for an additional five years. By that time, SPC had released over 200 titles, its films had been nominated for seventy-seven Academy Awards in various categories, and they had won nineteen times.[44]

## CONSERVATIVE EXPANSION

In terms of the division's mandate, SPC's new contract saw a more substantial degree of difference from the preceding two periods, though still adhering to some of the key principles that helped distinguish the company in the marketplace from the very beginning. First, the number of releases increased from between 9 and 14 to between 15 and 20 titles per year and on several occasions even went beyond the 20-film mark.[45] Second, for a distributor that had traditionally specialised in acquisitions of finished films targeted primarily at international film festivals, SPC was now geared more towards pre-buys through sole and co-financing deals, with almost two-thirds of its titles comprising films secured at various stages in their production process and before their festival premiere.[46] This was a result of the increased competition that SPC had been facing from the mid- to late 1990s onwards, when all the majors introduced their own specialty labels; this meant that renowned filmmakers were often being courted by a large number of financer–distributors willing to (co-)finance their films in exchange for the distribution rights.

An additional element of complexity here was added by the remarkable speed with which DVD technology entered the arena from the late 1990s to the early 2000s. The pervasiveness of this new technology created a brand new distribution outlet for films and benefited niche distributors like SPC immensely, especially from 2002 onwards, when it became clear that the DVD market would primarily be a sell-through market rather than a rental one.[47] With the DVD rights to many films that were available as negative pick-ups either pre-sold or retained by the producer, distributors who failed to secure the DVD rights stood to make the limited returns that the theatrical market normally allows. However, as an increasing number of films released by specialty distributors seemed to be returning more funds from DVD sales than from the theatrical box office, it made sense (and good business) for distributors to try to secure the DVD rights as well as the theatrical rights. In this respect, becoming involved from an early stage as a (co-)financer allowed these distributors to negotiate deals that included the rights for this lucrative new ancillary market. And with studio divisions like SPC having at their disposal the resources and clout of the parent company's Home Entertainment division, it made even more sense to target films whose DVD rights were still available and then to use the parent company's resources to exploit these titles fully. For example, Paul Schrader's film *Auto Focus*, financed by SPC, did little business at the US box office, recording a gross of $2.1 million. However, the same title brought in over $8.5 million from the DVD market,[48] thereby proving a commercial success for the division.

Arguably less visible but equally important, the other ancillary markets, and especially cable TV and foreign distribution, have constituted two areas in which SPC has seen a significant increase in terms of revenues in recent years.[49] While the division's reputation as an arthouse distributor of work by celebrated world cinema auteurs bumped up its revenue from distribution outside the US, SPC and the other specialty divisions did benefit substantially in the early to mid-2000s from the renewed interest of US cable television in niche filmmaking. According to reports in the trade press, in 2003 cable broadcasters were stepping up their support of indie cinema, often in dramatic ways, with Showtime 'becoming a major buyer of specialty indie films', and with niche cable distributors such as the Independent Film Channel and Sundance Channel buying an increasing number of pictures for their schedules.[50] With some of these channels being able to commit substantial funds for the cable rights to indie films, it was clear that this was one ancillary market that could prove particularly lucrative for a reputable niche distributor with a significant annual volume of films.

The division's now-stronger position in the 2000s marketplace was emphasised even further with its acquisition of a number of titles that had more crossover potential than its average pictures. For example, in 2004 the division had lined up Spike Lee's *She Hate Me*; Yimou Zhang's epic, *House of Flying Daggers*; the star-studded *Imaginary Heroes* (D. Harris) and *Being Julia* (I. Szabo); and the European co-production *Merry Christmas* (C. Carion, 2005), for which SPC paid $2 million for the US theatrical rights alone.[51] However, this obvious shift in gear did not necessarily mean a radical change in the division's low-risk philosophy. Rather, as I mentioned earlier, it meant an intensification of its focus on the type of film it normally targeted. And while, in the past, the finance deals tended either to be made with partners or to have a ceiling of $5 million if SPC was the sole financial backer, the division was now occasionally lifting this ceiling, as its $6 million finance package for Nicole Holofcener's *Friends with Money* (2005) demonstrates.[52]

The division's enhanced position in the marketplace can also be seen from its annual box-office performance. While, in 2004, SPC's films had grossed approximately $21 million for a 0.24 per cent share of the market, the twenty-one SPC titles of 2005 made for a combined gross of approximately $59 million, capturing 0.66 per cent of the market share; the two crossover hits it enjoyed, *Kung Fu Hustle* (S. Chow) and *Capote*, together grossed almost $30 million. This improved performance was replicated in 2006, when the division's eighteen films grossed a combined $60 million for 0.65 per cent of the market share, with $30 million again brought in by two films, *Capote* (which was released in September 2005 but played in cinemas until April 2006, grossing $29 million in total and becoming the division's second-highest-grossing film after *Crouching Tiger, Hidden Dragon*) and 'in-house' production *Friends with Money*, which took $13 million in the US.

These results were perceived by SPC and its parent company as an incentive to continue its conservative expansion. In January 2007, Michael Barker admitted that there was 'an organic change within the company' which coincided with 'an organic change within the marketplace'.[53] This change was caused by a constantly shrinking market for negative pick-ups, itself a product of the specialty labels' (including SPC's) involvement with films at an earlier stage, and often at script level. This means that most of the films with the potential for success were already attached to a distributor, leaving a very small pool of titles that could interest the studios' specialty arms. In this respect, SPC decided to 'shift its gameplan' and concentrate on 'board[ing] projects earlier, increase its financing role in films and up the budgets of the movies it distributes from an average of $6 million to as much as $15 million'.[54] These changes would place the division increasingly close to business practices associated with the leading divisions of the third wave of specialty labels, especially Focus Features and Fox Searchlight.

SPC's decision to shift its gameplan came at a time when the rest of the studio subsidiaries were undergoing major management changes that would eventually lead to a great shakeout of the sector in 2008 (see Chapter 9), especially immediately after the 'demise' of Miramax following the exit of Harvey and Bob Weinstein in 2005. However, the shift to product with more crossover potential was also prompted by SPC's parent company's decision to push for more films 'above and beyond the festival pickup model' that would contribute to the general revenue of Sony's various film divisions.[55] For that reason, and despite the parent company's respect 'for the Barker–Bernard charter of autonomy', SPC found itself in a position where it would itself have to release films that had originally been developed for its much larger sister label, Sony Pictures. One such title was *The Jane Austen Book Club* (R. Swicord, 2007), a film with a wider appeal than most SPC projects, which was produced by former SPE Chairman John Calley after he stepped down from his post and signed a production deal with Sony.[56]

Despite the nature of these changes and the seeming imposition from above of some principles that were foreign to the company's original philosophy, SPC's identity did not seem to alter drastically. The division's performance in the years 2007 to 2010 ranged from $40 million combined box office and a 0.41 per cent share of the market (2007) to $65 million and a 0.63 percent share of the market on twenty releases a year on average. As in 2005 and 2006, SPC's top earners during the closing years of the 2000s were films that broke the $10 million mark in terms of box-office gross – *The Lives of Others* (F. Henckel von Donnersmarck, 2007; $11.3 million), *Rachel Getting Married* (J. Demme, 2008; $12.8 million) and *An Education* (L. Scherfig, 2009; $12.6 million) – rather than turning out to be the next *Crouching Tiger, Hidden Dragon* or even coming close to the almost $30 million made by *Capote* and *Howards End*, which have remained the top three commercial successes for the division. Partly responsible for this has been SPC's persistence in using the same labour-intensive niche distribution marketing methods to push its films in the market, still refusing to buy television advertising and adopt other marketing strategies that have helped its rivals turn some of their low-budget properties into global hits.

Notwithstanding the failure to make a dramatic difference at the box office, the consistency of performance of their films in the last 6 years convinced Sony to renew Barker and Bernard's contracts as co-Presidents of SPC for an additional 4 years, extending their management term to 2013. With its films continuing to receive awards (most recently, the Oscar for Best Documentary for *Inside Job* [C. Ferguson, 2010] and Best Foreign Film for *Civilization* [S. Bier, 2010]) and providing the parent company with important diversity of product for its vast distribution pipelines,[57] it seems that SPC's place in the niche film market is secure; this is especially so as, post-2008, a number of its rivals have exited the field, leaving behind a consolidated specialty film sector.

## CONCLUSION

Sony Pictures Classics succeeded where all the classics divisions established before it failed. Having carved out a distinct identity from the start and through strict adherence to its low-risk philosophy, SPC refused to follow trends that emerged post-1995, when a new wave of studio film divisions entailed the commitment of increasingly large funds for production and distribution, and the gradual adoption of practices that, up until that time, had been strongly associated with the major Hollywood distributors (saturation releases, network television advertising and so on). Avoiding costly bidding wars and therefore missing out on the opportunity to distribute potentially more commercial fare, Sony's classics division specialised primarily in non-US arthouse films by renowned filmmakers; it had cultivated long-term relationships with the majority of these directors since the 1980s, when the company's senior executives were employed at UA Classics and Orion Classics. SPC also specialised in the finance and distribution of low-budget, homegrown films that had more points of contact with the low-budget, low-key independent films of the 1980s than with the star-studded indiewood films of the mid- to late 1990s and 2000s. In this respect, it managed to carve a niche for its films and to remain remarkably consistent in terms of commercial and critical success in the volatile and unpredictable specialty film market. Although the commercial success of its films never reached the same level as rival distributors such as Fox Searchlight and Focus Features, it was sufficient to convince the parent company's various management regimes to continue to support the division. As a result, SPC has retained the same management structure since its first year of operation and for the following nineteen years while, despite a slight expansion in the second half of the 2000s, it has also retained the same number of staff it had from inception.[58] If nothing else, SPC's example demonstrates clearly that a specialty arm with a clear business plan, stability in terms of management and vision, and a lack of interference from the parent company can both flourish in the marketplace and outlive the competition.

---

**Case Study: *Nueve Reinas* [*Nine Queens*]**
**(Fabián Bielinsky, 2000 [2002])**

Following the astonishing commercial success of *Crouching Tiger, Hidden Dragon* in 2001, Sony Pictures Classics kept to its long-established business model and emphasis on non-US arthouse film, though it did start targeting more commercially promising titles, often beating rivals to the acquisition of sought-after films such as Pedro Almódovar's *Talk to Her*. One of these titles was Argentine con game film, *Nueve Reinas*, which in 2000 became the highest-grossing film in Argentina for over a decade and which SPC had bought at the 2001 Cannes Film Festival.[59] The film was seen as part of a new breed of films from Latin American countries, which were 'more aware of the international market'[60] and therefore had attracted production and marketing funds from independent companies eager to invest in commercially viable filmmaking in the region. Films such as *Amores Perros* (A. G. Iñárritu, 2000), *Y Tu Mamá También* [*And Your Mother Too!*] (A. Cuarón, 2002) and *Diarios de Motocicleta* [*The Motorcycle Diaries*] (W. Salles, 2004) travelled outside their national and regional context particularly well, recording often-spectacular box-office figures in the US market and receiving rave reviews and Academy Award nominations.

In some ways, these films could be considered the indiewood equivalent of non-US arthouse films. In particular, they retained several elements associated with art cinema (emphasis on realism and ambiguity; a slower narrative and editing pace; a desire to trigger thought and, sometimes, shock; a tendency to unhappy endings and so on), as well as features that characterise filmmaking in their respective national and regional contexts. At the same time, they also demonstrated slick production values, made strong use of clear generic frameworks, often featured stars with some degree of international recognition and dealt with stories that would appeal equally to a Latin American and an international audience. According to Shaw, *Nine Queens*, specifically, was a film that '[could] be viewed as a generic scam movie, or it [could] be viewed as an Argentine film rooted in a national tradition and concerned with contemporary socio political issues'.[61] On the other hand, for SPC executive Dylan Lerner, *Nine Queens* was an appealing film as 'it broke the stereotype of traditional Latin American cinema',[62] which has been associated with explicitly political filmmaking that had little commercial appeal.

The film follows two con artists, Marcos (Ricardo Darín) and Juan (Gastón Pauls), in contemporary Buenos Aires over the course of twenty-four hours. Marcos saves Juan when a con trick at a petrol station goes wrong, with a view to recruiting him as his sidekick and potentially to conning him out of his money. As they go about performing a number of quick con tricks, they become involved in the sale of a counterfeit sheet of nine stamps, which are supposed to be extremely valuable, to a Spanish businessman. However, they lose the fake stamps and end up buying the original sheet at a reduced price with their own savings, with a view to making a profit from the Spanish businessman, who is willing to pay an inflated amount. It turns out that all these events were part of a trap for Marcos that was set by Juan, with the participation of a number of people that Marcos had fooled or mistreated over the years, including Marcos's own sister Valeria. The ending sees Marcos holding a cashier's cheque for hundreds of thousands of dollars from the sale but unable to use it, as the bank that underwrote it collapsed following fraudulent activities on the part of its board members.

Although the clear generic framework of the con game film within which the film operates allows for a very fast-paced and extremely entertaining story, *Nine Queens* also differs from US titles such as *The Spanish Prisoner* and *Confidence* (J. Foley, 2003) in significant ways. Arguably, the most important difference lies in the ways in which the film mobilises the discourse of corruption. While corruption is also instrumental in the Hollywood examples of the genre, it nevertheless either tends to be constructed in individual terms or is strictly contained within the microcosm in which the con artists operate, and therefore cannot be taken as indicative of the state of the US nation, as a signifier of a society in crisis.

In *Nine Queens*, however, the discourse of corruption – complete and total corruption – can be detected in almost every scene of the film and is mobilised as a key signifier of Argentina's problems. This is seen clearly in a montage approximately twenty-five minutes into the film, when Marcos shows Juan how pervasive corruption in the Argentine society is, how everyone around them is ready to make a move on other people, and how the Argentine capital is full of 'spitters, breakers, skin workers, blind fronts, hoisters, hooks, stalls, petermans, night raiders, grabbers, mustard checkers, fences, operators: swindlers'. Furthermore, the film's ending transfers this discourse of corruption from the diegesis to the real world, as the collapse of the bank at which Marcos was going to cash his cheque makes reference to a number of such instances during the major economic crisis in Argentina in the late 1990s and early 2000s. It is clear, then, that, despite its generic entertainment and commercial imperatives, *Nine Queens* does raise issues that are nationally and regionally specific and therefore maintains its kinship with earlier political filmmaking in the country.

SPC's marketing campaign steered clear of those issues. The division strongly emphasised the film's generic pedigree (obvious in the tagline 'If You Think You've Got It Figured Out . . . You've Been Conned) while ensuring that specific references to Argentina and its political problems were kept out of the advertising material. For instance, the film's poster focuses on the two main protagonists and the metropolitan area in which they operate, though any particular signifiers of locality are removed. Equally, the trailer created for the US market does not feature any Spanish-language dialogue, opting instead for brief scenes from the film that are presented under the authority of a voiceover. Despite this, the film made only $1.2 million at the US box office, proving the least successful of the group of prominent Latin American films of the period. Still, two years after its release, it was remade by Steven Soderbergh and George Clooney's production company, Section Eight, under the title *Criminal* and distributed by fellow studio specialty label Warner Independent Pictures. That film is discussed in the Case Study section for Chapter 9.

## NOTES

1. Bart, Peter, 'Sony Classics' Class Act', *Weekly Variety* (23 May 2005), 4.
2. Grove, Christopher, 'Crouching Indie', *Weekly Variety* (14 May 2001), 35.
3. Roman, Monica and Andrew Hindes, 'Classic Formula', *Weekly Variety* (3 August 1998), 7.
4. Thompson, Anne, 'Moving Pictures', *Hollywood Reporter* (17 October 2006), C1.
5. Biskind, *Down and Dirty Pictures*, 228.
6. Perren, 'Sex, Lies, and Marketing', 30–9.
7. Tzioumakis, *The Spanish Prisoner*, 62.
8. Unless otherwise stated, the figures relating to the division's distribution volume and box-office statistics were taken from *The Numbers*, http://www.the-numbers.com/market/Distributors/SonyPicturesClassics.php; accessed on 20 January 2011.

9. Prince, *A New Pot of Gold*, 58.
10. Medavoy with Young, *You're Only as Good*, 214.
11. Medavoy with Young, *You're Only as Good*, 284.
12. All figures for *Howards End* were taken from Box Office Mojo, http://boxofficemojo.com; accessed on 20 January 2011.
13. Prince, *A New Pot of Gold*, 60.
14. Mark Gill, President of Warner Independent Pictures, was quoted in Clark, John, 'To Promote Unusual Films, Try Uncommon Marketing', *New York Times* (16 January 2006), C5.
15. Thompson, 'Moving Pictures', C4.
16. Hernandez, Eugene, 'Decade: Michael Barker & Tom Bernard – Another Ten Years in the Classics World. Parts 1 & 2', *Indiewire* (20 December 1999), http://www.indiewire.com/article/decade_michael_barker_tom_bernard_-_another_ten_years_in_the_classics_world/; accessed on 30 January 2011.
17. Ibid.
18. Toumarkine, Doris, 'Sony Classics Gets "Vida Loca"', *Hollywood Reporter* (20 May 1993), 3.
19. 'Sony Pictures Classics', *Hollywood Reporter* (1 August 1995), 13.
20. Ibid.
21. 'About Sony Pictures Classics Large Format', Sony Pictures Classics, n/d, http://www.sonyclasssic.com/largeformat; accessed on 20 January 2011.
22. 'Sony Pictures Entertainment Announces New Long-term Agreement with Sony Pictures Classics', *Business Wire* (31 January 1997), n/a.
23. 'Sony Pictures Classics Awarded Top Prizes at Sundance Festival', *Business Wire* (6 February 1996), n/a.
24. 'Sony Pictures Classics Completes Deal with Producer Arthur Cohn to Re-release Vittorio de Sica's Oscar-winning "The Garden of the Finzi-Continis"', *Business Wire* (27 August 1996), n/a.
25. Griffin, Nancy and Kim Masters, *Hit & Run: How Jon Peters and Peter Guber Took Sony for a Ride in Hollywood* (New York: Simon & Schuster, 1996), 442.
26. 'Sony Pictures Classics', *Hollywood Reporter* (5 August 1997), 19.
27. 'Sony Pictures Classics', *Hollywood Reporter* (1 August 1996), 13.
28. Gray, Beverly, 'Sony Pictures Classics', *Hollywood Reporter* (1 August 1998), 13.
29. Roman and Hindes, 'Classic Formula', 7.
30. Ibid.
31. Ibid.
32. 'Sony Pictures Classics, Pandora Cinema Join Forces on Sandra Goldbacher's "The Governess"', *Business Wire* (16 May 1997), n/a.
33. Geier, Thom, 'SPC Compass Points "East–West"', *Hollywood Reporter* (13 September 1999), 10.
34. The figures were taken from 'The Distributors Summary' for 1999 in *The Numbers*, http://www.the-numbers.com/market/Distributors1999.php; accessed on 20 January 2011. Unless otherwise stated, the rest of the figures about the division's performance were taken from similar pages available at www.the-numbers.com and accessed on the same date.
35. 'Sony Pictures Classics' "Crouching Tiger, Hidden Dragon" Hits Over $13.5 Million Mark in its 4th Weekend of Release', *Business Wire* (3 January 2001), n/a.
36. Ross, Matt, 'Translating Foreign Pix to U.S. Hits: SPC Finds Creative Solutions to Bring Home Best in Overseas Fare', *Weekly Variety* (6 February 2006), B2.

37. Krenin Souccar, Miriam, 'Putting on the Indie Hits; Sony Pictures Classics Masters the Art of Finding Big Audiences for Small Films', *Crain's New York Business* (14 May 2001), 12.
38. Tzioumakis, *American Independent Cinema*, 283.
39. 'SPC Holding to Course after Healthy "Tiger" Run', *Hollywood Reporter* (4 January 2002), 16.
40. Ibid.
41. Ibid.
42. 'Viva la SPC', *Hollywood Reporter* (12 October 2001), 123.
43. 'Staying the Course at SPC: "Conversations" More than Idle Talk', *Hollywood Reporter* (5 September 2002), 17.
44. Rooney David, 'Classics Combo Stays at Sony', *Daily Variety* (13 May 2004), 21.
45. Ibid.
46. Thompson, 'Moving Pictures', C6.
47. Rooney, David and Anthony D'Alessandro, 'Discs Ease Risk: DVD is the Niche Player's Ace in the Hole', *Daily Variety* (17 August 2003), 5.
48. Ibid.
49. Rooney, 'Classics Combo Stays at Sony', 21.
50. Martin, Denise, 'Cable Coin Key for Title Wave', *Daily Variety* (17 August 2003), 51.
51. Roxborough, Scott, 'The Proof is in the Euro Pudding', *Hollywood Reporter* (7 June 2005), 10.
52. Mohr, Ian, 'SPC Coin Goes to Helmer's "Money"', *Daily Variety* (13 January 2005), 5.
53. Zeitchik, Steven, 'SPC Shifting its Gameplan', *Daily Variety* (5 January 2007), 1.
54. Ibid.
55. Zeitchick, Steven, 'Classy Classics Takes on New Role', *Weekly Variety* (15 January 2007), 1.
56. Zeitchik, 'Classy Classics', 49.
57. Fleming, Michael and Tatiana Siegel, 'Secure at Sony', *Daily Variety* (5 May 2009), 10.
58. Ibid.
59. Puente, Henry, *The Promotion of US Latino Films*, PhD dissertation (University of Texas, 2004), 392.
60. Shaw, Deborah, 'Introduction: A Qualified Success Story?', in *Contemporary Latin American Cinema: Breaking into the Global Market*, ed. Deborah Shaw (Plymouth: Rowman & Littlefield, 2007), 7.
61. Shaw, 'Introduction: A Qualified Success Story?', 7.
62. 'Fame, Glamour, Cash', *Latin Finance* (29 April 2004), http://www.latinfinance.com/DailyBriefArchivePrint.aspx?ID=63524; accessed on 1 March 2010.

# SECTION III
# Indiewood

CHAPTER 6

# Fox Searchlight (1994 to date)

INTRODUCTION

The company that spearheaded the third wave of the Hollywood majors' specialty divisions was Fox Searchlight. Established in January 1994 as a direct consequence of Miramax's increasing success in the early 1990s, which led to the latter's takeover by Disney in 1993, Fox Searchlight has been one of the most successful studio specialty arms, certainly in terms of box-office gross and market share, throughout its seventeen-year history. The division has been responsible for some extremely lucrative US 'quality indie blockbusters', including *Juno* (J. Reitman, 2007), *Sideways* (A. Payne, 2004), *Napoleon Dynamite* (J. Heder, 2004), *Little Miss Sunshine* (J. Dayton and V. Faris, 2006) and *Black Swan* (D. Aronofsky, 2010), as well as a number of less commercially successful canonical indie films, such as *The Brothers McMullen* (E. Burns, 1995), *Boys Don't Cry* (K. Peirce, 1999), *The Darjeeling Limited* (W. Anderson, 2007), *Crazy Heart* (S. Cooper, 2009) and many others. Fox Searchlight was also the distributor of British film *Slumdog Millionaire* (D. Boyle, 2008), which grossed over $140 million in the US and received seven Academy Awards, including one for Best Picture.[1] With the average Fox Searchlight title taking over $15 million at the US theatrical box office – compared, for example, with the $3.3 million average gross for Sony Pictures Classics films[2] – and with a total gross of over $2 billion from approximately 150 titles so far, it is clear that Fox's specialty division has been both a success story in the specialty film market and an extremely significant player in the US independent cinema sector. This partly explains why it remained untouched during the specialty division shakeout in 2008 and 2009, and is currently an industry leader in the much-consolidated post-2009 specialty film market.

Its solidity and its enviable success rate, however, were not present right from its inception. In its first six years, the division recorded only two major hits: *The Full Monty* (P. Cattaneo), which grossed $46 million in the US, and *Waking Ned* (K. Jones, 1998), which took $24 million. And while it also recorded a number of less spectacular successes, such as *The Brothers McMullen* ($10 million) and *Boys Don't Cry* ($11 million), it also released a significant number of films that underperformed at the box office, including the star-studded *Blood and Wine* (B. Rafelson, 1998 – $1.1 million), *Star Maps* (M. Arteta, 1997 – $0.6 million) and *The Imposters* (S. Tucci, 1998 – $2.2 million); on several occasions, it even attracted criticism from the trade press for the fluctuating performance of its titles.[3] As with other specialty labels, a change of management in 2000 proved instrumental in refocusing the division and helping it develop a clear identity. In this respect, during the first six years of its presence in the market, Fox Searchlight concentrated on both upmarket arthouse films and titles with more commercial potential, in a combination of cheap acquisitions and in-house productions with budgets that ranged between $3 and $13 million.[4] It also preferred to work with young filmmakers rather than with 'A-list' directors,[5] even though renowned auteurs like Spike Lee and Bernardo Bertolucci also had films distributed by the division.

Post-2000, however, and after a radical restructuring that saw a trio of executives (Peter Rice, Steven Gilula and Nancy Utley) brought in to run the division together, Fox Searchlight moved decisively to more commercial fare by 'cut[ting] down on the number of projects aimed at the traditional upscale arthouse audience and look[ing] for other filmgoers who [were] "underserved"', including teenagers, and African American and Latino audiences.[6] Despite this determination, the division's frequent choice of unusual subject matter and its collaboration with artistically minded filmmakers, such as Richard Linklater, Danny Boyle, Alexander Payne, Darren Aronofsky, Jason Reitman and a host of others, ensured that even its clearly commercial titles, like *Juno* and *28 Days Later* (D. Boyle, 2003), would be perceived as originating from the independent sector and therefore possessing a distinction that has been associated with independent cinema ever since the 1980s.[7] As Twentieth Century Fox Chairman Bill Mechanic put it in 2000, during the early months under the division's new management, 'the pictures may become "more pulpish" but they'll still have a "different sensibility".'[8]

For these reasons, this chapter will be divided into two main sections, each examining a distinct period in the division's history.

## 'A FORMIDABLE MARKETER AND DISTRIBUTOR OF SOPHISTICATED FILMS' (1994 TO 2000)[9]

The corporate takeover of Miramax by Disney in May 1993 took place weeks after the former had seen its low-budget British release, *The Crying Game* (N.

Jordan, 1992), which it had acquired for $4 million, become one of the most commercially successful specialty films of all time, taking over $62 million at the US box office.[10] While the spotlight was justifiably turned on this initially surprising corporate marriage, Twentieth Century Fox was also tracking the film's incredible success and planning its own move into the increasingly lucrative specialty sector.[11] While the box-office takings of Neil Jordan's film were certainly a crystal-clear indication of the potential for financial success that a single title could wield, the continuous rise in total theatrical earnings for specialty films as a whole in the US market was arguably more convincing. Specifically, for 1993, this figure had exceeded the $400 million mark, corresponding to a sizable 9 per cent of the total US box office (an increase of 4.7 per cent from 1992).[12] As one senior executive at Fox put it, 'as a business, we think it's something we haven't been taking advantage of and now we are saying "why are we out of that business?"'[13]

Indeed, only a few months later, in January 1994, Fox announced the formation of a new subsidiary with a view to it becoming operative by the end of the year. At that time, the parent company had not decided whether the new division would focus primarily on acquisitions (à la Sony Pictures Classics) or move immediately into production (more in the vein of Fine Line Features).[14] What was clear, though, was Fox's eagerness to emulate the Disney–Miramax model in terms of releasing specialised product through a 'separate, "classics" entity',[15] and not through the distribution apparatus of the main studio. In the next few months, Fox continued developing its subsidiary and looking for an executive to run it, and in July 1994, Tom Rothman, President of Production at the independent distributor Samuel Goldwyn Company, accepted the invitation to head the new division, which soon after was named Fox Searchlight.

Like Fine Line, the division did not feature the word 'classics' in its name, a designation that could have signified a more acquisitions-driven business model like the one followed by Sony's specialty label. Indeed, Searchlight seemed to be heading straight into the film production business, as one of the first projects Rothman initiated was a script-development deal with Sigourney Weaver and Jim Simpson's production company, Goat Cay, and the New Dramatists, a prestigious organisation of playwrights that seeks out promising young writers and helps them develop their writing skills.[16] Through that deal, Searchlight was looking for a source of properties over a 2-year period, with a view to turn the most promising ones into productions for the company.

However, Searchlight did not exactly ignore the acquisitions market. As a matter of fact, its first release was a negative pick-up that the division acquired at the 1995 Sundance Film Festival. Beating off competition from Miramax, New Line Cinema and the Samuel Goldwyn Company, the new studio division acquired Edward Burns's debut film, the micro-budgeted (production costs estimated around $25,000) *The Brothers McMullen*.[17] Searchlight acquired the distribution rights to the film before it went on to win the Grand Jury Prize at Sundance, the first of a number of awards it received in 1995 and 1996. The film, which is profiled in the Case Study at the end of this chapter, became a big commercial success for such a low-budget feature, grossing a little over $10 million at the US box office. Arguably more importantly, it became emblematic of Fox Searchlight's approach to specialty filmmaking, an approach that clearly centred on betting on films with obvious commercial potential and which often attracted criticism from the independent film community for 'selling out' or for lacking the 'authenticity' that (is supposed to) characterise(s) US independent cinema.[18]

Even before the release of Burns's film in late 1995, though, Fox Searchlight was moving in a number of directions in an effort to put together a substantial slate of films for release in 1996. Tom Rothman's reputation as an experienced executive with good knowledge of the specialty market, and the presence of a major like Twentieth Century Fox (and its resources) convinced a number of well-known filmmakers to collaborate with the as-yet-untested division. Accordingly, by February 1995, the company had almost a dozen projects in development with well-known directors such as Agnieszka Holland, Ang Lee, Lee Tamahori and Wayne Wang.[19] Although not all of these materialised, the activity gave the division a momentum that would help it establish itself in the marketplace. Arguably the biggest contributors to this momentum were the deals Searchlight made with celebrated independent filmmaker Spike Lee for the finance, production and distribution of his film *Girl 6* (1996), yet another independent picture with ample commercial appeal, and with French producer and distributor UGC for the production, finance and distribution of Bernardo Bertolucci's *Stealing Beauty*. The latter deal saw Searchlight exploiting a relationship between sister company Twentieth Century Fox and UGC that was formed in 1995, entailing the distribution of all Fox films in France by the new venture, UGC-Fox Distribution. With UGC also frequently functioning as producer and financial backer of specialty films, including US productions such as Hartley's *Amateur*, it was not surprising that the two players came together in an agreement to co-finance and produce films, with Searchlight obtaining distribution rights for English-speaking territories and UGC for the rest of the world.[20] *Stealing Beauty* was the first project to come out of this alliance.

Shortly after the successful release of *The Brothers McMullen*, and a little over a year after his appointment as head of the division, Tom Rothman moved to Twentieth Century Fox as the studio's new President of Production. Almost immediately, the parent company appointed Lindsay Law as Searchlight's new senior executive. With fourteen years' experience as President of American Playhouse – a PBS programme well known in the independent film sector, which was co-funded with the Samuel Goldwyn

Company and brought original US drama to TV in the form of mini-series, televised plays and films from the early 1980s to 1994 – Law had been involved with some of the best-known US independent film titles of the 1980s and the early 1990s,[21] such as *El Norte*, *Swoon* and *Safe*. Given his experience in film production and his knowledge of the independent film sector, Law seemed to be the right choice to lead Searchlight in its efforts to establish itself in an increasingly crowded specialty film marketplace. By the summer of 1996, Law had decided on the division's *modus operandi*: 10 to 12 releases a year, half of which would be generated 'in-house' and with budgets ranging between $3 and $13 million.[22]

By that time, specialty film, and especially US independent titles, had become increasingly popularised, presenting an excellent opportunity for the division's new president to steer the outfit to commercial success. According to film industry analysts and critics, 1996 was 'the year of the independents',[23] with export revenues for the 130 independent film companies represented by the American Film Marketing Association reaching an all-time high at $1.65 billion for the year;[24] with film festivals in Europe, once reserved for work by world cinema auteurs and a few prestigious American productions, becoming major destinations for American independent films; with cable television channels like the Sundance Channel being launched to meet the increasing demand for this type of filmmaking; and finally, with seven specialty distributors scoring forty-four Academy Award nominations with fourteen specialty films in the English language.[25]

In this seemingly golden hour for independent filmmaking, Fox Searchlight participated with five releases, all arranged by the short-lived Rothman regime and all having enormous potential to become commercial hits. In addition to *She's the One*, *Girl 6* and *Stealing Beauty*, the division also released Christopher Hampton's star-studded *The Secret Agent* and Al Pacino's study of Shakespeare's *Richard III*, *Looking for Richard*. However, none of the films proved to be the commercial success the division had hoped for; neither did the division contribute to the forty-four Academy Award nominations that went to films by specialty distributors, with *The Secret Agent*, in particular, becoming the first big miss for the division after a petty box-office gross of slightly over $100,000.

By 1997, when the first raft of Fox Searchlight films was put together by Law, the sector was going through a bad year, making the division's effort considerably more difficult. According to the *Los Angeles Daily News*, the first seven months of 1997 had been disastrous for the independent film business, as only one picture, Kevin Smith's *Chasing Amy*, had passed the $10 million mark at the theatrical box office, compared to the twenty specialty films that hit that landmark figure the previous year.[26] Indeed, by July 1997, Fox Searchlight had already distributed six films in an effort to meet its 10- to 12-release quota for the year. Three of these, the Australian *Love and Other Catastrophes* (E. K. Croghan), the British *The Van* (S. Frears) and the homegrown *Star Maps*, failed to reach $1 million gross each, with the first one recording just $200,000. However, it was the other three titles that proved more disappointing, as all featured big Hollywood stars such as Jack Nicholson and Michael Caine (*Blood and Wine*), Glenn Close and Frances McDormand (*Paradise Road* [B. Beresford]), and Julia Ormond (*Smilla's Feeling for Snow* [B. August]). The last title proved marginally more successful than the others, with a US box-office gross of $2 million, but all three represented major flops for the division.

However, the releases for the rest of 1997 told a different story. Despite an underperformance from *Oscar and Lucinda* (G. Armstrong) and the British *Intimate Relations* (P. Goodhew), Fox Searchlight also released *The Full Monty* and *The Ice Storm* (Ang Lee). And while the $8 million gross attained by the latter was also seen as a relative disappointment, given the presence of such established stars as Kevin Cline and Sigourney Weaver, and young newcomers Toby Maguire and Katie Holmes, the remarkable $46 million gross taken by *The Full Monty*, a film about unemployed British steel workers deciding to become strippers in an attempt to make some money, gave Searchlight its first crossover hit and covered the losses that the division's other releases incurred.

Searchlight had co-financed *The Full Monty* early during its production process after its executives had seen some of the dailies. With a budget of slightly over $3 million, it represented a safer bet compared to considerably more expensive US films such as *Blood and Wine* and *The Ice Storm*. After a careful marketing campaign that included the film's participation in the Sundance Film Festival, a number of free screenings targeting female audiences, cross-promotion deals with retail stores such as Ralph Lauren's Polo shops, and extremely effective teaser ads asking the question 'What is the Full Monty?', Searchlight platformed the film in New York, Los Angeles and San Francisco, with outstanding results. Five weeks later the film was playing on approximately 400 screens in seventy-five different markets, outperforming major Hollywood productions that were released around the same time and were playing on over 2000 screens.[27] After a nine-month run, which at its peak involved almost 800 engagements and four nominations for Academy Awards, the film joined a small group of British films, such as *The Crying Game* and *Four Weddings and a Funeral* (M. Newell, 1994), that became runaway successes; alongside the $46 million it recorded in the US, it even brought in another $150 million from its release in the rest of the world. Not surprisingly, one of the first steps the division's management took following the triumphant success of *The Full Monty* was to sign deals with its creative principals for future projects, especially the film's producer Uberto Pasolini. Like similar pacts between British production companies and specialty film distributors like Orion Classics and Fine Line Features, this agreement effectively gave

Fox's division 'a production base in the UK',[28] with Pasolini empowered to greenlight pictures for Searchlight. Furthermore, and given his previous work for Columbia Pictures, Pasolini was also contracted to develop properties for the rest of Fox's divisions, including the main studio.[29]

These deals demonstrate clearly that, under Law, Fox Searchlight was shifting more forcefully to production, as were the other specialty studio divisions (with the exception of Sony Picture Classics) during the late 1990s. According to the *Hollywood Reporter*, by 1998 a full two-thirds of Searchlight's annual output of 10 to 12 pictures were in-house productions,[30] with the division only opting for negative pick-ups for films with exceptional commercial potential. With production rates of US indie films constantly increasing, especially during the second half of the 1990s, the specialty film market had decisively become a buyer's market. This meant that the distributors, and especially the studios' specialty arms, were firmly in a position of power in terms of determining the prices paid for acquisition rights, with bidding wars ensuing only for pictures with outstanding commercial potential that were expected to return the distributor's investment, even if this was a sizable one.

The question of the return on a distributor's investment in specialty films had become particularly thorny during the late 1990s. Despite a growing number of box-office success stories, like *The Full Monty* and Fine Line's *Shine*, the financial returns for most films were constantly diminishing. This was because, during this period, the production costs of independent films – especially of those produced by the studios' specialty labels – often exceeded the $10 million mark. As the *Hollywood Reporter* put it, Fox Searchlight's production budgets 'can hit a very un-indie-like $12 million',[31] a far cry from the vast majority of the low-budget independent films of the 1980s but also from the budgets of many crossover hits like *sex, lies, and videotape* ($1.2 million) that were perceived as paradigmatic for the post-1990 indie film era.

But even if the large increase in budget levels could be factored in at a time when some specialty films had started grossing $100 million, the distributors of these films also saw a huge surge in advertising and marketing costs; alongside the inflated production costs, this was making the specialty film sector look like an increasingly uncertain business. According to Law, in the three-year period between 1995 and 1998 alone, marketing costs for independent films rose by an incredible 250 per cent, a direct result of the overcrowded marketplace and the need to commit more advertising and marketing funds to make a film stand out.[32] Even films with a theatrical box-office gross in the region of $10 million succeeded, according to Law, after their distributors had spent approximately $7 to $8 million on marketing. This included the purchase of advertising time on television, a practice that had been avoided by earlier incarnations of classics divisions (as we saw in previous chapters). In such a vastly changed specialty film landscape, even compared to just a few years earlier, Law continued, independent film 'now need[ed] to perform on opening weekend in the same way that studio films need[ed] to perform'.[33]

Besides the pressures of the reshaped specialty film environment, Fox Searchlight also had to face tensions inside the Fox family. As one of the four divisions of Fox Filmed Entertainment, which also included Twentieth Century Fox, Fox 2000 and Fox Animation Studios, Searchlight also had to perform financially in relation to its sister companies. This was particularly the case in relation to Fox 2000, another new division established around the same time as Searchlight, with a mandate to produce genre films and star vehicles in much lower-budget brackets than the blockbuster and franchise films released by Twentieth Century Fox. Under the management of Laura Ziskin, Fox 2000 occasionally encroached on Searchlight's turf with films such as *The Thin Red Line* (T. Mallick, 1998), *Fight Club* (D. Fincher, 1999) and *Anywhere but Here* (W. Wang, 1999), which have been celebrated either as examples of indie-wood, studio expeditions into the independent film arena (*Fight Club*, *Thin Red Line*), or as works by filmmakers more readily associated with independent film (*Anywhere but Here*).

Within this context, Law's approach continued to favour young filmmakers with its emphasis on commercially minded films and with its focus on film production supplemented by a handful of acquisitions. Like 1997, when *The Full Monty*'s success paid for all the division's underperforming films, 1998 brought a number of commercial disappointments (*Two Girls and a Guy* [J. Toback], *Shooting Fish* [S. Schwarz], *Cousin Bette* [D. McAnuff] and *Polish Wedding* [T. Connelly]),[34] but also a new crossover hit, *Waking Ned*. Searchlight acquired the US rights for the latter at the Cannes Film Festival for a reported cost of $4 to $5 million;[35] even if its US box-office gross was half that of *The Full Monty* (approximately $25 million), it gave the division a second commercial hit within the space of a calendar year, and placed it firmly within the leading group of specialty distributors which, by that time, included October Films, Gramercy, Artisan, USA Films and Trimark, along with the majors' divisions, Fine Line, Sony Pictures Classics and Paramount Classics.

However, the next two years (1999 and 2000) did not prove as successful for the division. Despite the continuation of a business formula that emphasised the release of films with clear commercial hooks, the division's most promising films failed to find a success to match that of *The Full Monty* and *Waking Ned*. For instance, *A Midsummer Night's Dream*, a film that cost $15.8 million to make,[36] boasted stars such as Kevin Kline and Michelle Pfeiffer, and had a tie-in deal with Max Factor,[37] grossed just $14.6 million. Similarly, in 2000, Philip Kaufman's *Quills* (2000), a $14 million adaptation of Doug Wright's play about the last days of the Marquis de Sade,[38] scored only $7 million at the US box office, despite the presence of stars like Kate Winslet, Geoffrey Rush and Joaquin Phoenix, three Academy Award nominations, and subject matter that could potentially attract audiences outside of the specialty film sector. With other titles such as *Among Giants* (S. Miller), *Dreaming of Joseph Lees* (E. Styles) and *Whiteboyz* (M. Levin) performing extremely poorly, the division's only solid success was Kimberly Peirce's controversial *Boys Don't Cry*, which recorded $11 million on a budget of $2 million and brought in an Academy Award for Actress in a Leading Role for Hilary Swank.

Not surprisingly, this kind of performance created considerable pressure for the division's management. After the success of *The Full Monty*, the division had found itself in twelfth place on the list of distributors, with a 0.76 per cent market share, but in the following two years it had slipped to seventeenth place and just a 0.34 per cent market share in 1998, and nineteenth place and a 0.27 percent market share in 1999. Amongst the established distributors during that period, only Fine Line was putting in a worse financial performance, while a host of specialty labels, such as USA Films, SPC, Gramercy, October, Lions Gate and Artisan, were all doing better. As for Searchlight's 'inspiration', Miramax was commanding eighth place on the list in 1999 with 4.33 per cent market share. With the division's performance on a downward spiral, the decision by the parent company to instigate a management shake-up in the early weeks of 2000 did not take anyone unawares. What was, perhaps, more surprising was the extent to which the new management team had established ties with Twentieth Century Fox, Searchlight's major sister company, rather than with independent filmmaking and the specialty film sector more generally.

## INDIE AND MAJOR CONVERGENCE

After the appointment of Nancy Utley, a veteran Twentieth Century Fox executive, as Searchlight's Head of Marketing in September 1999, Lindsay Law was replaced a few months later by another long-serving Twentieth Century Fox executive, Peter Rice, as Searchlight's new President of Production. With credits on big-budget Fox productions, such as *Alien Resurrection* (J.-P. Jeunet, 1997) and *Independence Day* (R. Emmerich, 1996), Rice had also been involved in more 'artistic' film productions by 'creative' filmmakers, such as Danny Boyle (*The Beach*, 1999) and Baz Luhrmann (*William Shakespeare's Romeo + Juliet*, 1996; *Moulin Rouge*, 1999). Both of these appointments were clear demonstrations of the parent company's intention to continue to support the specialty division, despite its unconvincing financial performance in the first 6 years of operations and in the face of intensified competition. Arguably more importantly, however, the appointments pointed to a future for Fox Searchlight that involved a firmer embrace of specialty films with clear commercial qualities, whether these originated in-house or were acquired at festivals and in other showcases. Two ways in which the new management would gauge the commercial potential of its future releases were the participation of big Hollywood stars and the presence of well-known filmmakers with successful track records, not only in the specialty film sector but also in more commercial circles. Given this new game plan, the two new executives' service at Twentieth Century Fox was certainly an advantage.

The first film to be greenlighted under Fox Searchlight's new management could not have sent a clearer message about the 'evolution' of the division.[39] Having started with Fox 2000 and after a long-winded development history, Steven Soderbergh's *Traffic*, a film based on the British television series *Traffik* (1989) about the global trafficking of drugs, became the flagship property in Searchlight's efforts to reinvent itself. Budgeted in the $30 to $40 million bracket, with a well-known director attached to the project and the rumoured participation of Harrison Ford in one of the leading parts,[40] it was clear that *Traffic* had few points of contact, if any, with earlier Searchlight fare. On the other hand, it seemed to be another clear example of indiewood, the newest phase in contemporary US independent film that was ushered in by aggressively expanding companies like Miramax in the late 1990s with films such as *Shakespeare in Love* and *Good Will Hunting*. Star-studded, narratively accessible and often benefiting from enormous budgets, these films represented an 'indie' cinema that retained a small number of qualities that characterised the films of the independent sector in the 1980s, while readily embracing elements and practices more characteristic of the output of the major studios.[41] It is not surprising, then, given the film's generous budget, that *Traffic* was greenlighted for Searchlight by executives formerly associated with the division's sister company, Twentieth Century Fox.

In the end, however, the film was not made by the division. Following the exit of the Chairman of Fox Filmed Entertainment, Bill Mechanic, from the company in 2000, the project was put into turnaround and eventually ended up at well-capitalised specialty producer and distributor USA Films. As a USA Films release, *Traffic* became another $100 million indiewood hit and received numerous Academy Awards for the 2000 to 2001 season. Searchlight, on the other hand, had its worst year yet, slipping a few more places down the distributors' list after the lacklustre performance of six releases – most of which had been arranged by the previous management team – that translated to a 0.23 per cent market share.[42]

Despite the division's failure to hang on to *Traffic* and the disappointing performance of its films in 2000, Fox Searchlight renewed its efforts to become competitive and establish a distinct identity in the marketplace. To help achieve both these targets, a third senior executive, Stephen Gilula, was appointed as President of Distribution. Unlike Rice and Utley, Gilula came to Searchlight from the specialty film sector and, in particular, from the arena of exhibition. As co-founder and President of the Landmark Theater Corporation, a company that, after twenty-five years of operations, had grown to become the biggest arthouse exhibitor in the US by the year 2000,[43] Gilula was in a position to channel the division's films to the right theatres, helping them achieve their full potential in terms of theatrical exhibition.

The change of regime at Searchlight was seen by the trade press as a clear indication of the parent company's intention to revamp its flailing division. Writing for *Variety*, Paul F. Duke summarised this new perception:

> Fox has revamped the shingle with a new lineup of top execs, and observers say Searchlight pics will go lighter on the Bard and heavier on the demo – a little more marketing-driven, keeping a core audience of ticket buyers in mind while also trying to maintain Searchlight's brief for artistically adventurous fare.[44]

The considerably more pronounced emphasis on making films for particular demographics that are much easier to market (compared to the upscale arthouse product that Searchlight often carried in the 1990s) has been perhaps the most distinct characteristic of the division post-2000. And while, for part of the trade press, a move in this direction would bring the division closer to genre labels such as Dimension Films and Screen Gems, and potentially steer it away from the 'sophisticated films' it had been known for in its pre-2000 history, the two were not necessarily mutually exclusive for the new management.[45] Indeed, the three executives were hoping to give the division a distinct character 'by marrying the best of its tradition of artistic risk-taking with more market awareness', ensuring that the division's films would find the particular audience they aimed to serve from the very beginning. As Nancy Utley stated about the division's new plans:

> It could be a film for a teen audience or the African-American or Latino audience. But the film will still have a filmmaker's voice. It wouldn't be exploitation films or simply a small version of a studio film.[46]

Although some of the films the division was associated with in later years tested Utley's description of the relationship of Searchlight films with small versions of studio films (for instance, *The Banger Sisters*, B. Dolman, 2002), the first examples of the division's output certainly fit the bill. For instance, the first 'in-house' production under the new regime, *Kingdom Come* (D. McHenry, 2001), clearly targeted the African American audience with the participation of an assortment of film and music stars, including LL Cool J,

Jada Pinkett-Smith, Toni Braxton, Vivica A. Fox, Cedric the Entertainer and Whoopi Goldberg. Focusing on the dysfunctional relationship of an extended family of African Americans who gather together after the death of a family member, the film also had clearly defined generic parameters, which made marketing it even easier and had the potential to bring in other demographics as secondary audiences. The division's first release in 2001, *Kingdom Come* grossed over $23 million on a budget of $7 million, giving Searchlight its third most commercially successful film to that date, and a rationale for building its business model in the same direction. In this context, the division's other releases in 2001 were also characterised by elements comparable to *Kingdom Come*, whether these were co-financed productions made by Searchlight (for instance, *Sexy Beast* [J. Glazer]) or negative pick-ups from Sundance and other festivals (*The Deep End* [S. McGehee and D. Siegel). On the other hand, though, another acquisition, Richard Linklater's pioneering rotoshop animation, *Waking Life*, grossed a marginal $2 million, despite excellent reviews and the presence of one of the key independent filmmakers of the 1990s and 2000s behind the camera.

The division's improved financial performance and shifting identity were also accompanied by stronger positioning within Fox Filmed Entertainment. With Fox 2000 producing only two or three titles annually in the first years of the decade, and with Fox Animation producing only two titles after its launch in 1997, Searchlight was the only other division alongside the main distributor, Twentieth Century Fox, to remain consistently active, while setting out to increase the number of its releases substantially (from six to 12) and to improve its financial performance further.[47] In this respect, by mid-2001, the division had already greenlighted a slate of films with very clear commercial elements, including Danny Boyle's post-apocalyptic British horror film *28 Days Later*; Jim Sheridan's period immigration drama *In America*; and Denzel Washington's therapist–troubled young man relationship drama *Antwone Fisher*. With the urban thriller *One Hour Photo* (M. Romanek), starring Robin Williams playing against type, already in production, Fox Searchlight was certainly gearing up for the full implementation of its revised business strategy. Output that year also included a number of arguably lower-profile acquisitions, including *Kissing Jessica Stein* (C. Herman-Wurmfeld); *Super Troopers* (J. Chandrasekhar); *The Good Girl* (M. Arteta); the above-mentioned *Banger Sisters*, featuring Goldie Hawn and Susan Sarandon in the leading roles; and *Brown Sugar* (R. Famuyima), the division's new offering to the African American audience.

Although not all these films were released in 2002 (a small number coming out the following year), the financial results for the division were a vast improvement on the previous years. Table 1 presents the division's 2002 releases and the US theatrical box-office gross for each film.

Table 1 Fox Searchlight's 2002 releases and their US theatrical box-office gross[48]

| Title | Release date (2002) | Box office ($ million) |
|---|---|---|
| *Super Troopers* | 15 Feb | 18.5 |
| *Kissing Jessica Stein* | 13 Mar | 7 |
| *The Good Girl* | 7 Aug | 16 |
| *One Hour Photo* | 21 Aug | 31.5 |
| *The Banger Sisters* | 20 Sep | 30.5 |
| *Brown Sugar* | 11 Oct | 27.5 |
| *Antwone Fisher* | 19 Dec | 21 |
| Total | | 152 |

One particularly interesting element in the list of releases was Searchlight's decision to eschew platform releasing for two of its titles, *The Banger Sisters* and *Brown Sugar*, opting instead – with the help of Twentieth Century Fox – to put them out wide, on 2,738 and 1,372 screens, respectively. Although a number of films released by classics divisions and specialty labels had been distributed wide in the past (*Crouching Tiger, Hidden Dragon*, *The Full Monty*), with the exception of Miramax titles (*Pulp Fiction, Beautiful Girls* [T. Demme, 1996] and a few others) this was always after they had 'proved' themselves in platform release for a few weeks and therefore had convinced their distributors to 'tap into' the financial and infrastructural resources of their respective parent or sister companies for a national release. While the other five Fox Searchlight releases followed this format of distribution, *The Banger Sisters* and *Brown Sugar* successfully demonstrated the benefits of a wide release for a specialty label. As Tom Rothman put it:

> It's not just the ability to take pictures wide, like *Antwone Fisher* and *The Banger Sisters*. It's also that there is a globally integrated campaign for movies. We're the only specialty company that doesn't have to go begging territory by territory . . . [Fox Searchlight] has the best of both worlds. That is, the risk-taking and flexibility of a specialty label and the power, leverage and scope of a major studio.[49]

On the other hand, the adoption by specialty labels of a distribution strategy so firmly associated with the major studio distributors (and often the major independents New Line and Miramax) blurred the line even further between the two, as it questioned the extent to which a distributor could be perceived of as a 'specialty' one if it utilised mass marketing methods.

Even discounting the box-office contribution of the two widely released films, the division's financial performance was vastly improved in the calendar year 2002, claiming 0.81 per cent of the US theatrical market with $75 million in box-office total and placing it ahead of the other specialty labels, as well as large stand-alone companies like Lions Gate, Newmarket Films and Artisan. If one also adds the $57 million brought in by *The Banger Sisters* and *Brown Sugar*, Fox Searchlight claimed approximately 1.4 per cent of the theatrical market with over $130 million combined gross. Along with its financial success, the division also had started convincing industry critics that it was 'forging a clear identity amid Hollywood's increasingly confused landscape' and that it 'ha[d] stabilised [its] inconsistent track record', bringing a vote of confidence for Rice and the new management team.[50]

Given the unmitigated success of the 2002 slate, 2003 was designed to maximise the new model further by offering more of the same. Apart from *28 Days Later* and *In America*, which had been greenlighted since 2001, the division had two additional significant titles that it had financed and to which it held the worldwide distribution rights: Merchant–Ivory's *Le Divorce* (starring Naomi Watts and Kate Hudson) and Alex Proyas's *Garage Days*. Furthermore, it had acquired Neil Jordan's *The Good Thief*, starring Nick Nolte, and Gurinder Chadha's *Bend it Like Beckham*, a British film that had already been a box-office smash in the UK and had the potential to repeat the level of business Searchlight had enjoyed with *The Full Monty*. Finally, after almost nine years in the specialty film market, the division also ventured its first non-English-language release, after deciding to distribute the French film *L'Auberge espagnole* [*Pot Luck*] (C. Klapisch).[51]

Despite the poor box office of some of the above titles, especially Alex Proyas's *Garage Days* (which grossed only $20,000 at the US box office on an estimated $6 million budget), Searchlight saw yet another year of solid success, thanks to the performance of three of its titles, whose combined box office approached the $100 million mark and therefore easily offset earlier losses: *In America*, contributing $15 million; *Bend it Like Beckham*, $32 million; and *28 Days Later*, $45 million. Reports were suggesting that the prestige earned by the division's titles and their box-office performance were fully appreciated by the very top echelons, not just the management at Fox but also at its parent company, News Corporation, and by the latter's Chief Executive, Rupert Murdoch.[52] Fox Searchlight thus began to enjoy a particularly enhanced status in the specialty film industry, just as this was being transformed yet again by the level of the commercial success attained by films like *28 Days Later*. With the trade press reporting that the division's box office had improved by over 200 per cent over just two years,[53] and labelling Searchlight as 'the very model of how a studio specialty division should operate', Fox's specialty division even started to be considered a challenger to Miramax's leadership of the wider specialty film market.[54]

The division improved its financial performance yet again in 2004 and further increased its market share from 1.34 per cent (2003) to $1.87 per cent, following the success of four titles that, by early 2005, had achieved a remarkable combined $170 million at the US box office (*Sideways*, *Garden State* [Z. Braff], *Napoleon Dynamite* and *Johnson Family Vacation* [C. Erskin]); taken together with the less commercially successful *I Heart Huckabees* (D. O. Russell) and *Kinsey* (W. Condon), this pushed the figure closer to $200 million, easily offsetting underperforming titles like Bertolucci's *The Dreamers* and the Robert Redford vehicle *The Clearing* (P. J. Brugge). Not surprisingly, in this period Searchlight arguably became the top destination for creative filmmakers, while the division itself aggressively pursued deals with production outfits, finance schemes and renowned directors around the world. For instance, in September 2003, Searchlight bought a 50 per cent stake in the British DNA Films, a company that was co-financed by significant British Lottery funds and which had so far produced commercially and critically successful films, including *28 Days Later* and *The Parole Officer* (J. Duigan, 2001).[55] A month later, the division made a co-finance and distribution deal with leading Hong Kong filmmaker Wong Kar Wai,[56] and by 2004 had first-look deals with *The Full Monty* producer, Uberto Pasolini, and key indie filmmaker David O. Russell.[57]

By early 2005, Fox Searchlight was at the pinnacle of its success, with *Sideways* approaching a $100 million take at the worldwide box office and receiving numerous Academy Award nominations, including one for Best Picture. Arguably, Searchlight's meteoric rise in the mid-2000s was also assisted by the decline of Miramax. In the spring of 2005, Bob and Harvey Weinstein announced that they would not renew their contracts with Disney, which were due to expire in September of the same year. A number of factors had stretched the relationship of executives at the parent company with the Miramax management to breaking point, including Disney's refusal to allow the Weinstein brothers to launch their own cable television station; the brothers' increasingly excessive spending on both production and marketing of Miramax films, some of which turned out to be financial disasters (*The Four Feathers* [S. Kapur, 2002], *The Human Stain* [R. Benton, 2003], *Proof* [J. Madden, 2005], *The Great Raid* [J. Dahl, 2005]); an acrimonious fight between parent company and subsidiary, with the former prohibiting the latter from distributing *Fahrenheit 9/11* (M. Moore, 2004); and corporate politics within Disney. With Bob and Harvey Weinstein walking out and starting anew with the establishment of stand-alone specialty production and distribution outfit, the Weinstein Company,[58] Miramax was entering a transitional period, at exactly the same time as Searchlight (and Focus Features, as we will see in Chapter 8) were increasing their dominance in the specialty film market.

Although 2005 did not prove as good a year for Searchlight, with only one film, *The Ringer* (B. W. Blaustein), recording a box-office gross similar to that of the division's earlier hits, the division's management acquired even more clout within Fox when they were assigned to a new specialty production and distribution outfit established within the larger Fox structure, which would specifically target 'teen and young adult audiences'[59] and would eventually become the short-lived Fox Atomic. And an additional factor that not only demonstrated the division's deeper integration within Fox and News Corporation, but also provided one of the first examples of synergies between film companies and social network media: Searchlight and the News Corporation-owned MySpace created a 'MySpace profile' for *The Ringer*, which, by January 2006, had attracted over 261,000 'friends'.[60] Although the embrace of social network media by film studios would very soon become one of the most important elements in film marketing campaigns, Searchlight developed a reputation as a pioneering studio subsidiary that had understood 'a cultural shift that [was] only gradually dawning on big media companies as they struggle[d] to connect with a generation of consumers spoon-fed on wireless technology'.[61]

All this activity produced a record slate of films for 2006 and 2007,[62] with twenty-three releases over the two-year period. Each of these years was anchored by titles that created an extremely strong presence at the box office – *Little Miss Sunshine* in 2006 and *Juno* in 2007 – the latter reaching blockbuster status after grossing $143 million at the US box office alone, and taking a similar amount in the rest of the world. The line-up consisted of an assortment of titles that included the successful reboot of Wes Craven's *The Hills Have Eyes* (A. Aja, 2006) and the critically acclaimed *Last King of Scotland* (K. MacDonald, 2006), as well as some expensive but underperforming productions (*Sunshine* [D. Boyle, 2007]) and the traditional offering to the African American demographic (*Phat Girlz* [N. Likke, 2006]); however, the majority of releases and the main distribution focus were clearly associated with the US indie scene, which, by that time, had become increasingly close to the Hollywood studios, both financially and aesthetically. *The Darjeeling Limited*, *Waitress* (A. Shelly, 2007), *The Savages* (T. Jenkins, 2007), *Fast Food Nation* (R. Linklater, 2006), *Trust the Man* (B. Freundlich, 2006) and *Thank You for Smoking* (J. Reitman, 2006), alongside the aforementioned *Little Miss Sunshine* and *Juno*, represented a formidable slate of indie films characterised by slick production values, accessible narratives, heavy dependence on genre, and the presence of a host of stars, including Adrien Brody, Bruce Willis, Julianne Moore, Katie Holmes, Robert Duvall and Steve Carell.

The scores of indie and indiewood titles that Searchlight produced and distributed, especially after the incredible success of *Juno* – which took $250 million gross worldwide, received seven Academy Award nominations and became a global pop phenomenon – attracted considerable criticism from both industry and cultural commentators. At the core of their 'attack' was the further 'mainstreaming' of US independent film. Driven by the numerous specialty labels of the studios, and in particular by Fox Searchlight, these divisions were seen, on the one hand, to replicate practices and borrow aesthetics from the expensive films normally associated with their sister or parent companies and, on the other, to 'water down' any controversial or sensitive issues that the films' narrative might tackle. Writing specifically on *Juno*, Gary Needham saw in it an 'indie-*lite*' independent film, the politics of which were lost in a maelstrom of excessive quirkiness and numerous pop references:

> [I]ndies like Fox Searchlight's *Juno* (Jason Reitman, 2007) try very hard to self-consciously inculcate the indie vibe for a general audience that is not especially attuned to the political, cultural and industrial nuances that have shaped Hollywood's other. *Juno* is a film that often feels forced in its attempt to cram as much alterity as is possible into ninety minutes. If abortion is the topic that gives *Juno* part of its edgy indie credibility then compared to the similarly-themed Todd Solondz's *Palindromes* (2004), *Juno* is, for want of a better expression, indie-*lite*.[63]

Such criticisms correctly identified the increasing convergence of independent film and Hollywood, with *Juno* and *Little Miss Sunshine* representing the product of such convergence, which is qualitatively different from more clearly independent films (in terms of economics, aesthetics, political positioning and so on) like *Palindromes*. The truth of the matter, however, is that the latter type of film (low-budget, aesthetically and narratively challenging, dealing with disturbing subject matter such as pederasty, abortion and exploitation, and featuring no known actors apart from Ellen Barkin in a brief supporting role) became increasingly marginalised in the post-*sex, lies, and videotape* era of indie cinema. This is clearly reflected in the theatrical box office of the two films, with *Palindromes* recording a little over $0.5 million in the US, compared to the $143 million brought in by *Juno*. In this respect, one could argue that Searchlight and the rest of the studio specialty labels were interested in and championed only very specific articulations of US 'independent' cinema – the more commercial ones associated with 'indie' and 'indiewood' filmmaking. From a financial point of view, this was certainly the right decision, as from 2006 onwards, the Fox specialty label found itself heading the studio specialty distributors in terms of market share in the US: 1.77 per cent in 2006, 1.41 per cent in 2007 and 2.51 per cent in 2008. As it happened, in 2008 the division had its best year ever yet again, with *Slumdog Millionaire* recording a worldwide box-office gross of $377 million and receiving seven Academy Awards, including one for Best Picture. Since then, Searchlight has remained at the pinnacle of specialty film production and distribution, with its focus tightly on US indiewood films (at the time of writing it has been enjoying another major hit with *Black Swan*) and with an assortment of other releases in the English language targeting particular demographics (*Notorious* [G. Tillman Jr, 2009 – African American audiences]; *My Life in Ruins* [D. Petrie, 2009 – Greek American audiences] and so on).

## CONCLUSION

Perhaps more than any other established studio division (with the possible exception of Focus Features), Fox Searchlight has been at the heart of developments in specialty filmmaking, and in US independent cinema in particular, that saw producers and distributors of such product becoming increasingly integrated with the processes and structures that characterise big media business, and especially the major studios. Steering clear of practices that defined the specialty labels of the early 1990s, such as releasing arthouse films in a language other than English, and opting instead to concentrate on an eclectic slate of narratively accessible US and British films that were characterised by obvious commercial hooks, the division became one of the key contributors to the transformation of independent into 'indie' and (later) 'indiewood' cinema. Such a cinema primarily became an industrial and marketing category, characterised by particular expectations and inviting particular viewing strategies, as opposed to the less institutionalised and infinitely more heterogeneous nature of independent filmmaking in the 1980s.

In the process, Fox Searchlight grew into a division that could boast a large number of extremely successful films in commercial terms, some of which redefined the level of revenues that 'indiewood' filmmaking could return to those who practise it. It also proved to be better equipped than many of the other studio divisions, and the major independents Miramax and New Line, to withstand the pressures of the rapidly changing specialty marketplace and the post-2008 global financial crisis. Having managed to keep the budget of even its most commercially successful films in check, and despite its substantial spending on marketing and advertising, Fox Searchlight has remained consistently profitable in the 2000s. Not surprisingly, it has been one of the three studio divisions to survive the shakeout in the sector, alongside Sony Pictures Classics and Focus Features.

### Case Study: *The Brothers McMullen* (Edward Burns, 1995)

*The Brothers McMullen* is an important film in the US independent cinema canon. First, it is the film that launched the career of actor, director, producer and star Edward Burns who, in the 'Cassavetes mould', became a prolific filmmaker in the independent sector with films such as *She's the One* (1996), *Sidewalks of New York* (2001) and *Ash Wednesday* (2002), while also starring in mainstream productions, including Steven Spielberg's *Saving Private Ryan* (1998) and *15 Minutes* (J. Herzfeld, 2001). Second, the film was one of the key 1990s 'no-budget' success stories that, alongside other similar examples such as *El Mariachi* (R. Rodriguez, 1992) and *Clerks* (K. Smith, 1994), helped create the myth that success could be achieved in the independent film sector without any significant economic risk,[64] as well as fostering the belief that any would-be director could easily make their own film, which saw its full expression in the 1990s.[65] Third, it became a Sundance Film Festival winner in 1995 (sharing the Jury Special Prize with Hal Selwyn's *Denise Calls Up*) at the peak of US 'indie' cinema popularisation, and its success influenced the future course of indie film both directly and indirectly. Fourth, it was characterised by an undisputed pedigree in terms of its production location, having been co-produced by Good Machine partners James Schamus and Ted Hope, a few years before Schamus ended up at Focus Features. Finally, it was also the film with which Fox Searchlight was launched at the end of 1995 and in many ways became emblematic of the division's philosophy, with its emphasis on commercial titles that could be marketed easily and therefore stood a good chance of crossing over.

Indeed, *The Brothers McMullen* fit the bill perfectly, both in terms of Fox Searchlight's stated focus on young filmmakers and talent-nurturing, and in terms of holding out considerable commercial potential. Made by a young, up-and-coming actor-writer-director, with the participation of physically attractive actors, and featuring a number of storylines that centred on romance and family, *The Brothers McMullen* seemed to be an easily accessible indie film that stood a good chance of tapping into the vast twenty-something audience that is often attracted to romantic comedies and dramas. Furthermore, as well as using these selling points in the marketing formula, the distributor could also target a sizable Irish American community, which could be mobilised because of the film's strong emphasis on that particular ethnic group.

Of all these elements, the most interesting one for the purposes of this study is the film's narrative accessibility. Focusing on three Irish brothers (two in their twenties and the oldest in his thirties) and on the anxieties and problems that their ethnic and cultural background seemingly creates in their relationships with a number of women, the film demonstrates few, if any, of the devices 'designed to deny, block, delay or complicate the anticipated development of narrative', which, according to Geoff King, tend to characterise the narratives of indie films.[66] Instead, the narrative of *The Brothers McMullen* is constructed according to principles that are quintessentially classical and which include cause–effect logic, psychological motivation, clear character transformation and the formation of three heterosexual couples by the end of the film. Even when some of the characters' decisions and actions are not particularly easy to defend or understand (Molly's reluctance to punish her husband and the eldest of the three brothers, Jack, for his marital infidelity; Barry's persistence in refusing to commit to Audrey until, literally, the last minute of the film), references to Irish traditions and family rituals, as well as popular interpretations of Catholicism, provide clear frameworks within which these actions are explained and understood. There is even a last-minute chase after one of the female characters by one of the brothers (played by Burns himself), which culminates in a kiss and the actual formation of the couple, marked stylistically by a conventional boom shot whereby the camera pulls back until the two protagonists disappear into the familiar Manhattan cityscape.

This narrative accessibility is compounded by a visual style that depends on conventional uses of *mise-en-scène*, cinematography, editing and sound. The only unusual stylistic technique is the occasional use of voiceover snippets by a number of characters, which allow the spectator momentary access to their innermost thoughts. But these revelations do not necessarily add to the spectator's understanding of the characters; rather they tend to emphasise the characters' perspectives on particular issues and concerns, while, in a couple of instances, functioning as comedic counterpoints.

The film's stylistic and narrative conservatism, in tandem with its thematic conventionality, made it the target of considerable criticism from both film critics and the independent film community, despite its otherwise undisputed financial credentials as a paradigmatic independent film that was shot at weekends over a long period of time in the filmmaker's family home and was partly financed by Burns's father. According to Levy, the film was a 'test case for films that are indie in budget and production mode but not in spirit or style',[67] while, for Merritt, it was 'the sort of movie that Hollywood makes with name actors and a budget hundreds of times larger'.[68] For some of Burns's contemporaries, his debut film signalled the beginning of a new era for independent cinema and its convergence with Hollywood. In the words of Kevin Smith, 'Ed Burns and *The Brothers McMullen* was the beginning of the end. It was a movie that absolutely could be made by a studio ... Everyone wanted to get a *Brothers McMullen* underway.'[69]

On the other hand, the film's numerous points of contact with commercial filmmaking, and the 'damage' it caused in terms of shaping expectations about what issues independent films should be dealing with and how they should look and sound, were welcomed by Fox Searchlight (and, by extension, by the other studio divisions in search of increasingly commercial properties). Following its acquisition, Fox Searchlight invested $500,000 in post-production work to polish the film and make it more attractive to audiences outside the specialty film sector.[70] Furthermore, in terms of marketing, the studio division focused on the attractive couple formed by Barry and Audrey (Burns and Maxine Bahns), smiling and surrounded by Barry's two other brothers, creating an effect of warmth, conviviality and family life that had the potential to attract audiences from outside the specialty film sector.

Searchlight's prediction of crossover success for the film proved correct. Following a platform release in seven theatres and with the help of many good reviews that celebrated the film's distance from trendier concerns with sex,[71] the film started to expand successfully, reaching a peak of 367 theatres in its seventh week. With a final gross of over $10 million at the US box office alone, and given its tiny budget, the film proved an unequivocal hit. Not surprisingly, Searchlight immediately made a pre-emptive bid for Burns's similarly themed second feature, *She's the One* (1996), which featured well-known female stars Jennifer Aniston and Cameron Diaz.[72] For the studio division, *The Brothers McMullen* not only was the perfect start, but also set the bar in terms of the kinds of projects with which it was going to be involved. These projects may often have attracted criticisms about the nature of their relationship to independent

> filmmaking (see in particular *Little Miss Sunshine* and *Juno*) but they also managed to achieve great commercial success. On the way, they helped the division establish itself as one of the leaders in the specialty film market.

## NOTES

1. Unless otherwise stated, all box-office figures for Fox Searchlight films were taken from The Numbers, www.the-numbers.com.
2. According to The Numbers, the average theatrical box-office gross for a Fox Searchlight film has been $15,155,454, compared to $3,279,679 for Sony Picture Classics. Even compared to Miramax, Fox Searchlight's performance is better, with Miramax films grossing approximately $12,396,739 on average (accessed on 1 February 2011).
3. Swanson, Tim, 'Rice Flexes Fox Arthouse Arm', *Weekly Variety* (25 June 2001), 9.
4. 'Fox Searchlight Pictures', *Hollywood Reporter* (5 August 1997), 20.
5. 'Fox Searchlight Pictures', *Hollywood Reporter* (1 August 1996), 13.
6. Duke, Paul F., 'The Recharge of the "Light Brigade"', *Weekly Variety* (1 May 2000), 9.
7. Tzioumakis, *American Independent Cinema*, 13.
8. Duke, 'The Recharge of the "Light Brigade"', 9.
9. This view of Fox Searchlight was expressed by the Chairman of Twentieth Century Fox, Bill Mechanic, when Lindsay Law was hired to run the division. See 'Lindsay Law Named President of Fox Searchlight', *Business Wire* (14 November 1995), n/a.
10. Parker, Donna, 'Fox Finds "Classic" Niche with New Upscale Division: *Crying Game* Success Inspires Another Studio', *Hollywood Reporter* (14 January 1994), 53.
11. Ibid.
12. Perren, *Indie, Inc.*, 109.
13. Parker, 'Fox Finds "Classic" Niche', 53.
14. Brown, Colin, 'Fox Seeks High Returns from Low budget Arm', *Screen International* (21 January 1994), 2.
15. Parker, 'Fox Finds "Classic" Niche', 1.
16. Toumarkine, Doris, 'Fox Searchlight Finds Goat Cay, New Dramatists', *Hollywood Reporter* (22 September 1994), 4.
17. The figure of $25,000 is provided by both IMDb (http://www.imdb.com/title/tt0112585/business; accessed on 1 February 2011) and The Numbers.
18. See, for instance, Newman's critique of Searchlight's *Juno*, in Newman, *Indie*, 232–46.
19. Parker, Donna, 'Fox Searchlight Finds Lee's "Girl"', *Hollywood Reporter* (24 February 1995), 83.
20. Ibid.
21. 'Lindsay Law Named President', n/a.
22. 'Fox Searchlight Pictures' (1996), 13.
23. Turner, Dan, 'For a Change Independent Films Get Both Acclaim and Good Box Office', *Los Angeles Business Journal* (3 February 1997), http://www.allbusiness.com/north-america/united-states-california-metro-areas/608029-1.html; accessed on 3 March 2011.
24. Quoted in Turner, 'For a Change Independent Films Get Both Acclaim and Good Box Office'.
25. Tzioumakis, *The Spanish Prisoner*, 16.
26. McNary, Dave, 'Anticlimax: Smaller Studios Seeking Sequel to Robust '96 Independent Hits', *Los Angeles Daily News* (29 July 1997), B1.

27. Weinraub, Bernard, '"The Full Monty" is by Far the Biggest Film Success at Fox Searchlight Pictures', *New York Times* (15 September 1997), 13.
28. Gray, Beverly, 'Fox Searchlight', *Hollywood Reporter* (1 August 1998), 14.
29. 'Producer Uberto Pasolini Signs Multi-Year Production Deal with Fox Searchlight Pictures', *PR Newswire* (21 May 1998), n/a.
30. Gray, 'Fox Searchlight', 14.
31. Ibid.
32. Perren, *Indie, Inc.*, 175.
33. Law was quoted in Gray, 'Fox Searchlight', 1.
34. Petrikin, Chris, 'Quartet Plays a Sweet Song for Fox', *Weekly Variety* (7 September 1998), 85.
35. Klady, Leonard, 'Late Noises Awaken Cannes Film Mart', *Weekly Variety* (25 May 1998), 7.
36. Harris, Dana, Thom Geier and Chris Gennusa, 'Fox Searchlight', *Hollywood Reporter* (1 August 1999), 10.
37. 'Max Factor Goes to the Movies', *WWD* (12 February 1999), 9.
38. Swanson, 'Rice Flexes Fox Arthouse Arm', 9.
39. The word 'evolution' was actually used by Rice himself. See Dana Harris and Claude Brodesser, 'Ford, Zeta-Jones Stop "Traffic"', *Weekly Variety* (21 February 2000), 26.
40. Ibid.
41. King, *Indiewood USA*, 3.
42. The percentage recorded by The Numbers for 2000 is for three releases: *Quills*, *Bootmen* and *Woman on Top*. However, the division put out three more pictures – *Chinese Coffee* (A. Pacino), *Soft Fruit* (C. Andreef) and *The Closer You Get* (A. Ritchie) – which are not acknowledged by The Numbers. Still, the latter three releases do not seem to have surpassed a combined gross of $250,000, with *Soft Fruit* grossing a mere $11,000 (http://www.imdb.com/title/tt0180181/business; accessed on 1 February 2011) and *The Closer You Get*, $220,000 (http://www.imdb.com/title/tt0218112/business; accessed on 1 February 2011). I have been unable to locate box-office figures for *Chinese Coffee*, which suggests either an extremely marginal or a straight-to-video release.
43. Duke, Paul F., 'Fox Searchlight Lands Gilula as Distrib Prexy', *Weekly Variety* (6 March 2000), 18.
44. Duke, 'The Recharge of the "Light Brigade"', 9.
45. Ibid.
46. Utley was quoted in ibid.
47. Swanson, 'Rice Flexes Fox Arthouse Arm', 9.
48. The figures in the table were taken from The Numbers (http://www.the-numbers.com/market/2002/FoxSearchlight.php; accessed on 1 February 2011) and represent the total box-office gross of the 2002 releases, irrespective of whether some of them continued their run in 2003. However, as The Numbers considers *The Banger Sisters* and *Brown Sugar* Twentieth Century Fox releases and not Fox Searchlight ones, the table was modified accordingly. The figures for these two films were also taken from The Numbers and were both accessed on 1 February 2011.
49. Brodesser, Claude, 'Fox: A Brighter Searchlight', *Weekly Variety* (7 April 2003), 55.
50. McNary, Dave, 'Searchlight: Low, Steady Beam', *Weekly Variety* (1 July 2002), 46.
51. 'Fox Searchlight Pictures Acquires Neil Jordan-Helmed Nick Nolte Starrer, a UK Smash Hit and Searchlight's First Foreign Language Film', *Internet Wire* (18 June 2002), n/a.
52. Brodesser, Claude, 'Taking a Risk, Checking it Twice: Smaller Edgy Fare Bolsters Tentpoles', *Weekly Variety* (11 August 2003), 8.

53. Ibid.
54. 'Searchlight Feasts with "28 Days"'; '"Beckham" Goals Ensure Fox Unit Has Momentum', *Hollywood Reporter* (4 September 2003), 13.
55. Dawtrey, Adam, 'Searchlight to Shine for British DNA', *Daily Variety* (5 September 2003), 1 and 18.
56. Kilday, Gregg, 'Searchlight, Wong Team Up for 3-pic Deal', *Hollywood Reporter* (6 October 2003), 1.
57. Dunkley, Cathy, 'Fox Searchlight', *Daily Variety* (8 September 2004), S16.
58. Perren, *Indie, Inc.*, 225–9.
59. 'Adding Multimedia: Fox Filmed Entertainment Establishes New Division to Target Teen and Young Adult Audience; Fox Searchlight Chief Peter Rice Appointed President', *Business Wire* (20 December 2005), n/a.
60. Bing, Jonathan, 'Friendship Has its Privileges for Brands, Pix', *Daily Variety* (31 January 2006), 4.
61. Ibid.
62. Snyder, Gabriel and Nicole LaPorte, 'Recharge of "Light Brigade"', *Weekly Variety* (13 February 2006), 1.
63. Needham, Gary, *Brokeback Mountain* (Edinburgh: Edinburgh University Press, 2010), 11.
64. Schamus, James, 'To the Rear of the Back End: The Economics of Independent Cinema', in *Contemporary Hollywood Cinema*, ed. Steve Neale and Murray Smith (London: Routledge, 1998), 98.
65. Kleinhans, Chuck, 'Independent Features: Hopes and Dreams', in *The New American Cinema*, ed. Jon Lewis (Durham, NC: Duke University Press, 1998), 310.
66. King, *American Independent Cinema*, 63.
67. Levy, *Cinema of Outsiders*, 213.
68. Merritt, *Celluloid Mavericks*, 372.
69. Biskind, *Down and Dirty Pictures*, 203–4.
70. Levy, *Cinema of Outsiders*, 214.
71. Ebert, Roger, '*The Brothers McMullen*', *Chicago Sun-Times* (18 August 1995), http://rogerebert.suntimes.com/apps/pbcs.dll/article?AID=/19950818/REVIEWS/508180301/1023; accessed on 1 March 2011.
72. Parker, Donna, 'Fox Searchlight on "McMullen"', *Hollywood Reporter* (25 January 1995), 6.

CHAPTER 7

# Paramount Classics / Paramount Vantage (1997 to 2008)

## INTRODUCTION

The next Hollywood major to enter the specialty film business through the establishment of a separate label was Paramount. Under the corporate umbrella of Viacom since 1993, Paramount had developed a reputation in the 1990s as an unadventurous film financer and distributor, characterised by the trade press as 'the most stolid of the major studios, known for its implacable leadership, fiscal conservatism and what some might say a rather narrow view of greenlight-worthy movies'.[1] In this respect, it is not surprising that it had made no prior efforts to trade in the specialty film sector. However, by 1997, all of Paramount's rivals had at least one specialty film label each: Columbia (Sony Pictures Classics), Fox (Fox Searchlight), Disney (an oversized Miramax), Universal (a controlling interest in October Films since 1997 – see Chapter 8) and Time Warner (which had merged with Turner Broadcasting System, New Line's parent company, and therefore had also acquired Fine Line). It is clear, then, that Paramount and its parent company had to make their move immediately or run the danger of being locked out of an increasingly lucrative theatrical market, as well as missing out on the additional benefits that came with the exploitation of these films in ancillary markets.

Paramount announced its new division in mid-1997 but, as with Fox Searchlight, it took more than a year for the new outfit to put out its first release, the documentary *Trekkies* (R. Nygard), in March 1999. However, unlike Searchlight, the new division did not shy away from world cinema arthouse titles, even though films in the English language would still make up the majority of its annual slate of releases. Furthermore, and again unlike the rest of its contemporaries, the division was launched with the designation 'classics' in its name, despite the fact that its business strategy did not include plans to rerelease old titles from Paramount's rich vault.

Given its emphasis on both homegrown and non-US arthouse films, Paramount Classics presented certain points of contact with the early 1990s studio divisions, especially Sony Pictures Classics. Additionally, one of the two senior executives chosen to lead the division was Ruth Vitale, former President of Fine Line Features, the other specialty label that was formed in the early 1990s. On the other hand, though, Paramount Classics was also established at a time when the ceiling for the commercial success of specialty titles, and especially of films associated with the US indie sector, was being radically redefined, while new stand-alone distributors and producer–distributor combinations like Artisan and Newmarket Films, alongside the existing powers, were increasingly opting to give financial backing to films with numerous and obvious commercial hooks in an attempt to maximise box-office returns. In this respect, Paramount Classics could not simply behave like a throwback to the early 1990s models of specialty film production and distribution, as it would have been extremely difficult to compete against the other studio divisions and consequently to justify investment from its parent company. Against this background, the appointment of former Miramax and Fox Searchlight executive, David Dinerstein, as Paramount Classics' co-President certainly sent a message that the division was also capable of handling indiewood titles.

The trajectory of Paramount Classics has been intricately linked with corporate politics within its sister company. Perhaps more than any of the other studio divisions of the 1990s and 2000s, Paramount Classics was the one closest to a major, with the trade press often commenting on its aversion to risk-taking and to deviation from its Paramount-set business plan, which made for a division that operated 'much like its parent'.[2] Furthermore, and in numerous interviews, the top echelons of the division's management readily admitted that they all really worked for the major,[3] which made Paramount Classics often look more like a marketing label inside the bigger studio than a fully-fledged autonomous division with its own objectives and identity. Indeed, as the ensuing account will demonstrate, the close proximity to the studio did not allow the division to create its own distinct identity in the specialty market.

This lack of identity is particularly evident in the division's history from its inception in 1997 till 2004, the year that the senior management team at the Paramount studio changed. During that time, the classics arm seemed to operate in the mould of Sony Pictures Classics, with a release schedule consisting almost exclusively of negative pick-ups and an eclectic array of different types of films, including US indies (*The Virgin Suicides* [S. Coppola, 2000]), arthouse films by celebrated world cinema auteurs (*Sunshine* [István Szabó, 1999]) and documentaries (*Trekkies*). However, the division also became involved with low-budget genre films (the remake of studio prison film *Mean Machine* [B. Skolnick, 2002]), while in 2000 it also ventured on to more commercial indiewood turf with Sam Raimi's star-studded *The Gift*, which none the less underperformed at the US box office, registering a gross of $12 million. Indeed, none of the other films mentioned surpassed the $10 million mark.[4]

The lack of identity in the marketplace was addressed in late 2004, when a new regime at Paramount (and Viacom) decided to 'beef up' and 'broaden' its classics arm.[5] Gradually, the division started turning to production, while its programme of acquisitions focused on more commercial properties, the cost of which was considerably higher than that of the division's negative pickups prior to 2004. With an accompanying change in the division's name from Paramount Classics to Paramount Vantage and the replacement of its joint presidents by former talent agent John Lesher, Paramount's specialty division became a radically different entity and was to be responsible for some significant critically, if not always financially, successful indiewood films, including the Academy Award winner for 2007, *No Country for Old Men* (Joel and Ethan Coen), *There Will Be Blood* (P. T. Anderson, 2007), both of these in collaboration with Miramax, and *Babel* (A. G. Iñárritu, 2006). This success, however, came at a price. As these films were much more expensive to market, and in a general climate of retrenchment, the studio decided that it did not need a separate division to release its specialty titles. Accordingly, in June 2008, Paramount Vantage was absorbed by the studio, and since then has continued to operate only as a marketing brand that has been attached to a handful of productions that are none the less distributed by the major. Given this trajectory, this chapter will be divided into two sections, the first one focusing on Paramount Classics until 2004 and the second looking at the rest of the division's history.

## 'WE'RE A SMALL COMPANY AND WE INTEND TO STAY THAT WAY'

Paramount's first move towards the establishment of a specialty label was initiated in the summer of 1997, when the studio assigned senior executive Rob Friedman to build a division from scratch and bring in a manager with 'acquisitions expertise and experience in marketing and distribution of specialized [pictures] to run it'.[6] With production expertise reportedly not part of the job description, it seemed that Paramount was looking more at the Sony Pictures Classics model rather than the Fox Searchlight one. This can be partly explained by the fact that the creation of the new division was set in motion by Jonathan Dolgen, a senior executive at Viacom Entertainment, who had come to the company from Sony where he was involved in setting up SPC in 1992.[7] With SPC very much defined as a fiscally conservative division that specialised in acquisitions of upmarket arthouse films and utilised practices that its managers had introduced and adopted during their years at UA Classics and Orion Classics in the 1980s, it was certainly surprising that an upstart division within the very different specialty film context of the late 1990s was being set up in that particular mould. What was perhaps less surprising was that, according to reports, Friedman had approached the SPC triumvirate of Tom Bernard, Michael Barker and Marcie Bloom as the ideal management team for Paramount's division but had failed to convince them to leave Sony.[8]

After a protracted period of searching, Paramount announced, at the end of February 1998, that its new division would be run jointly by former Fine Line Features President, Ruth Vitale, and former Fox Searchlight Senior Vice-President of Marketing and Publicity, David Dinerstein. The joint appointment reflected the two executives' main areas of expertise, seeking to marry Vitale's expertise in acquisitions and production (should the division venture into this area) and her experience of running a classics division with Dinerstein's knowledge of the distribution business.[9] On a closer look, however, the appointments of Vitale and Dinerstein arguably demonstrated Paramount's (and Viacom's) lack of clear objectives for the new division, given that the companies they had come from represented quite different approaches to specialty film, while the potential overall modelling of the division on SPC could stand to complicate the question of the identity of Paramount Classics even further.

Indeed, the first public expressions of the division's philosophy and key objectives by the new management seemed to confirm some of these problems. In a move that telegraphed the division as a new SPC, Dinerstein pitched Paramount Classics as a company that would fill 'a void in the market', as it intended to focus on its projects 'in a very labor intensive way that most other studios are incapable of doing', but would also be capable of 'step[ping] up to the plate when necessary' and using studio resources to achieve maximum returns on its properties.[10] With the rest of the studio divisions pushing more forcefully towards indiewood films, one could argue that Paramount Classics was indeed trying to emulate SPC and go for the smaller but steady profits that had been the staple of Sony's division since its inception. On the other hand, and shortly after its first releases in 1999, Vitale was quoted saying that Paramount Classics 'was part of a system to bring in new talent, new directors, new writers for Paramount proper',[11] a view that clearly presented the division as little more than a studio mechanism for the cultivation of relationships with talent and which had little to do with the philosophy of a division like SPC and its dedication to arthouse cinema. Finally, the division's budget range and level of investment in film acquisitions for 1998 was reported to be between $250,000 and $12 million, figures comparable to both Searchlight's $3 to $13 million (1997) and SPC's $250,000 to $5 million (1996).[12]

Vitale's admission that the classics division represented a training ground for young filmmakers who would be expected then to transfer smoothly to the main studio and work on its blockbuster and franchise films has been a major point of contention in scholarly approaches to specialty film, and especially to American independent cinema and the overall role of the classics divisions in it. As Emmanuel Levy argued in his comprehensive study *Cinema of Outsiders*, for many critics US independent cinema in the 1990s was not so much an alternative environment for young filmmakers as it was a contribution to talent cultivation for the major studios;[13] while Peter Biskind made the same point when he questioned whether the indie sector represented 'an autonomous world of its own, with its own values and aesthetic existing outside and thrusting against the gravitational pull of the system' or was simply 'a farm system for the majors'.[14]

While the emergence of the discourse of indiewood and its dominance over other forms of independent filmmaking in the late 1990s and 2000s arguably point towards the idea that the studio specialty film arms were indeed a training ground for directors before some of them moved to studio productions – an idea that Vitale's admission in 1999 seems clearly to support – one could argue that this was particularly the case once the studio arms started focusing on production rather than when they used to function primarily as distributors. This was because negative pick-ups tend to be determined by the amount of money committed to a film seeking distribution by the highest bidder, which does not easily encourage the cultivation of a relationship between talent and a particular distributor. On the other hand, the 'turn' to production of indie films in the 1990s, especially in the second half of the decade, contributed greatly to the cultivation of relationships, with several young filmmakers graduating to studio projects after one or two successful indie pictures for the studio subsidiaries.

If one accepts the above argument, Paramount Classics' initial emphasis on acquisitions was yet another questionable element in the division's stated objective to deliver new talent to the main studio. However, around the time of Paramount Classics' first release, its management announced that the division would also be venturing into production, with the aim of distributing six or seven films a year, including one or two productions.[15] Even though this plan did not materialise until much later in the division's history, it none the less showed that Vitale and Dinerstein were acutely aware of the limitations of a business model based exclusively on acquisitions, à la SPC, in the specialty film context of the late 1990s and the early 2000s.

The division's first releases came out in mid-1999; besides acquisitions, they also featured titles that had been passed on to Paramount Classics by the studio. In terms of acquisitions, Paramount Classics demonstrated that it would not only not shy away from arthouse films in languages other than English, but also that it would pursue properties that were characterised as 'unusually risqué' for a studio division.[16] One such title was Goral Paskaljevich's brutal *Bure Baruta* [*Cabaret Balkan*], a film about the extent to which violence permeated the lives of a group of people in former Yugoslavia, which at the time was being tested by the war in Kosovo. The film, however, did not attract significant box-office business, finishing with only $100,000 gross.[17] Perhaps more disappointing was the release of *The Adventures of Sebastian Cole* (T. Williams), which had attracted considerable attention at the 1999 Sundance Film Festival, during which Paramount Classics had bought the film for a reported sum of approximately $0.5 million.[18] Despite very positive reviews and a narrative that dealt with transgendered identities, which had the potential to be marketed as a serious film to a substantial audience, *The Adventures of Sebastian Cole* also grossed just $100,000 at the US theatrical box office. A similar fate awaited two more of the division's five releases in 1999, the documentary *Trekkies* (Paramount's Classics first release) and the mockumentary *Where is Marlowe?* (D. Pyne), both titles that originated in or had links to the main studio but which were eventually passed on to the specialty division for theatrical distribution. This left only one title, the British gay-themed *Get Real* (S. Shore), which passed the $1 million mark and became a very modest success.

With its first releases grossing less than $2 million combined, Paramount Classics found itself with a minimal market share in its first year of operations, far below the other studio divisions. Given this inauspicious start, and as the division was limited by the parent company in terms of bidding for the most commercial titles that were available in the acquisitions market, Vitale and Dinerstein quickly started looking into (co-)finance deals in order to secure more commercially promising product. In January 2000 they signed a deal with Total Film Group to distribute four of its productions, starting with Bruce Beresford's *Bride of the Wind* and Christine Lahti's *My First Mister*.[19] More importantly, the division became one of the backers of and arranged distribution for the supernatural thriller *The Gift*, written by actor–writer–director Billy Bob Thornton, directed by celebrated cult filmmaker Sam Raimi and featuring a stellar cast that included Cate Blanchett, Greg Kinnear, Keanu Reeves, Hilary Swank and Katie Holmes.[20] With these few deals in place, Paramount Classics also moved to acquire a number of films, including the French arthouse picture *La Fille sur le pont* [*The Girl on the Bridge*] by Patrice Leconte, renowned Hungarian auteur István Szabó's epic *Sunshine*, Kenneth Lonergan's Sundance winner *You Can Count on Me*, and Sofia Coppola's star-studded *The Virgin Suicides*, based on the celebrated novel of the same title by Jeffrey Eugenides (1993).

Although, of all these films, *You Can Count On Me* turned out to be the division's most profitable release (especially given its low $1 million budget) with a gross of slightly over $9 million,[21] *The Virgin Suicides* arguably became the most important film for Paramount Classics, both in the year 2000 and more generally in this first phase in the division's history. Despite the fact that upon its release it grossed a modest $4.9 million at the North American box office, Sofia Coppola's debut film received rave reviews, launched the career of one of the most promising female writer–directors in US indie cinema, and gave Paramount's division some much-needed visibility as a destination for young, hip, indie filmmakers. With *Sunshine* recording box-office takings of over $5 million, Paramount Classics enjoyed a financially much-improved second year of full operations, managing to climb to twenty-second place in the list of distributors in terms of market share, directly below all its major rivals.

This success, however, remained short-lived. From the next year on until 2005, none of Paramount Classics' twenty-five releases would achieve more than $5 million at the US theatrical box office, raising a lot of questions about the division's ability to compete with its rivals. Particularly telling were the distributor's results in 2001 (see Table 2). Six of the division's seven releases failed to reach the $1 million mark, grossing a combined total of $3.1 million, while the more commercially appealing *Sidewalks of New York*, Ed Burns's newest film about complicated romantic relationships, also failed to find an audience, grossing just over $2 million.

Table 2 Paramount Classics' 2001 releases and their US theatrical box-office gross[22]

| Title | Release date (2001) | Box office ($ million) |
|---|---|---|
| *Company Man* | 9 Mar | 0.1 |
| *Bride of the Wind* | 8 Jun | 0.4 |
| *American Rhapsody* | 10 Aug | 0.8 |
| *Our Lady of the Assassins* | 7 Sep | 0.5 |
| *My First Mister* | 12 Oct | 0.6 |
| *Focus* | 19 Oct | 0.7 |
| *Sidewalks of New York* | 21 Nov | 2.3 |
| Total | | 5.4 |

Such weak results clearly beg some questions about the division's sustainability, given that the figures translate to little, if any, income from the theatrical exploitation of its pictures in the theatrical market, especially at a time when rivals such as Sony Pictures Classics and USA Films were recording combined grosses of over $150 million (following the runaway success of *Crouching Tiger, Hidden Dragon* and *Traffic*, respectively). Despite a seeming inability to move in the right direction, however, Paramount Classics was in fact mediating its losses at the North American theatrical box office, primarily by exploiting Paramount's resources to push its most promising titles to markets outside the US. As Vitale put it:

We take a big footprint that extends beyond just North America. That spreads our risk greatly, so we can do a certain amount of business in the U.S., but it's not make-it-or-break-it based solely on a U.S. release.[23]

With stand-alone independents not being able to venture into worldwide distribution, studio divisions – even the underperforming ones, like Paramount Classics – were in a position to increase their profits or at least recoup part of their investment; this was the case with *The Gift*, which, apart from the $12 million it grossed in North America, also made an additional $32 million in the rest of the world.

Despite this additional income, it was clear that Paramount Classics was finding it difficult to establish a track record and, by the early years of 2000s, was being left behind by the other participants in the third wave of studio film divisions, who were moving increasingly to the production and distribution of indiewood titles. In this respect, it started attracting considerable criticism from the trade press,[24] which quickly spread in mainstream publications like the *Los Angeles Times*, and was directed towards Paramount Classics' chronic inability to generate revenues that were comparable to those of the other studio divisions.[25] By late 2004, however, changes at both Paramount and Viacom had already started putting in motion a radical reinvention of Paramount Classics. Instead of SPC, the inspiration for the division would be Fox Searchlight and Focus Features, while the designation 'classics' would disappear from its name in a bid to be rebranded as a serious player in the specialty film game.

## FROM INDIE TO INDIEWOOD

In July 2004, longstanding Viacom President and Chief Operating Officer Mel Camarzin and Viacom Entertainment Chairman Jonathan Dolgen left the company after a corporate shake-up in the top management tier of Paramount's parent corporation. Former MTV Chairman Tom Freston and former CBS Chairman Leslie Moonves took over their posts as co-Presidents and Chief Operating Officers, with Freston also in charge of overseeing Paramount and all the other film-related divisions.[26] Dolgen's departure immediate fuelled speculation as to whether Paramount and its classics arm would be changing their business philosophy and, in the case of Paramount Classics, whether it would be allowed to pursue more expensive films with more commercial potential.[27] The latter question was particularly pertinent, as Paramount Classics had started already showing some signs of change, even before Dolgen's departure. Specifically, it had moved to a few financing arrangements for films such as Patrice Leconte's *Intimate Strangers*, Roger Michell's *Enduring Love* and Mike Hodges's *I'll Sleep When I'm Dead* – all released in the second half of 2004 – prompting Vitale to acknowledge that Paramount Classics was, indeed, 'doing things a little bit differently'.[28]

Almost immediately, Freston announced that Paramount's specialty label was going to undergo a radical makeover 'as part of Paramount's push for fare that's riskier, more creative and aimed at a younger demo'.[29] Having been particularly impressed by the (still-fresh) success of Searchlight's titles *Bend It Like Beckham*, *Garden State* and *Napoleon Dynamite*, Freston planned to turn Paramount Classics into an outfit that was comparable to the leading studio divisions. According to some reports, Freston even toyed with the idea of creating a new specialty label from scratch, one 'that would have total creative autonomy and enough financial backing to produce a slate of modestly budgeted films with rising stars and gifted young filmmakers'.[30] In that scenario Paramount Classics might still continue to exist but would instead have to become a specialty marketing label for the more demanding arthouse product and thus operate within the structures of the new division. Finally, whether with a new division or with a revamped Paramount Classics, Freston was prepared to start committing funds for 'in-house' productions,[31] a strategy that had been absent from Paramount Classics' business plan under the parent company's previous management.

The first acquisitions of titles to be unveiled by Paramount Classics under the new corporate regime could not have sent a clearer message about the change of course on which the division would be embarking. Although a documentary, and therefore still firmly a specialty picture, *Mad Hot Ballroom* (M. Agrelo, 2005) focuses on New York public schoolchildren who try to learn ballroom dancing with a view to participating in a major competition. To market the film, Paramount Classics enlisted the help of fellow Viacom division, and one of the top brand names in children's entertainment, Nickelodeon. Despite them being under the same corporate umbrella since Paramount Classics' inception, this was the first instance of synergy between the two divisions and it proved an unmitigated success.[32] With a clever marketing campaign led by a poster that focused on two African American kids doing the tango and the Manhattan skyline in the background, and an aggressive tagline that read 'anyone can make it if they learn how to shake it,' the film attracted an audience substantial enough to make it Paramount Classics' third biggest hit after *The Gift* and *You Can Count on Me*, with a US box-office gross of over $8 million.

However, it was the second acquisition that made a much bigger splash and showed beyond any doubt that Paramount Classics was going to compete aggressively with the other studio divisions and independent distributors. After a screening of the John Singleton-produced *Hustle & Flow* (C. Brewer) at the 2005 Sundance Film Festival, Paramount's division thwarted competition in a reportedly fierce bidding war that involved all the key players in the specialty market and secured the rights of the $2 million-budgeted film by making an offer – in collaboration with MTV – of $9 million.[33] Although this move took the industry by surprise, given that the division suddenly jumped from bids of $2 to $3 million to one of the highest amounts in the history of the Sundance Film Festival, the film seemed to be fitting Paramount Classics' new business plan and providing promising opportunities for more synergies within Viacom. Featuring a story about a pimp who tries to change career and become a hip-hop artist, the picture looked like an ideal opportunity for the division to launch its collaboration with one of the key Viacom divisions, MTV, and its MTV Films label. With hip-hop music and the representation of African American culture having become mainstays of the music channel since the 2000s, Paramount Classics could count on constant and extensive advertising of its property to the right demographic without any additional marketing costs. Driven by an Academy Award-nominated performance by Terrence Howard in the main role, *Hustle & Flow* became easily the top-grossing title in the division's history, taking $22 million at the North American box office.

If *Mad Hot Ballroom* and *Hustle & Flow*, along with the synergies with Nickelodeon and MTV Films, telegraphed a new Paramount Classics that would market films to younger demographics, the inevitable next step was in-house production. Not surprisingly, the first production to be announced was a teen thriller with the title *Beneath*, which represented an extension of the division's relationship with MTV, and demonstrated beyond any doubt Paramount Classics' turn towards the youth market. Featuring attractive young actors and produced by the same team that produced *Napoleon Dynamite*,[34] the film provided evidence that the division was being reinvented in the mould of its main rivals, which also had been increasingly utilising synergistic approaches to filmmaking (see, for instance, Fine Line Features and HBO in Chapter 4, and Fox Searchlight and MySpace in Chapter 6).

With the division moving aggressively towards more commercial acquisitions, like *Winter Solstice* (J. Sternfeld, 2005), and making more production deals, such as Jonathan Demme's Neil Young performance film *Prairie Wind* and Craig Brewer's follow-up to *Hustle & Flow*, *Black Snake Moan*, industry perceptions of Paramount Classics started changing radically. In its report on the division's distribution activity for 2005, *Variety* characterised the specialty arm as being 'on steroids', having also managed to record its best financial performance since inception with $31 million in box-office revenues.[35] And even though this figure was still far below the revenues of Fox Searchlight, Focus Features and even Warner Independent (which had entered the marketplace only in the previous year – see Chapter 9), all of which recorded grosses of slightly over $100 million, it was sufficient to put a substantial distance between Paramount Classics and other stand-alone distributors that could not follow the indiewood trends.

In spite of this early success, the new Paramount Classics was only just starting to evolve as a division in search of a market identity, and in the minds of the management both of the main studio (which had also changed in late 2004) and of the parent company, the specialty division was in need of new leadership that would take it to the next level. That level, according to Eugene Hernandez of *Indiewire*, was clearly determined by the revenues associated with indiewood films. As he put it, 'studios have tasted the successes Indiewood hits can deliver and show no signs of retreating from capitalizing on those businesses.'[36] Accordingly, and despite the early success of *Hustle & Flow*, in October 2005 Paramount relieved Vitale and Dinerstein of their duties as the division's co-Presidents and instead hired John Lesher, a former talent agent, to run it. Even though Lesher had no previous experience in making films or running a film production and distribution organisation, he was none the less known for his relationship with a number of creative filmmakers, whom he was expected to attract to Paramount Classics (and the main studio). Significantly, many of these directors had already built their reputation on the specialty film circuit and their work had normally been distributed by the other studio divisions; they included Paul Thomas Anderson, Kimberly Peirce, David O. Russell, Alejandro González Iñárritu, Walter Salles and Fernando Meirelles.[37]

Despite Lesher's impressive credentials and contacts, his move to Paramount Classics raised a number of questions, especially within the context of the other appointments of senior executives at Paramount (especially its new Chairman Brad Grey), who had no prior experience in making films either.[38] As was later revealed, however, Lesher's established relationship with directing talent was key, not just for revamping the specialty label, but also for transforming Paramount too in an effort to break the perceptions of conservatism and become more competitive in the marketplace. Indeed, having purchased a number of 'edgier properties', including the horror-comic-book series *Damn Nation* and Charles Burns's graphic novel *Black Hole*, the main studio also needed younger, more creative filmmakers to make them into films that would appeal to the younger demographic that MTV would be delivering.

Lesher's contribution to these plans was immediate; he was instrumental in bringing Iñárritu's *Babel* to Paramount (and from there to the classics arm) for $20 million, a film that he had helped package while in his previous post as an agent at Endeavor Talent Agency.[39] With an ensemble cast that featured Brad Pitt, Cate Blanchett and Gael García Bernal, *Babel* was the clearest example yet of Paramount Classics' venture into indiewood territory. As for the division's plan of action under the new management, Lesher's intention was to pursue '"a healthy mix" of genres and innovative filmmakers', following similar trends in other studio divisions.[40] However, although divisions like Fox Searchlight, Focus Features and Miramax had established separate labels for the handling of genre films (Fox Atomic, Rogue Pictures and Dimension Films, respectively), Paramount had no plans to create a genre division.

Although 2006 was deemed a transitional year, as most of the division's line-up consisted of films arranged by the previous management team, Paramount Classics achieved the biggest hit in its history so far, thanks to another Sundance acquisition, the documentary film *An Inconvenient Truth* (see Case Study below). The success of the film, which grossed over $25 million, brought Paramount Classics enormous publicity and numerous awards, including an Academy Award for Best Documentary feature film. Yet, despite the unquestionable significance of the success of *An Inconvenient Truth*, it was the division's plans for 2007 that would completely redefine it; indeed, Lesher's relationships with some of the best-regarded creative filmmakers in the indiewood sector became the cornerstone for Paramount Classics' determined move in that direction.

The first production that Lesher arranged in January 2006, immediately after his appointment, was Paul Thomas Anderson's epic period drama *There Will Be Blood*. Having written and directed, among others, two of the most celebrated indiewood films in the history of the sector, *Boogie Nights* (1997) and *Magnolia* (2000), Anderson's new project, a loose adaptation of Upton Sinclair's novel *Oil!* starring Daniel Day-Lewis, did certainly fit the bill in terms of the direction Paramount Classics wanted to take. Following the setting-up of this project, Lesher convinced the main studio that the specialty division was a more appropriate distributor for *Babel*. Then, in February 2006, he announced another prestigious production, *No Country for Old Men*, by celebrated filmmakers Joel and Ethan Coen. With a career spanning over twenty years and with films ranging from canonical indie titles like *Blood Simple* (1984) and *Barton Fink* (1991) to more indiewood fare that featured global stars such as *Intolerable Cruelty* (2003, starring George Clooney and Catherine Zeta Jones) and *The Ladykillers* (2004, starring Tom Hanks), both of which grossed over $100 million worldwide, the Coens, like Paul Thomas Anderson, represented creative filmmakers at the pinnacle of their critical and commercial success, who were able to produce prestigious, often-demanding films without compromising their commercial potential. As both *No Country for Old Men* and *There Will Be Blood* were considerably more expensive productions than the average independent film, Paramount Classics co-financed them with Miramax in a fifty-fifty partnership.[41] For *Blood*, Paramount's division retained the US film rights while Miramax handled it in the rest of the world, while for *Country* the reverse distribution arrangement was agreed.

With additional commercially-minded titles on its roster, including Sean Penn's *Into the Wild*, Michael Winterbottom's *A Mighty Heart* (starring leading Hollywood actress Angelina Jolie) and Noah Baumbach's *Margot at the Wedding* (starring Nicole Kidman and Jack Black), it was clear that Paramount Classics was putting together an extremely ambitious programme of releases that were in no way comparable to the types of films it had handled in the pre-2005 period. The last piece in the jigsaw was revealed in May 2006 at the Cannes Film Festival, when Lesher announced that the rebranded division would also change its name to Paramount Vantage, with *Babel* becoming the division's first release under the new label in October 2006.[42] However, Lesher decided to retain the Paramount Classics brand as a distinct label that would distribute the artier films within Paramount Vantage.

In terms of prestige and critical success, the eighteen-month period between the division's rebranding as Paramount Vantage and March 2008 was on a par with the success of all the division's rivals. *An Inconvenient Truth* and *Babel* received eight Academy Award nominations in total, with the former winning its category and the latter also receiving one award. However, it was in the following film season that the division's success became most evident, with many industry critics admitting that the new management team had finally succeeded in putting Paramount's specialty label 'on the map'.[43] *No Country for Old Men*, *There Will Be Blood* and *Into the Wild* dominated the Academy Award nominations, receiving eighteen nominations in total, and *No Country for Old Men* receiving the Award for Best Picture.

The financial results of this slate of films, however, were not as high as anticipated. The strong theme of community and connection for humanity on a global level that permeated *Babel*'s multi-strand narrative held much more appeal outside the US, with only $35 million gross being taken in the North American market out of a worldwide total of $135 million. Owning only the domestic rights to *There Will Be Blood*, Paramount Vantage saw rentals of only $40 million domestic gross (from worldwide box-office receipts of approximately $76 million), a figure that was rather disappointing given the rave reviews and numerous awards the film had garnered. With *Into the Wild* and the British acquisition *The Kite Runner* also following the above pattern and grossing much less at the US theatrical box office than worldwide, it was clear that the division had enjoyed easily the best year in its history financially. This success became even more pronounced with the international box-office performance of *No Country for Old Men*, which grossed $85 million outside the US, and gave the division a hit that came close to the $100 million mark. However, as Miramax distributed the film in the North American market, *No Country for Old Men* became identified primarily with the Disney division rather than with Paramount Vantage.

## THE END (OF A NEW BEGINNING)

Although, within the context of the division's financial performance prior to 2006, the success described sounds extremely impressive, it was still found wanting in real terms, as well as in comparison with the performance of other key studio divisions. In terms of the latter, none of the division's titles approached the $140 million domestic gross that Fox Searchlight's *Juno* recorded, a film that was released around the same time as *There Will Be Blood* and *No Country for Old Men*. This was particularly significant, as *Juno* had cost an estimated $7 million, compared to the $25 million that each of the Vantage films reportedly cost to produce.[44] According to industry critic Anne Thompson, the above two Vantage titles and the majority of the division's releases after *Babel* (with the exception of *Son of Rambow* [G. Jennings], an early 2008 release) barely broke even, if they did not lose money,[45] a reality that put into question the business model upon which the rebranded division (and the other studio labels with the exception of SPC) operated.

That model, intricately linked with the US independent cinema's move to indiewood as its dominant expression since the late 1990s, depended on increasingly large budgets (to the extent that neither *There Will Be Blood* nor *No Country for Old Men* was eligible for the Independent Spirit Awards, their budgets being considerably higher than the $20 million ceiling set by Film Independent, which administers the awards) and therefore on an increasingly large financial commitment from the parent company; the attachment of well-known filmmakers and stars as a pre-condition for greenlighting and financing a film and for maximising returns from various ancillary markets; the choice of easily marketable subject matter that has the potential to create synergistic collaborations with other divisions within the same conglomerate in which a specialty label exists and to attract wider audiences than just the limited arthouse core viewers; an expensive marketing campaign that often included advertising spots on network television; and the eschewing of platform release strategies and the optioning of saturation releases that often saw such titles opening in over 1,000 engagements.

The above elements clearly demonstrate an approach to 'specialty' filmmaking that not only has few points of contact with the independent cinema of the 1980s, and even of the early 1990s, but also increasingly resembles studio filmmaking. According to Motion Picture Association of America data, the average cost of producing a specialty film had reached an incredible $49.2 million by 2007, an increase of 60 per cent over the previous year, when the cost was closer to $30.7 million. With marketing and advertising costs also increased by 44 per cent to $25.7 million for the same year, it made for a combined cost of a staggering $75 million to produce and launch a film in the specialty marketplace.[46] At the same time, the production and marketing costs for the average studio film totalled $106.6 million, only 45 per cent higher than their divisions' output.[47] And as Miramax, guilty of inflating production and advertising budgets in previous years, was in the process of being reinvented following the exit of the Weinstein brothers in 2005, it is clear that the companies responsible for this extraordinary rise in costs were the rest of the studio divisions, and especially

Paramount Vantage with its expensive slate of films. Given these figures, the commercial performance of the division's titles was not sufficient to recoup its costs. Accordingly, and following a similar decision at Warner in relation to its own specialty subsidiaries (see Chapter 9), on 3 June 2008 Paramount announced the closure of Paramount Vantage as a physical film production, distribution and marketing organisation; the label Paramount Vantage was to be retained as a production and marketing label that would operate within the studio, its films being distributed by Paramount itself.

Although the division's closure as a production–distribution organisation was also the product of a more general shakeout in the sector, which I discuss in more detail in Chapter 9, it was also a result of company politics that were specific to Viacom and Paramount. In particular, following Viacom's purchase of Dreamworks SKG in 2006, Viacom had found itself with three producing–distributing film divisions under the same corporate umbrella in addition to film-producing labels, MTV Films and Nickelodeon Movies, which belonged to different divisions. With the last two becoming increasingly active in the 2000s, both on their own merit and in collaboration with other Viacom subsidiaries, and with Paramount Vantage producing and releasing a number of expensive indiewood films, it made sense for Viacom to consolidate distribution and streamline marketing operations.[48] In this respect, the problems in the specialty sector created by the studio divisions' move to indiewood and the more general economic crisis that started to be felt in 2008 were not solely responsible for the radical redefinition of Paramount Vantage.

Since then, Paramount Vantage has been involved in a number of productions, including some notable indiewood titles such as *Revolutionary Road* (S. Mendes, 2008) and *Defiance* (E. Zwick, 2008), that were distributed by Paramount in 2008 and 2009. Yet again, though, corporate politics interfered with its efforts to maintain coherence and, eventually, its place within the increasingly large Paramount family. Specifically, after it had folded into the main studio, Paramount Vantage was given a mandate to develop, produce and acquire approximately six films per year, which the studio would then release.[49] However, following the establishment of the Paramount Worldwide Acquisitions Group in July 2008, 'a centralized acquisitions and local productions arm that [would] feed pics into the pipelines of Paramount Pictures [International] and Paramount Vantage',[50] the label's focus shifted accordingly to serve the needs of this initiative.[51] Since 2010, Paramount Vantage has been associated with only a handful of releases that were handled by the studio, the Renée Zellweger thriller, *Case 39*, being the most notable.

## CONCLUSION

Perhaps more than any of the other participants in the third wave of studio specialty film divisions, Paramount Classics / Vantage became a prime example of the necessity for a transition from indie cinema to indiewood, from relatively low-budget films that occasionally showed affinities with studio films to substantially financed productions that increasingly resembled studio productions and often recorded comparable box-office grosses – if the division were to survive in the 2000s. Conceived in the mould of SPC and Fine Line Features but having to compete with Fox Searchlight, Focus Features and even Miramax, Paramount Classics did not enjoy a high level of autonomy from the main studio. Instead, it was perceived as a smaller version of Paramount that was asked to operate under the same rules, policies and practices as the parent company, which did not allow it to follow the trends established by specialty film market leaders or, more importantly, to build a distinct identity in the specialty film marketplace. In this respect, the division seemed to be constantly underperforming financially, while its programme of releases did not appear to have the cohesion that characterised Fox Searchlight releases (films in the English language with clear commercial elements) or SPC (non-US arthouse and US independent films).

From 2004 onwards and especially after sweeping changes at its sister studio and parent company, Paramount Classics quickly dropped the more 'indie' Classics label and readily adopted practices associated with the dominant discourse in independent filmmaking in 2000s – indiewood. The division's foreign films, the openly arthouse titles and the low-budget indies all but disappeared, making way for expensive US films made by top directors and with the participation of major Hollywood stars. But the great critical and commercial success of films such as *Babel*, *No Country for Old Men*, *There Will Be Blood* and *Into the Wild* came at a price, as the funds invested for their production and marketing costs were often much higher than the returns from their commercial exploitation. With the global financial crisis necessitating a tightening of the purse strings and with the internal politics of studio and parent company often dictating the use of Paramount Vantage as a pawn in a much larger game, the division was quickly folded into the main studio in 2008, and from there to relative obscurity.

### Case Study: *An Inconvenient Truth* (Davis Guggenheim, 2006)

Feature documentaries have been a staple of contemporary American independent cinema, with studio divisions distributing such films from the very beginning (UA Classics' *From Mao to Mozart: Isaac Stern in China* and *Say*

*Amen* in the 1980s; SPC's *The Celluloid Closet* and Fine Line Features' *Hoop Dreams* in the 1990s), while *Trekkies* was one of the first releases for Paramount Classics in 1999. Given their extremely low budgets, they only need to attract small audiences to become profitable, while on occasion they have managed to generate substantial revenues, as was the case with the basketball-themed *Hoop Dreams* in 1994.

In the 2000s, however, feature documentaries became big business. Led by the astonishing commercial success of Michael Moore's *Bowling for Columbine* (2002), which became a crossover success after grossing more than $20 million, and especially the same director's *Fahrenheit 9/11*, which became a runaway hit in 2004, grossing $120 million at the US theatrical box office and an additional $100 million internationally, the format has enjoyed a rise in popularity with a host of titles finding both critical and commercial success; these include *Super Size Me* (M. Spurlock, 2004), *The Fog of War* (E. Morris, 2003), *Spellbound* (J. Blitz, 2002) and Paramount Classics' own *Mad Hot Ballroom*. Even documentaries made outside the US have also met with considerable international success, such as *March of the Penguins* (L. Jacquet, 2004), which became another runaway hit.

Following the considerable success of *Mad Hot Ballroom* and during a phase of 'radical makeover' designed to involve the division in riskier and more creative fare, Paramount Classics' new President, John Lesher, acquired Davis Guggenheim's climate-change documentary, *An Inconvenient Truth*. The film was based on a Powerpoint presentation that the former Vice-President of the United States, Al Gore, had been giving for a number of years in an effort to educate the public on the dangers of climate change. Made by Participant Productions, a new (in 2006) production company whose mission is to make entertaining films that engage with social and political problems, the film attracted considerable attention, mainly because of the participation of a political agent of Gore's stature but also because of the centrality of climate-change debates in everyday public discourse.

Following its premiere at the 2006 Sundance Film Festival, Lesher acquired the rights for the film in a deal reminiscent of the early UA Classics arrangements of the 1980s. Offering no fee upfront but agreeing to split all the rentals with Participant Productions fifty-fifty,[52] Paramount Classics convinced Participant to sign with them, while the success of *Mad Hot Ballroom* was still very fresh and the revamped division seemed to be both eager and able to market the film aggressively and turn it into a commercial success. Indeed, despite the fact that the film's marketing budget was just $4.5 million,[53] Paramount Classics orchestrated a huge public relations campaign that involved a large number of partners aiming 'to position [the film] as the take-action movie of the year'.[54] In this effort, the studio division was also supported by the production company itself, which had links with a strong network of charities and non-profit organisations that publicised the film to a very substantial global audience.[55]

Paramount Classics and Participant Productions' aggressive marketing and PR campaigns were essential for a documentary film that appeared to be difficult to categorise. At the core of the problem was the fact that the film had no interest in cinematic language or aesthetic experimentation and was instead focused on conveying a very particular message through the use of an aesthetically dry Powerpoint presentation – irrespective of the fact that Gore and his team had tried to make the presentation's graphics interesting.

> Here is a film [writes Jerry White] whose visuals mean absolutely nothing to its analysis of our global predicament and whose 'author' – clearly Al Gore, not director Davis Guggenheim – is every bit a man of politics and very far indeed from the *Homo cinematicus* that Truffaut longed for.[56]

Indeed, the film struggles to fit in any of the categories of documentary introduced by Bill Nichols.[57] Its closest links are with the expository documentary mode, in which a film aims to be descriptive and informative and to put forward a particular argument. However, this mode is characterised strongly by a disembodied and authoritative voiceover commentary that helps to communicate what is presented as 'objective truth'. But with Al Gore dominating most of the frames in *An Inconvenient Truth*, it is clear that the film goes beyond the expository mode.

These problems of definition are somewhat minimised by the inclusion of footage from Gore's personal life, career in politics and reflections on the subject of the film. These numerous short scenes regularly interrupt the flow of Gore's presentation and give the viewers an opportunity both to digest the hard data and to understand Gore's role better as an environmental activist at the very top level. Interestingly, these short scenes consistently emphasise the theme of loss (or near-loss) and the effect it has had on Gore (losing his sister to cancer, losing the 2004 elections to George W. Bush, almost losing his son in a traffic accident), which meshes well with the theme of loss (or near-loss) of our planet – unless we all act – as it becomes evident in the bulk of the film, Gore's presentation. In this respect, the film is structured coherently around a very specific theme, also invoked in the distributor's choice of taglines that clearly focused on warning people about the forthcoming disaster.

The film opened in May 2006 in platform release with extraordinary results, taking $400,000 from just four theatres. Following a gradual expansion, it peaked in its sixth week of release, when it played on 587 theatres. *An Inconvenient Truth* remained on release for an additional seventeen weeks, eventually taking over $24 million and becoming the fourth highest-grossing documentary in the history of US cinema to 2006. Despite no shortage of criticisms and a court decision that pinpointed a number of inaccuracies in its presentation of scientific fact,[58] on the basis of this film Gore was recognised by the international community as an extremely significant player in the efforts to reduce $CO_2$ emissions and in 2007 was awarded the Nobel Prize for Peace. As for Paramount Classics, the success of the film confirmed that the division was ready to go for more ambitious films, especially since, shortly after the release of *An Inconvenient Truth*, it was relaunched as Paramount Vantage and started trading in indiewood titles such as *Babel* and *There Will Be Blood*.

## NOTES

1. Harris, Dana, 'Classics' Simple Plan: Low Risk, High Art', *Weekly Variety* (15 July 2002), S18.
2. Ibid.
3. Ibid.; Tourtellotte, Bob, 'Paramount Classics, Nickelodeon Pair on Film Deal', *Reuters News* (28 January 2005), n/a.
4. Unless otherwise stated, all box-office figures for the division's films were taken from The Numbers (www.the-numbers.com) and were accessed on 1 March 2011.
5. McNary, Dave, 'Par Reinventing Classics: Freston Points Specialty Arm to Edgier Fare, Eyes Prod'n', *Weekly Variety* (4 October 2004), 5.
6. Hindes, Andrew, 'Gotham Dishes While Par Fishes for Classics Chief', *Weekly Variety* (21 July 1997), 2.
7. Goldstein, Patrick, 'New Indie Film Division Could Pump Up Paramount', *Los Angeles Times* (13 October 2004), http://www.azcentral.com/ent/movies/articles/1013paramount13.html?&wired; accessed on 1 March 2011.
8. According to reports, the health of Marcie Bloom, who had suffered an aneurysm, was a thorny issue in the negotiations and the trio decided to remain at Sony (Hindes, 'Gotham Dishes', 2).
9. Hernandez, Eugene, 'Paramount Unveils New Specialty Division; Co-Presidents Vitale and Dinerstein Discuss Plans', *Indiewire* (2 March 1998), http://www.indiewire.com/article/paramount_unveils_new_specialty_division_co-presidents_vitale_and_dinerstei/; accessed on 1 March 2011.
10. Hernandez, Eugene, 'A Conversation with Ruth Vitale and David Dinerstein, Co-Presidents of Paramount's New Specialty Film Division', *Indiewire* (2 March 1998), http://www.indiewire.com/article/a_conversation_with_ruth_vitale_and_david_dinerstein_co-presidents_of_param/; accessed on 1 March 2011.
11. Moerk, Christian and Claude Brodesser, 'Classic Startup', *Weekly Variety* (29 November 1999), 7.
12. For Paramount Classics figures see Beverly Gray, 'Paramount Classics', *Hollywood Reporter* (1 August 1998), 52; for Fox Searchlight see 'Fox Searchlight Pictures', *Hollywood Reporter* (5 August 1997), 20; for SPC see 'Sony Pictures Classics', *Hollywood Reporter* (1 August 1996), 13.
13. Levy, *Cinema of Outsiders*, 506.
14. Biskind, *Down and Dirty Pictures*, 470.
15. Harris, Dana, Thom Geier and Chris Gennusa, 'Paramount Classics', *Hollywood Reporter* (1 August 1999), 36.
16. Lorber, Danny, 'REVIEWS: A Violent, Gutsy "*Cabaret Balkan*", and "*After Life*" Vanishes', *Indiewire* (23 July 1999), http://www.indiewire.com/article/reviews_a_violent_gutsy_cabaret_balkan_and_after_life_vanishes/; accessed on 1 March 2011.
17. The box-office figure for this title was taken from IMDb, http://www.imdb.com/title/tt0169145/business; accessed on 1 March 2011.
18. Moerk and Brodesser, 'Classic Startup', 7.
19. 'Paramount Classics and Total Film Group Enter Distribution Deal', *PR Newswire* (14 January 2000), n/a.
20. 'The Gift Production Notes', *Cinema Review* (2011), http://www.cinemareview.com/production.asp?prodid=1250; accessed on 1 March 2011.
21. Talbert, Anita, 'Small Movies Getting Huge Oscar Push', *Los Angeles Business Journal* (25 December 2000), 24.

22. The table is a modified version of one that was published in 'Par Classics Plays It Quirky', *Hollywood Reporter* (4 January 2002), 19.
23. Vitale was quoted in ibid.
24. Dunkley, Cathy, 'Niche Unit's Exex Are Watching the "Detective"', *Daily Variety* (17 August 2003), 18.
25. Goldstein, Patrick, 'New Indie Film Division'.
26. Hay, Carla, 'Freston's Star Soars at Viacom', *Billboard* (12 June 2004), http://www.allbusiness.com/retail-trade/miscellaneous-retail-retail-stores-not/4652617-1.html; accessed on 1 March 2011.
27. Dunkley, Cathy, 'Paramount Classics', *Daily Variety* (8 September 2004), S20.
28. Quoted in ibid.
29. Quoted in McNary, 'Par Reinventing Classics', 5.
30. Goldstein, 'New Indie Film Division'.
31. McNary, 'Par Reinventing Classics', 5.
32. Tourtellotte, 'Paramount Classics', n/a.
33. Moss, Corey, 'Ludacris' "Hustle & Flow" Makes History at Sundance: Nine-Million-Dollar Purchase Biggest Ever at Film Festival', *MTV News* (24 January 2005), http://www.mtv.com/news/articles/1496196/ludacris-movie-makes-history-at-sundance.jhtml; accessed on 1 March 2011.
34. McNary, Dave, 'Par, MTV Dive "*Beneath*"', *Daily Variety* (27 June 2005), 5.
35. Ibid.
36. Hernandez, Eugene, 'New Studio Boss Shakes Up Paramount Classics, Vitale & Dinerstein Leaving Division', *Indiewire* (7 October 2005), http://www.indiewire.com/article/new_studio_boss_shakes_up_paramount_classics_vitale_dinerstein_leaving_divi/; accessed on 1 March 2011.
37. Gardner, Chris, 'Lesher Meshing with Par Classics', *Daily Variety* (3 November 2005), 20.
38. Gardner, 'Lesher Meshing with Par Classics', 1 and 20.
39. McNary, Dave and Chris Gardner, 'Extreme Makeover: The Par Edition', *Weekly Variety* (7 November 2006), 6; Gardner, Chris and Pamela McClintock, 'Par Classics digs "Dog"', *Daily Variety* (23 January 2006), 1 and 18.
40. Hernandez, Greg, 'Paramount Names Lesher President of Classics Label', *Daily News* (Los Angeles, CA) (10 November 2005), n/a.
41. Fleming, Michael, '"Country" Time for Coens', *Variety* (1 February 2006), http://www.variety.com/article/VR1117937286?refcatid=13; accessed on 1 March 2011. The co-financing arrangement was also influenced by the fact that both films were produced by Scott Rudin, who had a longstanding association with Paramount but was in the process of moving his production company to Disney and Miramax at the time.
42. McClintock, Pamela, 'Par Has a New Vantage Point', *Daily Variety* (19 May 2006), 2.
43. Thompson, Anne, 'Par Streamlines Specialty Arm', *Daily Variety* (5 June 2008), 24.
44. See Daniel Frankel, 'Fast, Cheap and in Control', *Daily Variety* (6 February 2008), A1 and A5.
45. Thompson, Anne, 'Niche Distrib Crunch Claims Par Vantage', *Weekly Variety* (9 June 2008), 6.
46. Miller, Winter, 'Indie Spirits Wade into Mainstream', *Weekly Variety* (10 March 2008), 53.
47. Motion Picture Association of America, 'Entertainment Industry Market Statistics' (2007), http://www.immagic.com/eLibrary/ARCHIVES/GENERAL/MPAA_US/M080925E.pdf; accessed on 1 March 2011.

48. Thompson, 'Par Streamlines Specialty Arm', 1 and 24.
49. Thompson, 'Niche Distrib Crunch', 6.
50. Jaafar, Ali and Tatiana Siegel, 'Far & Wide', *Daily Variety* (23 July 2008), 1.
51. Kay, Jeremy, 'Nick Meyer Leaves Paramount Vantage, Guy Stodel Stands In', *Screen Daily* (5 December 2008), http://www.screendaily.com/nick-meyer-leaves-paramount-vantage-guy-stodel-stands-in/4042259.article; accessed on 1 March 2008.
52. Thompson, 'Niche Distrib Crunch', 6.
53. Miller, Elizabeth, 'Building Participation in the Outreach for the Documentary *The Water Front*', *Journal of Canadian Studies* 43.1 (Winter 2009), 84.
54. 'News Analysis: Gore's "Truth" Finds Receptive Audience', *PR Week* (US) (29 May 2006), 8.
55. Participant Media: Our Mission, *Participant Media* (2011), http://www.participantmedia.com/company/about_us.php; accessed on 1 March 2011.
56. White, Jerry, 'Documentaries and Scenarios', *Velvet Light Trap* 60 (2007), 89.
57. Nichols, Bill, *Introduction to Documentary* (Bloomington: University of Indiana Press, 2001).
58. Adam, David, 'Gore's Climate Film Has Scientific Errors – Judge', in *The Guardian* (11 October 2007), http://www.guardian.co.uk/environment/2007/oct/11/climatechange; accessed on 1 April 2011.

CHAPTER 8

# Focus Features (2002 to date)

## INTRODUCTION

Focus Features, the specialty label established by Vivendi Universal in 2002, has been the one division from the group comprising the most recent wave of studio specialty film arms that succeeded in establishing a distinct and consistent brand identity from inception, while also sharing with Fox Searchlight the title of the most commercially successful studio division. Its key releases include iconic 'indie' and 'indiewood' titles – such as *Far from Heaven* (T. Haynes, 2002), *Lost in Translation* (S. Coppola, 2003), *Eternal Sunshine of the Spotless Mind* (M. Gondry, 2004), *Brokeback Mountain* (A. Lee, 2005) and *Milk* (G. Van Sant, 2008) – which prompted scholars to perceive the division as 'the definitive indie company in the 2000s, in the same way that Miramax once defined the 1990s independent landscape'.[1] Indeed, despite the company competing primarily with the other studio divisions, many of the business strategies Focus Features employed aimed to position it as the new Miramax, a studio division that transcended its specialty label status by gradually moving much closer to studio filmmaking than any of the other studio divisions, and which succeeded in building a strong brand identity in the 1990s that helped it define American 'indie' cinema and the specialty film sector more generally.

While the jury is still out as to whether Focus Features has become 'a major independent', a label that Justin Wyatt attached to Miramax and New Line Cinema after both companies were taken over by major studios and moved to a type of filmmaking that took them increasingly out of the specialty film market and closer to studio product,[2] Focus Features' immediate success and leadership in the specialty film sector attracted significant scholarly attention.[3] Indeed, with the exception of Miramax, which, not surprisingly, has attracted wide academic interest,[4] Focus Features is arguably the most discussed company in scholarly accounts of contemporary US specialty film sector.

Besides its immediate critical and commercial success, which has been sustained throughout its still-brief history, there are several other reasons for the level of attention Focus Features has received. Arguably the most important one is its identity, which, as I mentioned above, has been distinct from the start. Led by James Schamus, award-winning producer–screenwriter, film scholar and former senior executive in the well-established independent production, distribution and foreign sales company Good Machine, and by David Linde, former Miramax and later fellow Good Machine executive, as co-Presidents, the division's management made the establishment of a clear identity in the crowded specialty film marketplace a top priority. Specifically, Focus Features became known both for backing upscale, critic-friendly titles that were made by innovative US and world cinema auteurs and for not shying away from controversial subjects. Almost always, however, such risks have been cushioned by the presence of highly commercial elements, such as Hollywood stars and clear generic structures, which made Focus films easily marketable to substantial niche audiences.

Particularly prominent has been the division's emphasis on films by female filmmakers, with 12 of its 80 releases to 2010 directed by women. Furthermore, the impressive commercial and critical success of *Far from Heaven*, *Brokeback Mountain*, *Milk* and *The Kids Are All Right* (L. Cholodenko, 2010), all films exploring questions of sexuality and sexual identity, have also helped telegraph Focus Features as politically progressive, especially in terms of representation of gender and sexual politics. The division's identity was perhaps most succinctly described by the journalist who wrote that Focus Features 'are aggressive, they take big chances on little movies that have big payoffs, and they aren't afraid of dangerous ideas and rogue filmmakers',[5] though Schamus's own view that 'the definition of a Focus movie is one that will be hated by a large segment of the population' is also significant in any effort to understand the division's trajectory.[6]

Another factor responsible for the critical attention afforded to Universal's specialty division was its perceived central role in American independent cinema's firmer association with the labels 'indie' and 'indiewood', which, for Needham, represent 'an emergent and ongoing paradigm shift' in American independent cinema's definition of itself.[7] Although Needham uses the two labels interchangeably, the terms 'indie' and 'indiewood', as I have argued in this book, can be used to signify different expressions of, and arguably different periods in, post-1990 US independent cinema. However, they are both characterised by the studio divisions' shift from acquisitions to production (increasingly so since the mid- to late 1990s), which, Needham argues, 'is mirrored in the move from an American independent film (as separate from Hollywood and the media conglomerates) to indie film with its blatant ties to the major studios'.[8] Indeed, while Paramount Classics remained primarily an acquisitions-driven division until its revamp in 2006 and Fox Searchlight embraced indiewood production more readily after its 2000 management reshuffle, Focus Features entered the filmmaking business in 2002 with a splash by becoming one of the key financial backers of the $20 million, star-studded *21 Grams* (A. G. Iñárritu), without, however, ignoring acquisitions, not least Roman Polanski's *The Pianist*.[9] For all those reasons, it is not accidental that Focus Features is the only studio division, alongside Miramax, that is examined by Geoff King in the first major scholarly study of the indiewood phase of US independent cinema.[10]

Finally, the attention the division received from film scholars is also, without doubt, related to the presence of James Schamus, who has published substantial scholarly work in the area of film studies. With his essays usually appearing in well-known academic collections and focusing on questions of contemporary US independent cinema,[11] Schamus has contributed significantly to the study of independent film, especially as his 'inside knowledge' of the sector has provided scholars with rare insights into the industrial organisation of American independent cinema, its problems of sustainability and its relationship to the Hollywood majors.

Despite all this, detailed accounts of the division's organisation, the range of its business practices and its overall relationship to the other specialty labels have yet to be tackled, and therefore the present chapter focuses primarily on those questions. To help structure this exploration, I have divided the history of Focus Features into three sections. The first one deals with the division's 'prehistory', the years between 1997 and 2001, when the numerous companies that would eventually merge to form Focus Features came together in a complex and convoluted way under Vivendi Universal's aegis. This is followed by a second section that looks at the studio division's establishment and the practices that made it one of the leading players in the 2000s. The third and final section starts in 2006, when David Linde left his post as Focus Features' co-President for an executive post at Universal. Although Focus Features did not change drastically under Schamus's sole leadership, my study focuses on the ways in which the division overcame a couple of financially weak years and therefore avoided the fate of Paramount Vantage, Miramax and Warner divisions in the later years of the decade.

## PREHISTORY: THE COMING TOGETHER OF SIX COMPANIES

The origins of Focus Features reach back to 1997, five years before its official establishment in the spring of 2002. As well as Universal, the formation of the division involves its two successive corporate parents (Seagram and Vivendi) and a change in Universal's ownership from the former to the latter; a well-established independent film distributor (October Films); a Europe-based film production, finance and distribution organisation (Polygram Filmed Entertainment); a US distribution company created jointly by Polygram Filmed Entertainment and Universal (Gramercy Pictures); a US-based cable television network and its film production and distribution division (USA Networks and USA Films, respectively); an independent film packaging and production company (Good Machine); and an existing studio division within Universal (Universal Focus). Through a series of corporate mergers and takeovers during these five years, the status of all the above organisations was altered (often radically), to the extent that it became extremely difficult for scholars to continue to conceptualise US filmmaking in terms of labels such as 'studio' and 'independent'. And even if studio filmmaking could be relatively safely identified with the expensive films released by century-old major distributors such as Paramount, Warner Bros. and, in this case, Universal, the label 'independent filmmaking' was clearly impossible to defend in light of the participation of all these companies in the establishment of a studio specialty film division. Indeed, as the following chronicle of the establishment of Focus Features will demonstrate, it is very difficult to defend the proposition that this studio division (and by extension all the other producing–distributing studio arms that were established from the mid-1990s onwards) maintains any sort of contact with the concept of 'independence', as this has been defined in the early 1980s (see Introduction).

Following the formation in the mid- to late 1990s of Fox Searchlight and Paramount Classics, which joined the earlier-established Sony Pictures Classics, Fine Line Features and, of course, Disney's Miramax, all the major studios had established a strong relationship with the specialty market and its dominant US indie film submarket. Universal, which, by the late 1990s, was owned by Canadian liquor distributor Seagram, had not stayed out of those markets entirely. In 1997, the company had acquired a controlling interest in the well-established, stand-alone film distributor October Films for $14 million.[12] Having enjoyed an extremely successful year in 1996 to 1997 following the release of *Secrets and Lies* (M. Leigh, 1996) and *Breaking the Waves* (L. von Trier, 1996), October was given substantial funds by Universal with a view to co-financing and producing titles and to boosting its distribution slates still further. Almost immediately, the studio-backed October Films scored a big hit with Robert Duvall's *The Apostle* (1998), which grossed over $23 million after the company acquired it for $5 million.[13] However, problems between October and Universal quickly ensued when four October titles with controversial subject matter attracted a potential NC-17 rating, which would make their advertising and distribution problematic. One of them, *Happiness* (T. Solondz, 1998), became a victim of the strained relationship between division and parent company, with the latter forcing the former to sell the film back to its producer, Good Machine, which in the end had to distribute *Happiness* itself.[14]

In addition to having a controlling stake in October, Universal was also involved in a second specialty label, Gramercy Pictures, a distribution film company that Universal bankrolled together with Polygram Filmed Entertainment in order to distribute Polygram's significant number of titles in the US theatrical market. Specifically, the Europe-based Polygram would finance films and distribute them internationally, while Gramercy would utilise Universal's resources and market the Polygram product in the all-important North American theatrical market. This arrangement created a very strong specialty division for Universal, which, since the mid-1990s, had distributed a number of titles with strong commercial appeal, many of which proved lucrative at the theatrical box office, including *Four Weddings and a Funeral* (M. Newell, 1994), *The Usual Suspects* (B. Singer, 1995) and *Fargo* (J. and E. Coen, 1996). In this respect, Universal's association with October Films in 1997 meant that the studio now had two specialty film companies in its orbit, with October producing and distributing titles that were considerably more 'niche' than the ones carrying the Gramercy brand.

Around the same time (early 1998), Barry Diller, former Chairman of Paramount and later of Twentieth Century Fox, bought USA Networks from Seagram; this was an advertiser-supported basic cable network that he planned to use alongside existing assets, like the Home Shopping Network and several local TV stations.[15] As part of the general overhaul, Diller decided to expand into the area of film, as he wanted USA Networks to be able to supply a variety of product to its audience, including films. After an initial failed attempt to buy October Films from Seagram for $20 million, Diller succeeded in buying the studio division a few months later for $24 million,[16] thus acquiring an important library of sixty titles that October had accrued since 1990.[17] Furthermore, Diller also made a bid for Gramercy and its significant list of titles. By that time, Seagram had taken over Polygram, parent company of Polygram Filmed Entertainment and one of the largest music companies in the world, in a deal valued at over $10 billion.[18] With Seagram crumbling from the debt incurred by the deal and as they were primarily interested in Polygram's music-related interests, Seagram executives agreed to sell off some of Polygram's assets, including Gramercy Pictures. This meant that both Universal specialty divisions ended up with Diller, who merged them and created USA Films. This new company immediately entered the theatrical film production and distribution business as a specialty label and as a rival to the existing studio divisions and other well-capitalised independents of the time, such as Lions Gate and Artisan.

Universal, however, did not remain without a specialty label for long.

Towards the end of 1999, the major created Universal Focus, conceived as 'a marketing and distribution unit for "niche-oriented productions and acquisitions"'.[19] Staffed and managed by existing Universal executives, the new studio division seemed to be more in the mould of the early Paramount Classics with its emphasis on relatively low-budget acquisitions, rather than Fox Searchlight, which by that time was moving strongly into the business of film production. Universal Focus's first release, *Billy Elliot* (S. Daldry, 2000), became a considerable hit, with a gross of over $20 million at the North American box office,[20] while it was reported that the division had deals in place with a number of production companies.[21]

However, even before Universal Focus's first release, developments at Seagram set in motion a series of events that eventually led to the establishment of a very different specialty label for the studio. Specifically, in the summer of 2000, Seagram was taken over by Vivendi, a France-based, diversified conglomerate. Aiming to focus exclusively on media business, the new entity decided to rid itself of its non-media-related interests and was renamed Vivendi Universal.[22] Almost a year later, and as Universal Focus continued to operate as Vivendi Universal's sole specialty film distributor, the parent company took over Barry Diller's USA Networks in a deal valued at close to $10 billion.[23] This, of course, included USA Films, which – as we saw earlier – had been created largely by the merger of two former Universal specialty divisions, and meant that Vivendi Universal once again had two labels trading in the specialty film business. In this respect, it made sense for the parent company to combine the two in an effort to create a strong division that could compete with the established powers in the market. This was especially so as, in its brief 3-year history, USA Films had made quite a splash in the specialty film market following the critical and commercial success of several clearly indiewood titles, including *Being John Malkovich* (S. Jonze, 1999), *Traffic* (2000) and *Gosford Park* (R. Altman, 2001). In combination with Universal Focus's expertise in the release of niche titles, the new studio division would stand to compete across the spectrum of specialty releases, from the arty to the commercial.

The anticipated merger took a final twist in May 2002, when Vivendi Universal also moved to take over the well-established independent producer, film packager and occasional distributor, Good Machine. Having produced and co-financed some of the best-known indie titles of the 1990s, such as Todd Haynes's *Safe* and Ed Burns's *She's the One*, and fresh from the remarkable success of *Crouching Tiger, Hidden Dragon*, which was produced by the company and co-scripted by its Chairman, James Schamus, Good Machine had often attracted the attention of the majors,[24] but had managed to remain a stand-alone company since its inception in the early 1990s. However, in the months prior to the takeover by Vivendi Universal, Good Machine had struck an unusual – for such a company – deal with the main studio to produce the tentpole picture *Hulk* (2003), also co-written by Schamus and directed by Good Machine's frequent collaborator, renowned Taiwanese filmmaker Ang Lee. This partnership gave both parties the opportunity to assess the benefits of a corporate relationship that would bring the independent company into the studio's fold.

For Universal these benefits were clear. Besides its significant library of titles, Good Machine would provide the studio with one of the most established and prestigious producers of specialty films, which would stand to deliver even better results with the full financial backing of a major entertainment conglomerate. Perhaps less obviously but still very importantly, Good Machine would also bring to Universal its equally well-established international sales division, Good Machine International, which handled foreign sales for numerous independent companies, including USA Films.[25] In this sense, the combination of Universal's distribution resources outside the US and Good Machine's knowledge of the international specialty film markets would also stand to improve distribution for all Universal product and maximise returns on a global scale.

For Good Machine, apart from the apparent security that the backing of a major entertainment conglomerate would provide, the benefits were perhaps less obvious. What was clear at that point (2002) was that the company was becoming increasingly successful and its films substantially more expensive, which meant that they needed a strong push in the global market (and therefore a vastly increased print and advertising cost) to ensure maximum returns. In this respect, it made sense for them to be able to utilise the resources and funding of a globally established film finance and distributing organisation, especially after the breakthrough success of *Crouching Tiger, Hidden Dragon* and the almost certain blockbuster status that *Hulk* would stand to gain in 2003.

With Universal Focus, USA Films and Good Machine under the same roof, Vivendi Universal finally moved to the last chapter in the establishment of its specialty division. Under the new name Focus Features, the above three individual entities merged to create a particularly strong producing–distributing organisation, under the joint leadership of Schamus and Linde, while, as expected, Good Machine International became an important part of the new equation, under the new name Focus Features International. In creating Focus Features in this particular way, Vivendi Universal demonstrated clearly that it aimed 'to shake up the specialized film landscape – especially Miramax's leverage with top talent',[26] and went on to challenge the status quo straight away.

## 'THE ONE KIND OF MOVIE WE'LL NEVER MAKE IS THE MOVIE FOR EVERYBODY'[27]

Following the merger of the various Universal divisions, Focus Features instantly found itself with a number of commitments, especially in terms of releasing titles produced or acquired by USA Films. Most of these films were characterised by strong commercial elements, especially the presence of established filmmakers and bankable casts; they included Neil La Bute's *Possession*, starring Gwyneth Paltrow, and especially Todd Haynes's *Far from Heaven*, an unconventional pastiche of Douglas Sirk's well-known melodramas (made for Universal in the 1950s), starring Julianne Moore and Dennis Quaid. However, even before the division's first release which was another title inherited from USA Films, a documentary on legendary Hollywood producer Robert Evans – *The Kid Stays in the Picture* (N. Burstein and B. Morgen) – Focus Features announced two big deals, one in acquisitions and one in co-finance and production. The former involved the pick-up of Roman Polanski's *The Pianist*, which was awarded the *Palme d'Or* at the 2002 Cannes Film Festival and had been made on a very substantial (for a specialty film) budget of approximately $33 million.[28] Focus Features beat off the competition, securing the film's distribution rights for the North American market and, importantly, for several other large English-speaking markets such as Australia, New Zealand and South Africa.[29] These additional distribution rights would stand to increase the division's revenues from the film substantially, given that Polanski's pictures often performed better in the international market than in the US one (see, for instance, the example of *Death and the Maiden* given in Chapter 4). Following this, Focus also announced the co-financing of the $20 million picture *21 Grams* in exchange for the film's worldwide distribution rights.[30] The film had significant star power in Sean Penn, Naomi Watts and Benicio del Toro and represented Mexican filmmaker Alejandro González Iñárritu's highly anticipated follow-up to his extremely well-received debut *Amores Perros*, which had become a modest success for Lions Gate in 2001.

All these substantial deals clearly demonstrate the division's immediate emphasis on indiewood titles and its intention to compete with the very top distributors in the increasingly 'indiewoodised' specialty film market. According to Linde, Focus Features had the parent company's authorisation to finance films for up to $30 million, a ceiling that could be raised even higher if the division was able to secure partners to spread the risk.[31] In terms of distribution, Focus's annual slate was set in the region of 10 to 12 films and involved a mixture of acquisitions and productions. Focus International, on the other hand, received a mandate to sell the foreign rights to approximately 15 to 16 films per year, with the aim of forming 'long-term relationships with talent' which would help the division achieve 'worldwide presence', while also underscoring its ethos 'as a filmmaker-based company'.[32] To confirm these objectives, and even before the end of its first full year of operation, Focus Features already had deals in place with US and international production companies, including Michael Bay's genre film company Platinum Dunes; Pedro and Augustin Almodóvar's El Deseo; and former Studio Canal senior executive Stephane Sperry's Liaison Films.[33] Finally, despite the emphasis on indiewood titles, and in order to compete more directly and 'on multiple fronts' with both Miramax and New Line Cinema, Focus Features also decided to branch out into cheap genre films, with particular emphasis on horror, urban films and comedies.[34] Even though this diversification would not take place until 2004 with the formation of Rogue Pictures, it was clear that Focus Features had been developing a strategy that took into consideration all areas of the specialty film market.

*Far from Heaven* and *The Pianist* spearheaded the seven releases the new division put out between July and December 2002 in its first year of operation. Apart from *The Kid Stays in the Picture*, the line-up also included the aforementioned *Possession*; Ed Burns's *Ash Wednesday*; post-9/11 drama *The Guys* (J. Simpson); and all-star French crime comedy *8 femmes [8 Women]* by well-known arthouse filmmaker François Ozon. Despite two major box-office disappointments (*The Guys* and *Ash Wednesday*), which failed to reach even the $100,000 mark each, and moderate results for *8 Women* and *Possession*, the division made a substantial splash with its two banner films, *The Pianist* and *Far from Heaven*, which jointly recorded approximately $50 million at the US box office and received eleven Academy Award nominations (with *The Pianist* alone being responsible for over $30 million and receiving three Oscars, including one for Best Director). In this respect, Focus Features managed to have a first year that was financially successful overall, as losses on the majority of their releases were offset by the success of *The Pianist*. Furthermore, the awards and critical recognition ensured ample publicity for the new division, which immediately found itself one of the top destinations for creative filmmakers.

Focus Features' reputation was augmented further at the end of 2002, when it announced a series of deals with celebrated filmmakers for a number of films with remarkable commercial potential. Thus, besides the expensive *21 Grams* which had been announced earlier in the year, Focus Features would also finance and produce Sofia Coppola's second feature, *Lost in Translation*, starring Bill Murray; Michel Gondry's *Eternal Sunshine of the Spotless Mind*, written by celebrated screenwriter Charlie Kaufman and starring major Hollywood stars Jim Carrey and Kate Winslet; and renowned female Indian filmmaker Mira Nair's adaptation of *Vanity Fair*, starring Reese Witherspoon.[35] With the addition of the Sylvia Plath biopic, *Sylvia* (C. Jeffs), starring Gwyneth Paltrow, and playwright-turned-filmmaker Neil La Bute's adaptation of his own play, *The Shape of Things*, Focus Features was lining up an impressive list of indiewood titles for release in 2003 and 2004, clearly demonstrating that it was aiming to transcend the specialty market and operate as a major independent in the way Miramax had been operating since the mid- to late 1990s. Furthermore, and as King has noted, almost all of the above titles and several of its less commercial ones 'exhibit[ed] artistic, literary or intellectual dimensions of one kind or another that seemed clearly available to viewers as markers of prestige / distinction for both themselves and the work in question'.[36] As well as contributing to the building up of Focus Features' distinct identity in the specialty film marketplace, this particular characteristic also helped the division become 'a favourite' with the critics, who also tended to identify Focus Features films as quality titles.

By the time of its first anniversary in May 2003, the division's films boasted a combined worldwide gross of $250 million. In terms of market share in the US, for the calendar year 2003 Focus Features achieved box-office revenues of $107 million from eight releases, which corresponded to a 1.14 per cent share of the market. Only Miramax and Fox Searchlight achieved better results in the specialty marketplace that year, though Searchlight's revenues of $125 million were the product of eleven releases. To these impressive financial results one should also add the significant income from premium cable channels, as sister company Universal handled the sales of Focus Features titles as part of bigger packages that included Universal's own titles to leading cable broadcasters Starz Encore and HBO.[37] This arrangement was mutually beneficial for the two film divisions; on the one hand, Universal had much more leverage in sales negotiations than Focus Features and therefore was able to achieve much higher prices for the films it represented than if the specialty division had to do the negotiations itself. On the other hand, the prestigious award-winning Focus Features films added significantly to Universal's titles, at a time when Universal was lagging consistently behind competitors such as Warner Bros., Disney and Sony / Columbia.[38]

By 2004, Focus Features had reached the apex of its critical success. Within the space of one year (September 2003 to September 2004), it had released a series of films, all of which attracted great publicity and a number of awards, while the majority also found considerable commercial success; *21 Grams*, *The Motorcycle Diaries*, *Eternal Sunshine of the Spotless Mind* and *Vanity Fair* achieved a combined gross of over $80 million at the US box office and a similar figure in international markets, prompting industry insiders to acknowledge that Focus Features had 'hit a rhythm where its approach of identifying quality projects with the right directors [was] connecting well with the critics and the marketplace'.[39] However, despite the industry buzz, the undisputed critical attention and the considerable commercial success of its titles, the division was still perceived in some industry circles as 'underperforming' and as unable to achieve the $100 million hits that its main competitors had already pulled off by that time. In this respect, even the division's greatest success during this period, *Lost in Translation* – a film that had cost only $4 million to produce,[40] had brought in $44 million at the US box office and over $60 million in the rest of the world, had attracted an enormous amount of publicity and received over seventy awards, including an Academy Award for Best Screenplay – was seen as lagging behind runaway successes like *Shakespeare in Love* and *My Big Fat Greek Wedding*.[41] Such a view made it clear, beyond any doubt, that the stakes in the specialty film market of the early to mid-2000s had reached unprecedented heights in terms of what was deemed a good commercial performance for a film and for a distributor.

Given its inability to increase profit margins drastically with its indiewood titles, Focus Features swiftly resorted to the creation of a genre-film-producing and distributing division as an alternative provider of supplementary income. Equally importantly, this was another move that aimed to position the division on the same level as Miramax and New Line, given that both major independents' releases 'span the spectrum from arthouse to mainstream fare',[42] with the genre / mainstream fare divisions always outperforming their indie sister labels.[43] Having a distinct label with marketing expertise for low-budget genre films meant that Focus would either be able to bid for these films itself if they were produced with outside money; produce them itself 'in-house'; or have them supplied on a regular basis through deals with production companies that specialised in such fare – for example, Michael Bay's Platinum Dunes, with which Focus already had a relationship. In this respect, creating this label made sense from all possible angles.

Rogue Pictures was announced in March 2004 with a mandate to release 'upscale action, thriller and urban fare with franchise potential'.[44] Like its sister label, Rogue was conceived of primarily as a production-driven label, as opposed to an acquisitions-focused organisation, but had no fixed annual quota of titles. Furthermore, and unlike Dimension and New Line Cinema, who were managed and serviced by different teams of executives and staff from the ones running 'quality' brands Miramax and Fine Line Features, Rogue Pictures was placed under the same management as Focus Features. This was because the business of cheap genre films was perceived by Schamus and Linde as an extension of specialised filmmaking, and one that was targeted none the less at a different audience demographic.[45] Indeed, Rogue Pictures' first release had nothing to do with 'the literate films with impressive talent rosters and awards cachet' that had become the hallmark of Focus Features' brand identity.[46] It was, instead, *The Seed of Chucky* (D. Mancini), a sequel to the 1998 horror film, *The Bride of Chucky* (R. Yu), which was followed by the British zombie spoof *Shaun of the Dead* (E. Wright, 2004). Both were moderately successful at the box office but did not prove to be the kind of hit Focus and Rogue were hoping for; and neither did the four releases of 2005, with the exception of the low-budget *Cry Wolf* (J. Wadlow), which grossed $10 million on a budget of $1 million.[47]

The emergence of genre divisions such as Dimension, Rogue and, later, Fox Atomic and Paramount Insurgent, as sister labels to specialty film studio divisions and as 'an organic growth' of the specialised film business begs the question of the nature of their relationship with US independent cinema.[48] After all, it was 'independent' genre films, especially horror pictures, and their *dependence* on the commercial elements of sex and violence that early critics of contemporary American independent cinema found questionable and wanted excised from the emergent independent film canon (see Introduction). However, as stand-alone companies and studio divisions alike started increasingly to embrace pictures with commercial potential, genre became significant in expressions of 'indie' filmmaking, while the representation of (often gratuitous) sex and violence became intricately linked with indie cinema (see, for instance, the films of Quentin Tarantino). Despite the fact that all these 'commercial' elements were often cleverly and creatively treated in stories narrated with great visual flair (*Pulp Fiction*), were placed at the service of formal play (*Memento*) or used in an attempt to explore significant social or political issues (underage sex in *Kids* [L. Clark, 1995]), on many occasions they were also used conventionally, replicating structures and aesthetics that are associated with studio filmmaking (for instance, the use of romantic comedy in *The Brothers McMullen*). With the concept of an alternative or resistant 'independence' quickly giving way to a hip 'indie' filmmaking practised within the studios, there was no reason for low-budget genre filmmaking, especially horror and thriller films, to take place only outside the majors. In this respect, it became an integral part of the widely expanded indie cinema.

By the beginning of 2005, Focus Features had continued to grow and had attracted an impressive stable of producers, with some formalising their relationship with the division through the signing of first-look deals.[49] These arrangements suggest that Focus Features always had access to a large number of projects at various stages of development, which meant that it could choose the most promising titles that would help continue its 'connection' with audiences and the market. As it turned out, 2005 proved to be another 'best year yet' in the history of the company; two of its films went beyond the $30 million gross mark at the US box office (*Pride & Prejudice* [J. Wright] and *The Constant Gardener* [F. Meirelles]), and *Brokeback Mountain* finally provided the runaway indiewood hit the division was looking for, grossing $83 million in the US and an additional $100 million in the rest of the world.

*Brokeback Mountain* was another extremely important film in the creation of the division's identity. Besides its commercial success – at the time of writing, the film remains Focus Features' biggest box-office hit – *Brokeback Mountain* underscored the division's commitment to backing progressive films, especially ones that deal with questions of gender and sexual politics, and clearly exemplified the definition of the Focus Features film given by Schamus a couple of years later as 'one that will be hated by a large segment of the population'. Celebrated for its representation of the relationship of two gay lovers within what is usually the strictly heteronormative world of the western genre, the film was hailed by some reviewers as 'a shift in scope and tenor so profound as to signal a new era'.[50] And while scholars like Needham have questioned the extent to which the success of the film and the 'ample visibility and exposure to the gay community' it offered have indeed signalled a new era,[51] few critics would question the film's place in the list of canonical 'indiewood' films and its contribution to Focus Features' brand identity.

## FOCUS FEATURES AND THE EXPANDED SPECIALTY MARKET

The critical and commercial success of *Brokeback Mountain*, which was released in December 2005, brought even more publicity and attention to the division. Despite the fact that the film lost out on the Academy Award for Best Picture to Lions Gate's *Crash* (P. Haggis, 2005), Focus Features was finally starting to be perceived by the trade press as a financially successful studio specialty division, the 'most stable hitmaker in the last few years', for General Electric, the division's new parent company following the merger between General Electric's NBC and Vivendi Universal in 2004.[52] Writing for *Variety*, Ian Mohr called Focus Features' 2005 to 2006 season 'a banner year', which placed the company at the very top of specialty distributors, adding that 'if three years ago specialty divisions imitated Miramax and two years ago it was Searchlight, now it [was] Focus.'[53] However, it was exactly at that point that the first major change in the division's management structure took place. In March 2006, it was announced that David Linde's duties as co-President of Focus Features would become part of a much-expanded role that would also include a senior executive post at Universal, accompanied by a 'transfer' from New York (where Focus Features was based) to Los Angeles and Universal's headquarters.[54]

Perhaps more significant than the surprising nature of the reorganisation of a division that seemed to be at the top of its game, was the decision to unsettle the successful team of Linde and Schamus by giving the former an additional role, which was widely anticipated to minimise his association with the day-to-day affairs of Focus Features. Although Linde and Schamus were equally responsible for running the division, it was often assumed in the trade press that Linde oversaw the business side of things, while Schamus was perceived as the 'creative nerve center', given his numerous credits on films as both writer and producer.[55] In this respect, industry critics were beginning to wonder whether NBC Universal was 'messing with Focus mojo'[56] and if Linde's move to Universal would 'tip the balance of power in the specialty sector'.[57]

Following Linde's departure, Schamus was swiftly promoted to the post of the division's Chief Executive Officer, overseeing Focus, Rogue and Focus International. Under his sole leadership, Focus Features did not change its philosophy or its objectives and continued its mission to attract creative filmmakers to its fold, with Woody Allen becoming the first new addition.[58] Furthermore, Linde's presence at Universal gave Schamus access to the very top management echelons at the major's studio, which proved particularly useful for the arrangement of deals between Universal and Focus Features. For instance, the two NBC Universal film divisions came together for a first-look production pact with Brazilian filmmaker Fernando Meirelles, who would develop films with other Brazilian directors in both Portuguese and English for the two companies.[59] Additionally, Schamus extended a deal Focus had made in 2005 with Bertelsmann's giant publisher Random House for the film adaptation of certain of the publisher's properties, with an agreement to co-finance, co-produce and distribute *Reservation Road* (T. George, 2007).[60] Despite all this activity, Schamus's main deals revolved around Focus Features' entry into the distribution of animation film, with the distribution of Portland-based Laika Productions' *Coraline* (H. Selick, 2009), and Rogue Pictures' stronger emphasis on horror films, following deals with filmmaker Wes Craven and production company Platinum Dunes, extremely important players in the field of horror cinema.

The deal for *Coraline* represented a gamble for the division, as the film was the first production of a new animation studio bankrolled by former Nike senior executive Peter Knight, who, in an effort to build an organisation to rival market leader Pixar, invested the vast sum of $65 million in Laika's first production.[61] After a successful release in 2009, *Coraline* became Focus Features' second-biggest box-office hit in its history, having grossed $75 million in the US and an additional $50 million in the rest of the world. On the other hand, the deals with Craven and Platinum Dunes represented much safer bets, even though the terms of both deals seemed to be much better for the producers than for the distributor. Writing specifically on Focus's deal with Platinum Dunes, *Variety*'s Michael Fleming suggested that the production company's 10 per cent participation in the gross was 'one of the richest producer deals in town' and 'frighteningly lucrative' in a climate of cutbacks and retrenchment, even though, according to Focus, the terms were similar to those Platinum Dunes enjoyed in its deal with Miramax and Dimension, which preceded that with Focus and Rogue Pictures.[62]

Despite the perception that the specialty division played 'second fiddle' in the above deals, its financial performance in 2006 made it clear to Schamus that Focus Features and Rogue Pictures needed production deals with filmmakers and companies with established track records – irrespective of how expensive these would be – if the two divisions wanted to remain at the top. While Focus Features' market share in the calendar year 2006 was 1.32 per cent, up from 1.20 per cent in 2005, the truth was that the vast majority of the division's box-office revenues were from the release of *Brokeback Mountain* in late 2005. Moreover, none of Focus Features' seven releases in 2006 made more than $15 million in the US theatrical market, which demonstrated beyond any doubt the importance of both indiewood and genre films with commercial potential if the company were to survive in the volatile specialty market.

As it turned out, 2006 was just a bad year in the division's history. For 2007, Schamus had orchestrated a programme of ten releases for both divisions that aimed to return Universal's specialty labels at the top. Central to his strategy was the fact that all titles were in-house productions, which Focus International could also exploit in world markets and therefore contribute substantially to the division's bottom line.[63] Indeed, despite the fact that some of its titles seemed to underperform at the North American box office – with some important and expensive productions such as *Reservation Road* and Ang Lee's *Se, Jie* [*Lust, Caution*] grossing only $100,000 and $4.6 million, respectively – this had no impact on the division's investment. The co-finance deal for *Reservation Road*, which came part and parcel with a number of presales, minimised the division's exposure to the extent that it lost very little money, while the $50 million gross that *Lust, Caution* took outside the US produced a handsome profit for the division. Furthermore Focus Features enjoyed another big success with *Atonement* (J. Wright), which grossed $130 million worldwide, while Rogue's *Balls of Fury* (R. B. Garant), *Hot Fuzz* (E. Wright) and *The Hitcher* (D. Meyers) also proved commercially successful, demonstrating the viability of the two divisions under Schamus. Finally, in the same year, Focus announced a huge finance deal with German hedge fund company Dresdner Kleinwort worth $200 million, which would stand to finance the next twenty to twenty-five of its pictures. The deal was among the first of its kind for a specialty label and was hailed as 'the biggest slate financing deal for a specialty-film division'.[64]

Given the healthy state of affairs at Rogue Pictures, Focus Features' ability to generate at least one big success per year that could offset the losses of its other productions, Focus International's continued activity in worldwide sales and distribution, and the presence of equity finance for its productions, it was clear that the Focus edifice was well cushioned to avoid the problems that most of the other divisions, bar Fox Searchlight and Sony Pictures Classics, had started to face. Indeed, while news of the closures of Paramount Vantage and the Warner divisions was still fresh, Focus Features proceeded to its most expensive acquisition – after a two-year period during which it traded only in 'in-house' productions – paying $10 million to secure the rights of *Hamlet 2* (A. Fleming) and sending a clear message that it was not facing the same problems as its competitors.[65] And while *Hamlet 2* proved to be a box-office failure, the success of more indiewood titles such as *Milk* and *Burn After Reading* (J. and E. Coen), which together grossed $90 million at the US and over $120 million at the international box office, as well as Rogue Pictures' *The Strangers* (B. Bertino), which took $80 million worldwide, put the division in the top ten US distributors, with a record market share for the company of almost 2 per cent. Under these circumstances, it is not surprising that Universal's division remained unscathed during the 2008 studio division shakeout.

Despite these clear signs of success, however, Focus Features' parent company sold Rogue Pictures in January 2009 to finance and production company Relativity Media for $150 million. The sale, sparked by General Electric's pressure on all its divisions to increase profitability, even if that meant the sale of assets, was part of a large reconfiguration within NBC Universal, following a partnership deal between Universal and Relativity Media that would see the latter contributing up to $3 billion in co-financing deals for Universal pictures till 2015.[66] This meant that, despite the sale, Universal and Focus Features would continue to benefit from Rogue Pictures' films, especially as they would retain their interest as international co-distributors and would stand to collect a 10 per cent distribution fee.[67]

Not surprisingly, the sale of Rogue Pictures did have a substantial impact on Focus Features' revenues, as the division's box office and market share for the calendar years 2009 and 2010 were much lower than the record 2008 figure ($159 million and 1.50 per cent, and $74 million and 0.72 per cent, respectively, as opposed to $193 million and 1.94 per cent in 2008). A significant contributor to this revenue slump was the poor box-office performance of a number of indiewood titles, especially during 2010, including Noah Baumbach's *Greenberg* ($4.2 million US gross - see Case Study) and Sofia Coppola's *Somewhere* ($1.8 million gross). This significant drop in the division's performance had few repercussions in terms of its overall position in the specialty market, as 2010 was a bad year for the sector overall, with Focus Features' main rival, Fox Searchlight, experiencing a similar drop in market share (1.53 per cent in 2010, down from 2.51 per cent in 2008). With *Variety* predicting in mid-2011 that the specialty market 'is coming back at a healthy rate after a disastrous couple of years', Focus Features is still in pole position to exploit the renewed opportunities for more commercial success. However, the recent purchase of NBC Universal by cable giant Comcast might put increased pressure on Focus Features to perform more strongly financially, which might entail an even stronger emphasis on indiewood pictures.

## CONCLUSION

Following its extremely complex inception in 2002, Focus Features quickly established itself as a specialty studio division with a strong brand identity, staking a particularly strong claim in taking the place of the rapidly declining Miramax. Alongside Fox Searchlight, Universal's specialty label became an undisputed leader in the specialty film market through its tripartite emphasis on indiewood productions and their non-US equivalent (*The Motorcycle Diaries*; *8 Women*); on moderately budgeted genre films that were almost mathematically guaranteed to return a profit (sometimes a substantial one); and, crucially, on international sales and distribution of its productions and other companies' specialty titles. This last business strategy allowed Focus Features a healthy income from the international markets, which cushioned the division from the losses made by titles that underperformed in the US market. Even in the case of *Hamlet 2*, which, as noted earlier, the division had acquired for $10 million and which grossed less than $5 million at the North American box office, Focus Features stood to lose very little, as 'much of the pickup price was offset with territorial distribution deals' that Focus International had arranged long time before the film opened in the US.[68]

The profit from genre fare and the income from worldwide sales provided the division with sufficient margin to exercise 'its trademark risk-taking' with more arty and ambitious productions, which provided Focus Features with the kind of distinct brand identity that its rivals, including Fox Searchlight, have yet to achieve. On the other hand, this distinct identity and the division's continued emphasis on films that 'will be hated by a large segment of the population' have not allowed it to produce the increasingly exorbitant profits that the specialty divisions' parent companies have come to expect from their subsidiaries. In this respect, Focus Features' future can only be as good as its new parent company's commitment to support the division and to be happy with the relatively small profits it generates.

---

**Case Study:** *Greenberg* **(Noah Baumbach, 2010)**

Despite the emphasis of most specialty film divisions and many stand-alone companies on indiewood titles with considerable commercial potential, US specialty filmmaking also continued to witness the making of large numbers of low-budget films, the majority of which have failed to secure theatrical distribution. However, in the latter half of the 2000s, a group of performance-based, digital video-driven pictures that were characterised by 'low key naturalism, low fi production values and a stream of low value chatter' that gave them collectively the title 'mumblecore films',[69] attracted significant attention in the specialty film market. None of the twenty or so films that fall under that label

– which include, among others, *Funny Ha Ha* (A. Bujalski, 2002), *Kissing on the Mouth* (J. Swanberg, 2005), *Four-Eyed Monsters* (S. Buice and A. Crumley, 2005), *The Puffy Chair* (J. Duplass, 2005), *Hannah Takes the Stairs* (J. Swanberg, 2007) and *Baghead* (J. Duplass and M. Duplass, 2008) – achieved theatrical box-office success beyond $200,000, and only a handful secured theatrical distribution by one of the established distributors, and yet the majority have had substantial presence in some ancillary markets and alternative distribution outlets.[70]

With some of these films costing as little as $2,500 and $3,000 to make, it is clear that they operated at a small but sizable profit that allowed their creators to pursue filmmaking as a viable career option, while staying away from corporate Hollywood. Indeed, their inability to generate a substantial box-office gross from a theatrical release immediately means that these films are not easily amenable to Hollywood cooptation, as the majors have religiously followed a logic in film distribution that sees a film being distributed theatrically and advertised globally to achieve maximum exposure before moving to other ancillary distribution channels that supplement theatrical box-office revenues. Furthermore, the harsh aesthetic created by the use of digital video, and their subject matter, which in some instances has flirted with pornography, have located them far away not only from Hollywood, but also from the studios' specialty labels that have focused primarily on indiewood titles.

However, in 2010, and after the mumblecore film cycle seemed to have reached an end of sorts in late 2008,[71] the release of *Greenberg* was hailed as an example of 'mumblecore meet[ing] the mainstream'.[72] Given that it was produced and directed by established independent filmmaker Noah Baumbach and financed and distributed by Focus Features, the characterisation of *Greenberg* as mainstream filmmaking raises a number of issues about the types of films that are considered 'truly' independent and the perception of studio divisions as extensions of their parent companies, and therefore an integral part of mainstream Hollywood. Indeed, compared to the micro-budgeted mumblecore films of the mid-2000s, *Greenberg* was a big-budget production; featured a major Hollywood star, Ben Stiller, in the unconventional titular role and other well-established actors in secondary parts (Jennifer Jason Leigh, Rhys Ifans); was shot, not on digital video, but on film; and was certainly characterised by slick production values that included a music score from James Murphy and his acclaimed dance-punk band, LCD Soundsystem. It was also produced by Scott Rudin, one of the most accomplished and acclaimed figures in both studio and independent film (with credits on such indiewood titles as *There Will Be Blood*, *No Country for Old Men* and *Revolutionary Road*).

Despite the clear indication that the film was conceived as an indiewood exercise, *Greenberg* was also characterised by a number of elements that had more points of contact with less dominant forms of independent filmmaking. These included a narrative that was conveyed primarily in fragmented conversations and encounters that end abruptly, and consisting mostly of a large number of brief scenes that were often only loosely connected; a downbeat story that revolved around the relationship of a 40-year-old man, recently released from a psychiatric hospital, with a much younger woman, both of whom seem to lack direction in their lives; and a visual style that occasionally attracts attention to technique and therefore creates a certain distance between spectator and narrative. All these elements seem more at home with the 'indie' mode of filmmaking that was popularised in the 1990s and allowed filmmakers to present both new types of stories and new ways of filming them. Furthermore, the casting of Greta Gerwig in the female lead in a role reminiscent of the ones she had played in mumblecore films, and a cameo appearance by actor–filmmaker Joe Swanberg, who had also been a key figure in the mumblecore movement, suggested that *Greenberg* was willing to take chances with less commercial choices. In this respect, the film's reception by the popular press as 'mumblecore going mainstream' is somewhat problematic. Instead, one could argue that *Greenberg* tried to marry the independent, the indie and the indiewood in one picture.

This effort, however, did not prove financially successful. Despite a strong marketing campaign that focused mainly on Ben Stiller playing against type (especially as he was coming hot from the big box-office successes *Tropic Thunder* [B. Stiller, 2008] and *Night at the Museum 2* [S. Levy, 2009]), and on the film's director, Noah Baumbach, whose film *The Squid and the Whale* (2005) is part of the US indie film canon, *Greenberg* created little appeal at the US box office, grossing just $4.2 million. As a matter of fact, it proved to be the first of a number of underperforming titles for Focus Features, which, in 2010, experienced its worst year in terms of market share. If nothing else, the financial failure of the film suggests perhaps that film production in the age of indiewood requires a coherent approach to filmmaking, one that avoids mixing elements from disparate articulations of specialty filmmaking.

## NOTES

1. Needham, *Brokeback Mountain*, 10.
2. Wyatt, 'The Formation of the "Major Independent"', 84–7.
3. King, *Indiewood USA*, 235–77; Needham, *Brokeback Mountain*, 8–30; King, Geoff, *Lost in Translation* (Edinburgh: Edinburgh University Press, 2010), 13–18; Davis, Glyn, *Far from Heaven* (Edinburgh: Edinburgh University Press, 2011), 11–20.
4. See, in particular, Wyatt, 'The Formation of the "Major Independent"', 75–90; Berra, John, *Declarations of Independence: American Cinema and the Partiality of Independent Production* (Bristol: Intellect, 2008), 161–77; McDonald, Paul, 'Miramax, "Life is Beautiful", and the Indiewoodization of the Foreign–Language Film Market in the USA', *New Review of Film and Television Studies*, 7.4 (December 2009): 353–75; Biskind, *Down and Dirty Pictures*; King, *Indiewood USA*, 93–140; Perren, *Indie, Inc.*
5. Tom O'Neil, quoted in Souccar, Miriam Kreinin, 'Focus Features Translates Buzz into Oscar Edge; Wins Kudos with "*Lost in Translation*"', *Crain's New York Business* (23 February 2004), 4.
6. Schamus was quoted in Miller, 'Indie Spirits Wade into Mainstream', 54.
7. Needham, *Brokeback Mountain*, 8.
8. Needham, *Brokeback Mountain*, 21.
9. Fleming, Michael and Claude Brodesser, '"Grams" Finding Focus', *Daily Variety* (16 July 2002), 1; Rooney, David '"*Pianist*" Banks on Voter Response', *Weekly Variety* (10 March 2003), 46.
10. King, *Indiewood USA*, 235–77.

11. See, for instance, Schamus, 'To the Rear', 91–105; and Schamus, James, 'A Rant', in *The End of Cinema As We Know It: American Film in the Nineties*, ed. Jon Lewis (London: Pluto, 2002), 253–60.
12. Biskind, *Down and Dirty Pictures*, 274.
13. Biskind, *Down and Dirty Pictures*, 301 and 326.
14. Merritt, *Celluloid Mavericks*, 381.
15. Hoffmeister, Sallie, 'USA Networks CEO Kay Koplovitz Resigns', *Los Angeles Times* (10 April 1998), http://articles.latimes.com/1998/apr/10/business/fi-37857; accessed 1 April 2011.
16. Biskind, *Down and Dirty Pictures*, 351 and 362.
17. The number of October films was cited in Lyons, Charles and Dan Cox (2000), 'United Slates of USA', *Weekly Variety* (14 February 2000), 1.
18. Anon. (1999), 'Seagram Selling Some Film Assets', *New York Times* (8 April 1999), http://www.nytimes.com/1999/04/08/business/the-media-business-seagram-selling-some-film-assets.html?src=pm; accessed on 1 April 2011.
19. Goodridge, Mike, 'Universal Dubs Specialised Arm Universal Focus', *Screen Daily* (29 June 2000), http://www.screendaily.com/universal-dubs-specialised-arm-universal-focus/402834.article; accessed on 1 April 2011.
20. The figure was taken from The Numbers (www.the-numbers.com). Unless otherwise stated, all box-office and market share figures were taken from this database.
21. Goodridge, 'Universal Dubs Specialised Arm'.
22. Saint Marc, Françoise Meaux, 'Vivendi Universal Merger Deal Only Days Away', *Screen Daily* (15 June 2000), http://www.screendaily.com/vivendi-universal-merger-deal-only-days-away/402696.article; accessed on 1 April 2011.
23. Brown, Colin, 'Diller Thriller for Vivendi Universal', *Screen Daily* (17 December 2001), http://www.screendaily.com/diller-thriller-for-vivendi-universal/407799.article; accessed on 1 April 2011.
24. Brown, Colin, 'Universal Buys Good Machine and Merges it with USA Films', *Screen Daily* (3 May 2002), http://www.screendaily.com/universal-buys-good-machine-and-merges-it-with-usa-films/409083.article; accessed on 1 April 2011.
25. Ibid.
26. Hayes, Dade and Charles Lyons, 'Banner Days for USA', *Weekly Variety* (4 March 2002), 3.
27. Schamus, quoted in Rooney, David, 'Focus Takes Rogue Turn with Launch of a Genre Arm', *Daily Variety* (25 March 2004), 29.
28. The Pianist – Wladyslaw Szpilman – Homepage (2006), http://www.szpilman.net/framemovie.html; accessed on 1 April 2011.
29. 'Palme d'Or Winner Lands a US Distributor', *Studio Briefing – Film News* (28 May 2002), http://www.imdb.com/title/tt0253474/news?year=2002; accessed on 1 April 2011.
30. Fleming and Brodesser, '"Grams" Finding Focus', 1.
31. Rooney, David, 'Niche Biz Comes into Focus: U Specialty Label Marries Taste with Overseas Savvy', *Weekly Variety* (2 August 2004), 15.
32. 'Universal's Independent Movie Operation Combines U.S. Distribution, Foreign Sales', *Deal Memo* (19 May 2003), 10.
33. Ibid.
34. Ibid.
35. Dawtrey, Adam, 'Focus Finds 'Lost' Nights', *Daily Variety* (2 October 2002), 3; Bing, Jonathan, 'Lion Alum Falls into Focus as Original Slate Ramps Up', *Daily Variety* (10 January 2003), 6.

36. King, *Indiewood USA*, 249.
37. Anon., 'Universal's Independent Movie Operation', 10.
38. In the calendar years 2002, 2003 and 2004, Universal was ranked fifth, fourth and sixth, respectively, in the list of the Big Six distributors.
39. Steven Beer, quoted in Souccar, 'Focus Features Translates Buzz', 4.
40. This figure was taken from King, *Lost in Translation*, 8.
41. Souccar, 'Focus Features Translates Buzz', 4.
42. Rooney, 'Focus Takes Rogue Turn', 1.
43. Biskind, *Down and Dirty Pictures*, 430.
44. Rooney, 'Focus Takes Rogue Turn', 1.
45. Ibid., 29.
46. Rooney, David, 'Focus Features', *Daily Variety* (8 September 2004), S16.
47. The figures were taken from IMDb (http://www.imdb.com/title/tt0384286/business) and were accessed on 1 March 2011.
48. Rooney, 'Focus Takes Rogue Turn', 29.
49. Rooney, 'Focus Features', S16.
50. Rich, quoted in Kaufman, Anthony, 'Rogue Rovers: Subversive Western Poses Special Challenge for Ang Lee and Focus', *Daily Variety* (27 October 2005), A2.
51. Needham, *Brokeback Mountain*, 22.
52. Rooney, David, 'Is Studio Messing with Focus Mojo?', *Daily Variety* (17 March 2006), 1.
53. Mohr, Ian, 'U Moves Put Lens on Focus: Linde's Rise Places Schamus in Spotlight and Starts Rivals Jostling for Dominance', *Weekly Variety* (27 March 2006), 6.
54. Ibid.
55. Rooney, 'Is Studio Messing with Focus Mojo?', 21.
56. Ibid., 1.
57. Mohr, 'U Moves', 6.
58. Mohr, Ian, 'Focus Scoops up Woody Pic', *Daily Variety* (21 April 2006), 1.
59. Mohr, Ian, 'U Digs "Gardener" Guy', *Daily Variety* (27 July 2006), 1.
60. Fleming, Michael, 'Focus on the "Road"', *Daily Variety* (16 August 2006), 1.
61. 'Oscar or Not, "*Coraline*" is a $65-Million Gamble that Paid Off for Phil and Travis Knight', *Fast Company* (5 March 2010), http://www.fastcodesign.com/1572170/oscar-or-not-coraline-is-a-65-million-gamble-that-paid-off-for-phil-and-travis-knight; accessed on 1 April 2011.
62. Fleming, Michael, 'Dunes Digs a Rich Rogue Deal', *Daily Variety* (6 October 2006), 1.
63. Snyder, Gabriel, 'Focus Looks to Regain its Fire', *Weekly Variety* (15 January 2007), 49.
64. Zeitchik, Steven, 'Focus Secures Slate Coin', *Daily Variety* (26 January 2007), 39.
65. Hayes, Dade, 'Focus Features: Showmanship Pairs with Cineaste's Taste', *Daily Variety* (8 September 2008), A5.
66. Cieply, Michael, 'Universal Sells Rogue for $150 Million', *New York Times* (4 January 2009), http://www.nytimes.com/2009/01/05/business/media/05rogue.html; accessed on 1 April 2011.
67. Siegel, Tatiana, 'Relativity Goes Rogue', *Daily Variety* (5 January 2009), 6.
68. Hayes, 'Focus Features', A5.
69. Hernandez, Eugene, 'SXSW '07 Daily Dispatch: Mumblecore Movie? Swanberg, Bujalski, Duplass and Others Unveil "Hannah Takes the Stairs"', *IndieWire* (15 March 2007), http://www.indiewire.com/article/sxsw_07_daily_dispatch_mumblecore_movie_swanberg_bujalski_duplass_and_other/; accessed on 1 April 2011.
70. Van Couvering, Alicia, 'What I Meant to Say', *Filmmaker Magazine* (Summer 2008), http://www.filmmakermagazine.com/spring2007/features/mumblecore.php, accessed

on 1 April 2011; and O'Hehir, Andrew, 'Beyond the Multiplex: Don't Call it Mumblecore', *The Salon* (11 October 2008), http://www.salon.com/ent/movies/btm/feature/2008/10/11/nights_weekends/index.html, accessed on 1 April 2011.
71. Kohn, Eric, 'Greta Gerwig is a Mumblecore Prop in "Arthur"', *Indiewire* (8 April 2011), http://www.indiewire.com/article/review_greta_gerwig_is_a_mumblecore_prop_in_mainstream_comedy_arthur/; accessed on 1 April 2011.
72. 'Mumblecore Meets the Mainstream', *The Economist* (22 April 2010), http://www.economist.com/node/15949109; accessed on 1 April 2011.

CHAPTER 9

# Warner Independent Pictures (2003 to 2008) and Picturehouse (2005 to 2008)

INTRODUCTION

Out of all the major studios, Warner has been the one with the least presence in the specialty film market. Having resisted the trend of establishing a classics division in the 1980s, it continued to stay away during the boom years of the indie film in the early and mid-1990s. Despite its change of ownership in 1989, following the merger of Time and Warner, and the increased presence of the new conglomerate in various media and entertainment sectors, specialty film continued to remain a field outside its interests. Even after the 1996 Time Warner merger with Turner Broadcasting System, the parent company of New Line Cinema and Fine Line Features, Warner's relationship with Fine Line was more evident in the annual financial report of what was then the world's largest entertainment conglomerate than in more practical or meaningful terms. This was because Fine Line continued to enjoy a close relationship with its immediate parent company, New Line Cinema (see Chapter 4), which also continued to produce, distribute and acquire films under the expanded Time Warner banner. This status quo, and Warner's protracted absence from the specialty market, continued after the ill-fated 1999 takeover of the company by AOL and well into the early years of the 2000s. In this respect, it seemed rather surprising that, within the space of two years in 2003 and 2005, the entertainment giant would move to create an upstart specialty film division in close contact with its main studio, Warner Independent Pictures (WIP), and replace Fine Line Features with yet another division, Picturehouse, which would have corporate links with both New Line Cinema and an HBO that was increasingly oriented towards film production.

The reasons behind Warner's absence from the specialty film market are not clear. Arguably, one of the factors is related to Warner Bros., the main film finance and distribution organisation within Time Warner, and its expertise in handling franchise blockbusters such as the *Harry Potter* and *Batman* films, distributed in saturation release and carrying enormous print and advertising costs. Indeed, the studio has been one of the most financially successful distributors in contemporary US cinema, ranked first in terms of total US theatrical box-office revenues for the period between 1995 and 2011.[1] Given its great emphasis on tentpole films and the handsome payoffs its franchises have generated, it is certainly tempting to argue that running a specialty division, which, under the best of circumstances, would only produce a fraction of the main studio's profits, would be deemed not worth the investment and commitment of resources from the corporate parent.

Furthermore, the fact that Warner did not establish a separate division to finance, produce / acquire, market and distribute 'independent' films does not necessarily mean that it did not trade in them. Since 1995 and until the establishment of Warner Independent in 2003, the main studio released a number of films that one would normally associate with the specialty film sector and with any of the studio divisions examined in this study. Some of the most obvious of these titles include *Empire Records* (A. Moyle, 1995), *Surviving Picasso* (J. Ivory, 1996) and *Welcome to Collinwood* (A. and J. Russo, 2002), while *Three Kings* (D. O. Russell, 1999) has been discussed by film scholars as one of the key early indiewood titles, despite its finance, production and distribution by a major studio.[2] With the exception of *Three Kings*, all the above titles opened in platform release but failed to find a substantial audience, with *Welcome to Collinwood*, and *Empire Records* in particular proving major disappointments after registering a combined theatrical US box-office gross of less than $1 million. *Three Kings*, on the other hand, was released ultra-wide in approximately 3,000 theatres and grossed over $60 million on an estimated budget of $48 million.[3]

Although the box-office performance of these films did little to ignite the studio and parent company's enthusiasm for plans to expand to the specialty film market in a more forceful manner, the enormous revenues of the first key indiewood titles in the late 1990s and early 2000s, Fox Searchlight's increasing success with more commercial and genre-specific films like *Antwone Fisher* in 2002, and Universal's 2002 entry into the specialty market as an instant top producer–distributor prompted Warner to reconsider. With approximately 13 per cent of all ticket sales in the US during the 2002 to 2003 film season coming from the specialty market,[4] the right time for the establishment of a specialty division by the major seemed finally to have come. Thus, in August 2003, Time Warner formally established Warner Independent Pictures.

Picturehouse, on the other hand, represented both an extension and a rebranding of Fine Line Features. As we saw in Chapter 4, New Line Cinema's specialty label was facing an uncertain future in the 2000s, after enjoying critical and some commercial success in the 1990s as a top distributor (and financer–producer later in the decade) of specialty fare, especially of US indie films. This uncertainty was partly due to the division's lack of clear identity in the 2000s in the face of compromised leadership, following the long-term secondment of its senior executive, Mark Odersky, as New Line's supervisor of the production of the *Lord of the Rings* trilogy, between 1999 and 2003. During that time, Fine Line's slate of releases had been reduced drastically, raising numerous questions about its future. However, in the summer of 2003, Fine Line signed a deal with fellow AOL Time Warner division HBO that seemed to provide hope for the specialty distributor's survival. Under the terms of the deal, the key HBO film productions and acquisitions would be distributed theatrically by Fine Line in an effort to enhance their visibility and market value before finding their place in the leading cable channel's schedules. This agreement seemed to have secured Fine Line's short-term future, at the exact same time as Warner was establishing WIP. However, despite the release of multi-award-winning films that, critically, were extremely well received, such as *American Splendor* and *Elephant*, the theatrical box-office revenues were disappointing for both parties. Following a handful of releases in 2004, the division was finally closed as a freestanding producer–distributor and instead became a specialty marketing label within New Line.

However, HBO, which by the 2000s had become a global brand of quality in several entertainment areas, not just television, was still in need of a pact with a strong specialty distributor that would push its film product in the film market. While a deal with WIP was certainly an option, Warner's new specialty film label seemed to be moving rapidly in the indiewood direction with the release of *Good Night, and Good Luck* (G. Clooney, 2005) and with other titles that had clear commercial hooks, such as *A Scanner Darkly* (R. Linklater, 2005). Such a direction could have proved problematic, given the 'idiosyncratic' nature of many of the HBO titles, which would require a more focused, grassroots type of marketing strategy.[5] Rather than seek such a partner outside Time Warner, HBO and New Line Cinema decided to continue their collaboration through the establishment of Picturehouse. Utilising many of Fine Line's existing resources and merging them with formerly independent production company Newmarket Films, which the two partners took over in order to secure the services of Newmarket's senior executive Bob Berney as the new division's President, Picturehouse was established as a jointly owned distribution subsidiary. Despite being established primarily as a distributor for HBO film product, Picturehouse was also envisaged as a distributor of films from a number of sources and suppliers, with a focus on the acquisition of arthouse films from around the world, making for a very different specialty division from WIP, which mainly concentrated on US film titles. Indeed, Picturehouse's greatest commercial successes would prove to be non-US films, with Guillermo del Toro's *El Laberinto del Fauno* [*Pan's Labyrinth*] (2006) becoming its top box-office attraction.

Given the short-lived history of both labels, the rest of the present chapter is divided into three sections, with the first one focusing on Warner Independent, the second on Picturehouse and the third on Warner's decision to shutter both divisions in 2008.

## WARNER INDEPENDENT PICTURES: 'DEVELOPING ORGANICALLY' IN THE SPECIALTY SECTOR

Warner's decision finally to establish a specialty label in August 2003 came at the end of yet another 'banner' year in the history of studio divisions and, to a lesser extent, stand-alone companies. In a virtual repeat of 1996, when films released by companies other than the major studios dominated the Academy Awards, the quintet of films nominated for Best Picture for the year 2002 to 2003 included four titles released by studio subsidiaries – *Chicago* (R. Marshall) and *Gangs of New York* (M. Scorsese) by Miramax; *The Pianist* by Focus Features; and *The Lord of the Rings: Two Towers* (P. Jackson) by New Line Cinema – with the Miramax–Paramount co-produced and co-distributed *The Hours* (S. Daldry) completing the list. While these Miramax and New Line titles were far removed from the type of modestly budgeted specialty fare that has been discussed in this book, and also from pricier indiewood titles such as *There Will Be Blood* and *No Country for Old Men*, the presence of other, decidedly niche titles in the other Academy Award categories was another cause for celebration for indie and indiewood filmmaking. These titles included New Line Cinema's more modestly budgeted *About Schmidt* (A. Payne); Miramax's *Frida* (J. Taymor) and *The Quiet American* (P. Noyce); Screen Gems' *Adaptation* (S. Jonze); IFC Films' *My Big Fat Greek Wedding* (J. Zwick); and Focus Features' *Far from Heaven*. By the end of the season in August 2003, it was evident that this was a particularly good period for the specialty sector, a view that was confirmed, as mentioned earlier, by the fact that approximately 13 per cent of all ticket sales during that period were generated by specialty titles.

Within this climate of renewed optimism about the future of specialty filmmaking, Time Warner's slice of this 13 per cent market share was close to nothing. This was because Fine Line Features had just two releases in 2003, with only *American Splendor* generating a modest box-office gross. Realising that the specialty film market had become far too big to ignore, even at this late stage when all its competitors had already established their own divisions in the sector, Warner finally decided to make the move it had resisted for years. Announcing the establishment of WIP, the studio's senior executives placed clear emphasis on targeting 'all potential audiences' thereby staking their claim to the significant part of the market that was served by specialty labels. As they put it:

> For strategic and creative reasons, we have long felt that in order to truly be a 'full-service' studio, we need to produce, distribute and market all genres of films, with all size budgets to all potential audiences and not be limited by traditional, mainstream definitions of a 'studio' film.[6]

A less obvious reason behind this decision had also to do with Warner's eagerness to keep creative filmmakers within the studio fold by providing them with a distribution apparatus that could market their films effectively – irrespective of budget, content and target audience – in an increasingly competitive marketplace. Like all the other studios, Warner had a number of development and distribution deals with several production companies and filmmakers, including some of the most creative film directors, producers and stars often identified with independent cinema, such as Steven Soderbergh and George Clooney (Section Eight), film producer Christine Vachon (Killer Films) and Robert Redford (Wildwood).[7] While Redford was making films irregularly and Vachon's films rarely proved box-office champions, Soderbergh and Clooney were considered major players at Warner, after the first Section Eight production, *Ocean's Eleven* (2001), turned out to be a global commercial success, grossing over $450 million worldwide. With their second production, Christopher Nolan's *Insomnia* (2002), also returning a respectable level of rentals, Warner was eager to keep Section Eight within the fold. This meant, however, that it would need to be prepared to bankroll and market a range of films made by the company, including a number of low-key and considerably cheaper productions than *Ocean's Eleven* and *Insomnia* (see Case Study).

In order to ensure parity with its competitors, the division's physical establishment was entrusted to executives with prior experience in other studio specialty labels, with former President of Miramax LA, Mark Gill, who had experience in both the production and marketing sides of the specialty business, assuming the senior executive post.[8] The division's mandate involved the production or acquisition of up to ten titles per year with production budgets of up to $20 million,[9] a budget range that clearly put WIP on a level comparable to Fox Searchlight and Focus Features. Furthermore, and like its competitors, Warner Independent would focus primarily on production, with a proposed 8/2 split between producing its own films and acquiring other titles, including ones in languages other than English.[10] Finally, and more in the mould of Focus Features, Warner's division would be solely responsible for its own distribution and marketing apparatus, though in terms of greenlighting productions, Gill would need to seek permission from both the President of Warner

Bros. Entertainment Group (the group of divisions within which WIP was placed) and the President of Warner Bros. Pictures (the main studio).[11]

With its organisational structure still at inception stage, WIP moved immediately to put together a slate of releases. The first title to be associated with the division came from Christine Vachon's Killer Films co-production, *A Home at the End of the World* (M. Mayer, 2004). Starring Colin Farrell, the film was another one of Vachon's modestly budgeted films that were well known in the US independent film sector for tackling 'issues of queer identity and politics'.[12] Given that such films (pre-*Brokeback Mountain*) were traditionally treated as niche entertainment, it made more sense for Warner to pass the distribution and marketing of this title to its new division, ensuring that the film remained within Warner's fold. This was especially important as Farrell had starred in a number of high-profile productions in 2002 and 2003, following his breakthrough role in Spielberg's *Minority Report* (2002), and his emerging stardom could help the film cross over.[13]

The division then moved into production with the finance of two titles that offered considerable commercial potential. *Around the Bend* (J. Roberts, 2004) was a low-budget family drama with substantial star power in the form of Michael Caine, Christopher Walken and Josh Lucas. In contrast, *Every Word is True* (2006) represented a $12 million production investment in a film that dealt with Truman Capote's relationship with killers Dick Hickock and Perry Smith while researching his well-known book, *In Cold Blood*. Featuring a host of stars, written and directed by Douglas McGrath, a filmmaker with a pedigree in adaptations of literary classics such as *Nicholas Nickleby* (2002), and co-produced by Killer Films, the film clearly represented a prestige project with considerable potential for awards and box-office success.[14]

Despite these early finance and production deals, the division did not ignore the acquisitions market; *We Don't Live Here Anymore* (J. Curran, 2004), a drama with substantial star presence in Laura Dern, Naomi Watts, Mark Ruffalo and TV star Peter Krause, became its first pick-up from the 2004 Sundance Film Festival, for approximately $2 million.[15] Finally, the division made a deal with production company Big Beach to co-finance actor Liev Schreiber's directorial debut *Everything is Illuminated* in exchange for distribution rights,[16] and after signing an agreement with fellow Time Warner production label Castle Rock, was granted distribution rights for *Before Sunset*, Richard Linklater's eagerly anticipated sequel to his commercially successful indie film *Before Sunrise* of 1994.[17]

With such a substantial volume of product already secured, WIP started planning its first releases for the summer of 2004, almost a full year after its establishment. *Before Sunset* became the division's first release in early July, followed by *A Home at the End of the World* later in the same month and *We Don't Live Here Anymore* in mid-August. WIP's slate of releases at the peak of the summer blockbuster period was part of a more general trend of 'counterprogramming' that also characterised the release schedules of the rest of the specialty distributors, studio divisions and stand-alone independents alike.[18] Rather than targeting the autumn months, which have traditionally been the time that the major studios released their less commercial fare and therefore were widely perceived as the best time for smaller films to compete for the attention of the cinema-going public, distributors were convinced by the increased success and visibility of a number of specialty titles in the 2002 to 2003 season to use their new titles as counterprogramming to the barrage of sequels and franchise reboots that characterised the 2004 summer release schedule in the US. This distribution strategy, however, proved a disappointment, as the overall marketplace had become so congested with releases from specialty distributors that, effectively, the various specialty films in release were not competing against the studio films but against each other. According to *Variety*, the weekend in which *Before Sunset* opened also saw the release of three other key specialty titles, including Searchlight's *The Clearing* (P. J. Brugge), MGM / UA's *De-Lovely* (I. Winkler) and Disney documentary *America's Heart and Soul* (L. Schwartzberg),[19] while *A Home at the End of the World* opened in an equally busy marketplace 3 weeks later.

Given these circumstances, WIP's first results were not particularly encouraging. *Before Sunset* ended its run with a US box-office gross of slightly less than $6 million. If this figure can be perceived as a very modest success, this was not the case for the $1 million and the $3.3 million that *A Home at the End of the World* and *We Don't Live Here Anymore*, respectively, grossed worldwide. Furthermore, WIP's other three 2004 releases also proved commercial failures. Despite its star power, *Around the Bend* took a meagre $200,000, representing a major disappointment for the division. *Criminal*, a faithful remake of the Sony Pictures Classics-released con game film, *Nueve Reinas* [*Nine Queens*], took only $1 million (see Case Study). Finally, *A Very Long Engagement*, an expensive French production that had grossed over $60 million in the rest of the world, managed only $6 million at the US theatrical box office and, moreover, failed to become the major Academy Awards contestant that WIP (and Warner) hoped it would.[20]

Despite these early box-office disappointments, which placed the division far below its main rivals in terms of market share, WIP had a solid chance to establish itself in the next 2 years, as it had already received its parent company's financial support for an additional fifteen productions and acquisitions in 2005 and 2006.[21] With the division's President subscribing fully to the idea of one major box-office hit that would offset losses from other releases, WIP moved with a programme of releases that included several titles with strong crossover potential. Besides the previously mentioned *Every Word is True*, the division could also bet on *The Jacket*, starring Adrien Brody and Keira

Knightley, and Christopher Guest's Hollywood satire, *For Your Consideration*, as well as on *The Painted Veil*, a period costume drama set in China boasting the star presence of Edward Norton and Naomi Watts.

However, the division's most prominent properties were two films that could be considered its first foray on to indiewood turf. Based on the titular novel by Philip K. Dick, *A Scanner Darkly* was the result of the pioneering rotoshop animation that the film's writer–director Richard Linklater had used in his more modestly budgeted *Waking Life* (2001). Starring Keanu Reeves and Robert Downey Jr, the film had the potential to appeal to a variety of audiences and prove the crossover hit the division wanted. In contrast, *Good Night, and Good Luck* was actor–director–producer George Clooney's labour of love. Taking place during the early days of television, the film dramatised the public feud between CBS journalist and broadcaster Edward R. Murrow and Senator Joseph McCarthy. Shot in stark black and white and starring David Strathairn and George Clooney, the film was clearly a prestige project, while the presence of Clooney as both writer–director and star gave it ample commercial appeal, despite its 'heavy' political subject. With well-established production companies 2929 Entertainment and Participant Productions co-financing this $7.5 million Section Eight production,[22] WIP's risk was, in any case, limited should the film not prove successful at the box office.

Indeed, 2005 proved to be a good year. Despite many of the above films not being released till 2006, WIP managed a solid hit in *Good Night, and Good Luck*, which grossed over $54 million worldwide, with $31 million at the North American theatrical box office. The film also attracted rave reviews and six Academy Award nominations, including one for Best Picture and two for Clooney's contribution as co-screenwriter and director, encapsulating the type of film that Warner Independent's parent company had envisaged when creating its specialty division. However, the film's success was overshadowed by a second crossover WIP title, one that became an unexpected commercial triumph, not only for the division but also for specialty film more generally. WIP paid just $1 million to secure US theatrical rights for French documentary *La Marche de l'empereur* [*The Emperor's Journey*] (L. Jacquet), after the film was screened at the Sundance Festival in January 2005.[23] Produced by French production company Bonne Pioche in collaboration with Disney's Buena Vista France for approximately $3.5 million and directed by a former scientist,[24] the film showed the annual journey of the Emperor penguins in Antarctica in order to mate and breed. Following the purchase of the film's rights, WIP added a new voiceover narration by Morgan Freeman, along with a musical score, changed the film's title to *The March of the Penguins*, and partnered up with *National Geographic* in the marketing of the film. After a careful 4-week platform release, *March of the Penguins* expanded nationwide, reaching a peak of 2,500 theatres in its eleventh week. Its crossover success was primarily explained by its educational value that appealed to family audiences, while the film was also endorsed by Christian organisations, thus providing additional audience groups.[25] After twenty-five weeks on release, *March of the Penguins* ended its run with $77.5 million, becoming the 'the sixth most successful independent film in history', according to some sources.[26]

With two of its six releases for 2005 surpassing the $100 million mark in combined box office and compensating handsomely for the division's losses from the release of its other titles, Gill's business philosophy seemed to be paying dividends. This was especially important as, prior to the success of both films, he was reported to be under substantial pressure,[27] given the overall underperformance of the division's releases. Nevertheless, towards the end of the year and as WIP's key films had proved their commercial value, both the division and the main studio found themselves victims of cost-cutting exercises on the part of the parent company, with over 300 employees fired, including several senior executives at the specialty division. Despite the healthy level of revenues generated, not only by WIP but also by Warner Bros., as several of its summer films had proved hugely successful commercially, there was a substantial problem with the studio's level of income from DVD sales, which had started to decline. Specifically, Warner Bros. had been at the forefront in terms of supporting DVD technology since its introduction in 1997 and in making its titles available in that format. According to reports, the studio was the undisputed leader in the sell-through market during the early years of the DVD, being responsible for approximately half of all DVD sales in the first half of 1998.[28] By the mid-2000s, however, and within a general slowdown in the DVD market due to the emergence of alternative forms of digital film delivery, Warner was seen as the company with the most to lose, given that it had peaked in 'home video sooner than some of the others ha[d]'. In anticipation of substantially reduced profits in the following financial year, and irrespective of the box-office success of both the studio and the specialty arm, the parent company decided to implement cuts across the board in order to balance its books.[29]

Despite the trimming-down of its staff and operations, Time Warner's financial backing of WIP seemed to continue without any problems in 2006. However, its first releases that year once again failed to register at the box office. Albert Brooks's *Looking for Comedy in the Muslim World* scored less than $1 million at the US box office. *Temporada de Patos* [*Duck Season*] (F. Eimbcke), a Mexican film that WIP distributed in collaboration with renowned filmmaker Alfonso Cuarón's company, Esperanto Films, grossed only $150,000,[30] while Kaige Chen's *Wu ji* [*The Promise*] took a little over $650,000. With combined box-office revenues below the $2 million mark in the first half of 2006, it was evident that WIP had not reached the levels of stability and success its parent company had expected. Furthermore, there were reports about clashes between the division's management and the executives of the main studio that oversaw WIP, which were exacerbated by the weak financial results of the division. Within this climate, and citing '"irreparable divergent views" as to the course Warner Independent Pictures should follow', Mark Gill resigned in May 2006, a little over two-and-a-half years after the establishment of the division.[31]

Gill's exit flagged up a number of issues that had been problematic in Warner's specialty division and that also characterised the other studio divisions. First, it revealed the absence of a concrete plan as to the direction of the company and its identity in the market. By the time of Gill's resignation, WIP had made only a couple of forays into indiewood filmmaking. On the other hand, it seemed to have a substantial focus on more upscale, arthouse films, including several world cinema titles, a trend that was not subscribed to by leading studio divisions like Fox Searchlight and Focus Features. In this respect, WIP appeared to have more similarities with Paramount Classics, before its revamp as Paramount Vantage and its full entry into indiewood with films like *Babel* in 2006, and also with Fine Line Features and its efforts to produce and acquire films that were still relatively cheap. This absence of clear direction and identity was arguably evident right from the beginning, even during the announcement of the division's establishment. As Jeff Robinov, President of Warner Bros. Pictures and the main executive with whom Gill later had 'irreparable divergent views', stated:

> Warner Independent will operate as a true independent film company with its growth and direction *developing organically* . . . While it might be *difficult to precisely define* or label Warner Independent, our purpose couldn't be more clear. We want to create a home for director-driven films that don't fit into, or are simply not suited for, the distribution patterns, marketing budgets and commercial pressures that are inherent to mainstream studio films.[32]

The plan for organic development and the difficulty in defining the division in precise terms can be read as shorthand for a lack of clear direction at a time when the level of investment in the production, acquisition and marketing of specialty films, and especially of US titles, was rising exponentially as the studio divisions and the well-capitalised, stand-alone companies were increasingly embracing indiewood filmmaking. With WIP setting itself up to follow neither Fox Searchlight and Focus Features in their emphasis on indiewood fare, nor Sony Pictures Classics in its focus on acquisitions of moderately priced arthouse and indie titles, the division's plan for organic development certainly seemed to be questionable.

Perhaps not surprisingly, Gill's replacement came from the ranks of Warner Bros., with Polly Cohen, a production specialist, taking over the reins of the division. Cohen's appointment represented both a closer relationship between specialty label and major studio, and a more concerted effort on WIP's part to emphasise production as its main business in the specialty film market. While production was also at the core of the division's mandate under Gill, the former WIP President did not stick to the 8/2 production/acquisitions ratio, with a number of US indies and world cinema pick-ups featuring on the division's annual slates. However, Cohen's expertise in production and her close ties with the studio conveyed a renewed emphasis on production, which was welcomed by a number of established independent producers who were hoping to make films for the division.[33] On the other hand, it also conveyed a different approach to the selection of properties and to filmmaking more generally, one that seemed very similar to studio filmmaking. As Robinov clearly stated:

> The company started out as a place to bring new filmmakers into the Warner Bros family and we want to build on that ... We want it to operate a little bit more like Warner Bros and want to make movies in a more collaborative way with the filmmakers.[34]

Warner's close check on its specialty division clearly suggests that Cohen's efforts to build a distinct identity for WIP were doomed to fail right from the beginning. In addition to the identity problem, Cohen had to deal with the repercussions from the box-office performance of the rest of WIP's 2006 releases. Not only did the division fail to produce any crossover hits of the magnitude of *March of the Penguins*, but also it failed to produce any film with a US box-office gross of more than $8 million. This meant that even its two titles with the most commercial potential, *There Is No Word* (Douglas McGrath; released as *Infamous*) and *A Scanner Darkly*, turned out to be box-office disappointments, with the latter grossing around $7.5 million worldwide and the former $1 million, an extremely low figure for a film with such prestige qualities.

Such a performance raised numerous questions about the division's future, despite the fact that, upon Cohen's arrival, the parent company had allocated to WIP a new corporate development fund in order to help it identify key properties and turn them into productions.[35] Furthermore, the increasingly close ties between studio and specialty division, which had started to become evident through the exchange of projects between the two organisations (for instance, Mark and Michael Polish's *The Astronaut Farmer* started as a WIP production but its release was taken over by Warner Bros.; Paul Haggis's *In the Valley of Elah* started out in the studio before becoming Warner Independent's key release in 2007),[36] also raised doubts about whether WIP had a future in the Time Warner family.

The performance of the division's films certainly did not improve in 2007, when only one of its releases (*In the Valley of Elah*) grossed more than 1 million while the five other titles it distributed recorded a combined gross of less than $1.5 million. Even *In the Valley of Elah*, written and directed by Academy Award-winner Paul Haggis and having the star power of Charlize Theron, Tommy Lee Jones and Susan Sarandon, grossed just $6.7 million at the US box office and therefore proved a commercial disappointment. Adding together the revenues from all its titles on release during 2007, WIP finished the year with just $15.6 million. This compared to $136.2 million for Fox Searchlight and $124.8 million for Focus Features, while, crucially, fellow Time Warner specialty film division Picturehouse also did much better, taking $58.3 million for the year.[37]

With this level of performance, the future of WIP became untenable. After only two releases in 2008, Michael Haneke's US remake of his own *Funny Games* (1997) and David Gordon Greene's *Snow Angels* (the combined box office of which was approximately $1.5 million), the parent company decided to close the division, and also Picturehouse, which at the time was doing much better financially than WIP. Given Time Warner's decision to close both its specialty film divisions at the same time, I will discuss their closure at the end of this chapter.

## PICTUREHOUSE: 'FILMS THAT YOU REALLY FEEL LIKE YOU HAVEN'T SEEN BEFORE'

While Warner Independent was realising its first titles in 2004 to 2005, Time Warner's other specialty label, Fine Line Features, was all but inactive, following its change of status from a 'freestanding division' with its own distribution staff and facilities to a 'specialty marketing label' within New Line, using its personnel and distribution network to release a few titles that were too specialised for its immediate parent company.[38] Its change of status also put an end to the agreement Fine Line had made with fellow Time Warner subsidiary HBO, under which Fine Line would distribute a small number of HBO Films titles theatrically before these were shown on the HBO movie channels. Through that agreement Fine Line was supplied by HBO Films with some of its most critically praised titles in the 2000s (*Elephant*, *Maria Full of Grace*), even though the box-office results were uneven, *Elephant* in particular performing very poorly at the US box office.

The end of this agreement forced HBO Films to look elsewhere for a theatrical distributor. With Warner Independent trading in films which were arguably more commercial in nature than the offbeat, arthouse HBO titles, the cable division looked outside Time Warner for a partner. In early 2005, it was already in talks with stand-alone company Newmarket Films, which had been enjoying remarkable success following the release of Mel Gibson's *The Passion of the Christ* (2004), the highest-grossing specialty film in the history of the sector with over $370 million from the US theatrical market alone. On the other hand, HBO was also in talks with New Line Cinema for the creation of a new specialty subsidiary in which both Time Warner divisions would be partners and which could be much more attuned to the needs of HBO Films than Fine Line had been.[39]

The lynchpin in all these discussions was Bob Berney, one of the three partners in Newmarket Films, a company that had started as a 'boutique financier' of US independent productions but by the 2000s had expanded its operations to the business of film acquisition, production and distribution.[40] For its first theatrical release, *Memento* (C. Nolan, 2000), Newmarket had brought in Bob Berney as marketing consultant; two years later, Berney joined the company as head of distribution operations. Under Berney's leadership, several Newmarket titles crossed over, with the New Zealand film *Whale Rider* (N. Caro, 2003) and the US production *Monster* (P. Jennings, 2003) jointly grossing over $60 million, before the astounding success of *The Passion of the Christ*. Furthermore, Newmarket Films had also distributed the HBO Films production *Real Women Have Curves*, before HBO decided to make the agreement with Fine Line for the distribution of future projects. During the negotiations, Newmarket's theatrical distribution arm became available for sale to HBO, with Berney open to a move to a new structure under the auspices of HBO. However, HBO was not prepared to branch out into the theatrical distribution business on its own and therefore sought to bring in New Line Cinema as a partner. With New Line still interested in the specialty market and employing a small number of Fine Line employees,[41] the deal made sense for all parties. In May 2005, the new specialty label was officially unveiled under the name Picturehouse and with Bob Berney as its President.

Picturehouse's mandate seemed to be markedly different from the rest of the third wave of specialty labels, in terms of both the types of pictures it would be working with and where these films would come from. In terms of the latter, Picturehouse was in the rather enviable position of having at least one key supplier, HBO Films, widely considered as a financer and producer of 'some of the indie world's most critically praised product'.[42] This arrangement, however, also meant that the new division, in the first instance, needed to be geared towards distributing films that were often offbeat, with few clear commercial elements, and more often than not without any stars. For that reason, Picturehouse was betting on Berney's 'eye-catching' track record,[43] as he had been involved in successfully marketing films with no obvious commercial qualities, often through the use of grassroots marketing techniques. Most notably, Berney had been credited with the hugely successful marketing campaign for IFC Films' *My Big Fat Greek Wedding* (J. Zwick, 2002), which in 2002 became the most commercially successful independent film, grossing over $242 million at the North American box office. Berney's other, less spectacular successes, as well as his own predilection for 'arthouse fare', then, telegraphed a division that seemed to be made more in the mould of Sony Pictures Classics than the rest of the studio divisions.

However, the similarities with Sony's specialty division ended there. Whereas SPC started out with an emphasis on acquisitions and, later, co-finance deals, before entering on a few production deals (see Chapter 5), Picturehouse already had HBO Films as a supplier of product but, crucially, could also count on at least three other sources to meet its proposed annual quota of eight to 10 releases a year.[44] These included New Line Cinema productions that were too specialised for the major independent, which, after the success of the *Lord of the Rings* trilogy, had been focusing almost exclusively on expensive properties that were distributed in saturation releases; productions to be jointly funded by New Line Cinema and HBO Films, specifically for the theatrical market; and, finally, acquisitions.[45] In this respect, the new division seemed to have a substantial part of its product secure and therefore had to resort to acquisitions only to complete its slate; this made it more comparable to specialty divisions such as Fox Searchlight and Focus Features, who were relying mostly on production for their line-ups.

This interesting launching position, rather unique in the specialty film industry, that characterised the new division did not go unnoticed by the trade press. In a *Variety* article, tellingly entitled 'Picturehouse Revs Up Specialty Biz; Distrib's Leisurely Launch Leaves Strategy Questions', Ian Mohr questioned Picturehouse's emerging identity, calling its launch 'ambitious but also a bit confusing, perhaps even to those announcing it', labelling the division 'a work in progress', and asking a number of questions pertaining primarily to its business strategies and its relationship to the other studio specialty labels.[46] Perhaps the most important question was whether HBO and New Line would be willing to commit the level of marketing funds necessary to allow the division to compete against the market leaders, a question that also extended to Time Warner's overall degree of commitment to the specialty sector. Still, the *Variety* article suggested that Berney seemed to have a substantial degree of freedom to shape the division, which confirmed the fact that he had played an extremely significant role in its establishment.

Given all the suppliers of product for the division, which, for its first line-up, also included a number of Newmarket Films titles that Berney brought with him when New Line and HBO Films bought Newmarket Films' distribution division, Picturehouse found itself with no shortage of releases. Unlike WIP, which had to wait almost a year to put out its first picture, Picturehouse announced the release of no fewer than nine titles during the division's launch. These can be divided into four categories:

- Newmarket Films productions brought in by Berney: *Rock School* (D. Argott), *The Chumscrubber* (A. Posin) and *A Cock and Bull Story* (M. Winterbottom)
- Picturehouse acquisitions: *The Thing About My Folks* (R. De Felitta) and *Ushpizin* (G. Dar)
- Picturehouse prebuys before production commenced: *Fur* (S. Shainberg)
- HBO Films (production and acquisitions): *Last Days* (G. Van Sant), which became the first film to be released as a Picturehouse title, *The Notorious Betty Page* (M. Harron – in collaboration with Killer Films) and *As You Like It* (K. Brannagh – in collaboration with BBC Films).[47]

Furthermore, only a few weeks after its announcement, Picturehouse acquired an additional title, *Factotum* (B. Hamer), while also entering into a co-finance deal for an expensive international co-production about the life of Genghis Khan, *Mongol* (S. Bodrov).[48]

With all these titles, Picturehouse devised an intensive distribution schedule of one release per month between June 2005 and January 2006, followed by a slightly less strenuous programme for 2006, managing to release twelve pictures altogether in its first eighteen months of existence. Despite the questions about its identity in the trade press, Picturehouse remained pretty consistent in the type of films it handled, with arguably only one picture falling into the 'indiewood' category, Steven Shainberg's *Fur*, a biopic about renowned photographer Diane Arbus, starring Nicole Kidman and Robert Downey Jr. Even this film, though, reportedly cost less than $10 million and was therefore much cheaper than other indiewood titles released by Picturehouse's rivals.[49] The rest of its films had more points of contact with the more offbeat and quirky type of filmmaking that characterised indie cinema before inflated budgets, the participation of stars and the focus on more commercial storylines, often within strong generic frameworks, made a lot of specialty filmmaking resemble the films of the major studios.

Despite all this early activity, the first box-office results were far from encouraging. None of the division's first seven releases passed the $1.5 million mark at the US box office, with *The Notorious Betty Page* proving the most commercially successful with a little over $1.4 million. Van Sant's *Last Days* was a box-office disappointment, grossing less than $500,000, while the first two Newmarket titles, *Rock School* and *The Chumscrubber*, jointly brought in a meagre $110,000. Finally, even its more upmarket (and expensive) film, *Fur*, which was finally released in November 2006, crashed in the marketplace, recording a petty $200,000, despite its hefty budget and the presence of major stars.

This level of underperformance certainly raised a number of questions both about the division's viability and, more generally, about the relevance of Picturehouse's business model, during a year when Fox Searchlight and Focus Features enjoyed box-office revenues of over $100 million each, thanks to the impetus of indiewood titles such as *Sideways* and *Brokeback Mountain*. And while Berney must have felt some pressure from his corporate parents after Picturehouse found itself in lowly thirty-ninth place in the list of the US theatrical distributors with a market share of 0.03 per cent for the calendar year 2005, he was none the less adamant that there was a place in the market for a distributor like Picturehouse that resisted the indiewood trend. This was especially so, as Paramount Classics, which had also largely stayed away from indiewood productions, was in the process of being reinvented as Paramount Vantage and therefore providing reduced competion. As he explained:

> While many of the titles don't have an automatic or easy marketing hook, the slate also means the company has diversified its bets. Even if a movie struggles to find an audience, the next release is so radically different that it basically gives the company a shot at a fresh start.[50]

In this respect, so long as the division was able to keep the marketing costs low, one successful film would be able to pay for a substantial number of underperforming releases, as has been the case with other studio specialty labels.

Indeed, Picturehouse had two commercially successful films released in 2006, which easily offset the losses of its early releases. The first was Robert Altman's *A Prairie Home Companion*, which was based on a long-running, Minnesota-based radio variety show. Featuring a trademark Altman ensemble cast that included stars such as Kevin Kline, Meryl Streep and Tommy Lee Jones, the film attracted several specialty distributors but Picturehouse secured the US rights for a fee of $3.75 million.[51] Given the show's substantial fan basis, Picturehouse had an established primary audience, which it hoped would respond to the film following a 'grassroots-oriented' campaign that the division planned to design.[52] Specifically, and given the radio show's popularity in the National Public Radio network of stations, Picturehouse decided to screen the film to the employees of 100 such stations with a view to creating word of mouth before the film's release.[53] The results justified the campaign. Opening in 760 theatres over the summer period, *A Prairie Home Companion* worked successfully as counterprogramming against Pixar's *Cars* (J. Lasseter and J. Ranft) and Twentieth Century Fox's *The Omen* (J. Moore), bringing in over $4.5 million on the way to a $20 million US box-office gross and becoming the first big hit for the division.

The success of *A Prairie Home Companion* signalled a change of gear for the division in terms of the types of product it would be involved with, films that would be considerably more expensive than its early titles and with more commercial elements. For instance, in January 2006, Picturehouse announced the acquisition of distribution rights for the period costume drama *Silk* (F. Girard, 2007), a $20 million international co-production. This was followed by the acquisition of the North American rights for Guillermo del Toro's $17.8 million *Pan's Labyrinth*, for which Picturehouse paid $6 million, a price that compared with those paid by the division's rivals for several high-performing specialty titles.[54] Later in 2006, Picturehouse bought the US theatrical rights for two expensive biopics that had great commercial potential: Oliver Dahan's Edith Piaf biopic with Marion Cotillard,[55] and the $18 million, Jennifer Lopez-produced biopic of Puerto Rican salsa singer Héctor Lavoe, *El Cantante*, which Picturehouse bought for between $4 and $5 million.[56] Finally, following the investment of this substantial capital on acquisitions, Picturehouse's joint parent organisations announced that the division post-2007 would start to be 'involved in projects earlier in their development – possibly with the help of outside financiers',[57] a move that would effectively launch the division in the production business.

The initial results were no less than spectacular. Released in the last week of 2006, the dark fantasy *Pan's Labyrinth* proved to be a crossover hit, grossing over £37 million in the US market and being nominated for six Academy Awards, eventually winning three. This was followed by the Edith Piaf biopic, *La Vie en rose*, which scored over $10 million at the North American box office and also received great reviews and an Academy Award for Actress in a Leading Role. The almost $50 million in box-office revenue from these two titles certainly offset some misfires, especially *Silk*, which grossed only $1 million, and *El Cantante* (L. Ichaso), which also proved a disappointment, bringing in only $7.5 million. With approximately $60 million in combined US box office for the calendar year 2007, Picturehouse found itself in the same place as revamped Paramount Vantage and much higher in terms of market share than SPC and fellow Time Warner division WIP, as we saw earlier.

Picturehouse's improved performance pointed to a more secure future, especially as it had lined up several commercially appealing titles for 2008, including *The Mongol* (which the division had acquired in 2005), *The Women* (an all-star remake of George Cukor's celebrated film by Diane English) and the Guillermo del Toro-produced *Orfanato* [*The Orphanage*] (J. A. Bayona). However, the underperformance of some of its titles, and especially the ones supplied by HBO Films, became a thorny issue for the future of the division. *Starter for Ten* (T. Vaughan) and *Rocket Science* (J. Blitz) brought in less than $1 million in combined box-office revenues, while reports suggested that other HBO titles selected for theatrical release never reached the theatres.[58] These included Kenneth Brannagh's *As You Like It*, which had been announced as one of the original nine Picturehouse titles in 2005 but was never released theatrically. Not surprisingly, HBO Films started to reconsider the benefits of its collaboration with New Line Cinema, especially when a new management team was installed at the cable broadcaster. Despite HBO deciding to continue its support of Picturehouse – and despite Picturehouse finally providing the distributor with a title that proved a commercial success in 2008, *Kit Kittredge: An American Girl* (P. Rozema, 2008) – Picturehouse started to be increasingly associated with the other partner in the venture, New Line Cinema, inviting critics to compare it with Fine Line Features.[59]

HBO's half-hearted support of the division post-2008 was a sign of worse things to come; in May of the same year and after only two releases, Time Warner announced the termination of its own support, not only of Picturehouse but also of WIP. The rest of Picturehouse's titles were released in the second half of the year as the division was being dismantled. Ironically, 2008 turned out to be the division's best year, with $63 million in box-office revenues from only six releases, compared to a similar figure from nine releases in the previous year.

## 'THE GREAT STUDIO PULLBACK OF 08–09'[60]

At the beginning of 2008, a number of issues pointed towards a difficult year for specialty filmmaking. First, the level of box-office revenues for films by specialty distributors took a significant dip, from $1.32 billion in 2006 to $1.16 billion in 2007 (down 11.9 per cent), while 350 of the 530 films released by all specialty labels failed to surpass the $250,000 mark. This was despite the fact that the overall theatrical box office had increased slightly during the same period.[61] Part of the reason for this failure was a particularly congested marketplace that saw the release of several specialty titles every week, making it extremely difficult for more than just a few titles to assert themselves. According to *Variety*, on the weekend of 7 to 9 December 2007, specialty distributors released *Juno* (Fox Searchlight), *Atonement* (Focus Features) and *Grace is Gone* (The Weinstein Company). These immediately came up against *The Diving Bell and the Butterfly* (Miramax) and *The Savages* (Fox Searchlight), which had been released the weekend before; Todd Haynes's *I'm Not There* (Focus Features), released two weeks earlier; and *No Country for Old Men*, which was still expanding following a successful platform release.[62] Such a cluttered schedule could not sustain more than a handful of commercial successes, and only *Juno*, *Atonement* and *No Country for Old Men* managed to cross over, despite the fact that films like *The Savages* and *I'm Not There* were also pushed aggressively and received strong reviews.

Such a crowded marketplace was also the outcome of a considerable increase in the number of both distributors and specialty films. As regards the number of films, the responsibility lay not only with the studio divisions, but also with numerous newcomers, production and distribution companies eager to test the specialty film business model. Indeed, the number of distributors had been growing steadily since the 2000s, from 75 releasing organisations in the US in 2002 to 153 in 2007, an increase of over 100 per cent. This was because, during that period, Wall Street finance was readily available, with a number of investment banks and hedge funds willing to invest in a film business model that was initially characterised by 'low risk' and had the potential for huge payoffs.[63]

As well as competing for theatre bookings with titles from the established stand-alone companies and the studio divisions, the product glut also drove advertising and marketing costs to stratospheric heights. As I mentioned in Chapter 7, by 2007 the average marketing costs for a specialty release had reached $25 million, going up 44 per cent from the previous year. In extreme cases, studio divisions found themselves spending this amount of money on print and marketing costs for films that had cost only $5 or $10 million to produce, making it almost impossible to break even.[64] With almost all the studio divisions eventually turning to production and with the average production costs hitting $49.2 million in 2007, it was clear that a film needed to reach $100 million minimum to return a profit. Despite the emphasis on commercially driven indiewood filmmaking, $100 million hits were the exception rather than the rule, with only Fox Searchlight surpassing this at the US box office in 2007. Furthermore, the availability of such enormous amounts of marketing funds encouraged a number of these divisions to utilise increasingly wide release methods, prompting their corporate parents to question their *raison d'être*. Why should they maintain two different divisions with their respective infrastructures and overhead costs if both used the same distribution methods?

The box office slump, overproduction, increased competition, the cluttered released schedule, the huge rise in production and marketing costs, and the increasing excursions of specialty labels into studio release methods represented a significant cluster of problems for the studio divisions and their corporate parents. At the same time, though, these companies had to face three additional issues that were also contributing factors to the changing rules of the game in specialty filmmaking. The first of these was the deterioration of the acquisitions market, which, during the 1990s in particular, had been the main provider of specialty product. Although this market had been expanding as an increasing number of films was being produced globally, the acquisition prices of films with the biggest commercial potential had been driven to stratospheric heights, often reaching $10 million and therefore representing a huge investment for a distributor. In the face of such exorbitant prices, often driven by bidding wars, studio divisions either embraced film production, which allowed them to control the level of their investment and to ensure quality, or arranged finance deals in exchange for rights to a film before it was submitted to the festivals. In this respect, the most commercially appealing specialty films were already attached to a distributor, leaving the less appealing ones vying for the distributors' attention at the festivals. With almost all the studio divisions on the lookout for a small number of acquisitions to complete their line-ups, the product acquired failed on many occasions to live up to expectations, in spite of the often-hefty price tag attached to it.

Second, the studio divisions did not only have to compete against newcomers for theatre bookings. Arguably, a bigger threat was posed by their sister companies and their blockbusting franchise films, which, year by year, were claiming an increasing number of theatres and screens. Sony's *Spider-Man 3* was released on 4 May 2007 in over 4,200 theatres and on approximately 10,000 screens.[65] This accounted for over 25 per cent of all existing indoor screens in the US market, the total number of which, according to the Motion Picture Association of America, was 39,347.[66] With other releases from the majors claiming a comparable number of theatres and screens, and with the more commercial films promising exhibitors a higher volume of ticket sales than the specialty films, it is clear that this was also a substantial problem.

Finally, both the studios and the specialty divisions had to deal with the alarming slowdown of DVD sales, after a particularly successful six-year period in the early 2000s when this particular ancillary market supplied a significant part of a film's profit. However, after a few consecutive years that saw huge increases in penetration levels, the new technology quickly reached saturation point, and this affected all companies, especially Warner and its divisions (as we saw earlier). With no alternative home delivery technology advanced enough to anticipate a turnaround, both studios and specialty labels would see diminishing returns from their biggest ancillary market, which was often powerful enough to transform a theatrical financial failure into a success. This was especially the case with independent films that did not have time to assert themselves in the theatrical marketplace and had hopes of 'being discovered' in the home video market a few months later.

This complex picture provides the background for Warner's decision to shutter its two divisions. Indeed, the parent company had already started exploring the possibility of merging WIP and Picturehouse as far back as early 2007, almost a year and a half before the final decision. However, its proposal was met with resistance from both New Line Cinema and HBO Films,[67] whose Picturehouse was then in only its second year of operation and had just released its box-office champion *Pan's Labyrinth*. Seeing the success of Picturehouse in 2007, Warner decided to shelve its plans for a merger and to continue to operate both divisions, despite the fact that WIP had started to become a particularly costly enterprise. With its few releases in 2007 grossing a combined $8.9 million and with overheads running at $7 million,[68] it was clear that WIP had become a money-losing venture as early as 2007.

In February 2008, only a few weeks after the re-evaluation of Picturehouse's relationship with HBO Films and its increasing attachment to New Line Cinema, Time Warner announced the merger of its main studio, Warner Bros., and New Line. The merger, the first move by a newly installed regime at the parent company, took place following New Line's failure to launch an expensive franchise based on Phillip Pullman's trilogy, *His Dark Materials*.[69] Given New Line's almost exclusive focus on wide releases during the 2000s, the need for a separate global distribution network under the same corporate umbrella was questionable. After the merger, it was envisaged that New Line would still continue to produce and distribute a few films a year but use Warner Bros.' resources to put them in the marketplace.

The end of New Line as an autonomous division within the Time Warner structure immediately signalled the beginning of the end for Picturehouse, especially as its relationship with HBO had not proved commercially successful. Indeed, in the next 2 months, the merger of the two specialty divisions resurfaced, with the expectation that Warner would continue backing the newly merged entity.[70] However, on 8 May 2008, the corporate parent announced the closure of both divisions. The move caused shockwaves throughout the industry, especially as this was the first major conglomerate to exit the specialty film business. According to the President of Warner Bros., Alan Horn, the closure reflected 'the reality of a changing marketplace',[71] where the model of producing or acquiring a film cheaply, marketing it with limited resources, and letting it find its place in the market was no longer a reality. This was also coupled with a cost-cutting exercise that aimed to discard 'duplicate production, marketing, and distribution infrastructure' and increase efficiency.[72] In this respect, and as in the case of Paramount Vantage, the closure of the two divisions was both a product of the impact of all the key issues that troubled the specialty labels and the outcome of corporate politics, in tandem with more specific cost-cutting measures.

Although this move signalled the end of both divisions, Warner was reluctant to admit that it was getting out of the specialty film business entirely. Accordingly, it also announced that its much leaner New Line Cinema, which had had some experience in distributing niche films before focusing almost exclusively on the development of franchises such as the *Austin Powers* and *Rush Hour* trilogies, would be undertaking the distribution of any specialty titles, especially indiewood films, that ended up at Warner. Given the increasing access to such titles via multiplexes rather than arthouse theatres, the argument went, it would make the distribution and marketing of such titles a much easier prospect compared to previous years.[73] However, by 2010, the division had not been involved with any specialty films, suggesting that Time Warner did, in fact, withdraw completely from the specialty film business by the end of 2008.

## CONCLUSION

For a number of film industry critics Time Warner was a 'Johnny-come-lately' to the specialty film business, and its level of commitment to both of its specialty divisions was always questionable. Indeed, both divisions entered the marketplace at a time when the costs of producing, acquiring and marketing films were much higher compared to the 1990s, the decade in which most of the second- and third-wave studio labels were established. Given that neither Warner Independent nor Picturehouse was built on the frugal arthouse release model pioneered by SPC (though Picturehouse seemed to start life like this) or on the much more commercial, indiewood-led model championed by Fox Searchlight and Focus Features, the two Warner divisions occupied variations of a middle ground that did not seem to be stable enough to help them find their niche in the market. For instance, WIP had one, rather accidental, hit with *March of the Penguins*, and only three strongly commercial (for the specialty sector) pictures in *Good Night, and Good Luck*, *A Scanner Darkly* and *The Valley of Elah*, the rest of its releases being an amalgam of documentaries, non-US arthouse films and low-budget pictures that were difficult to market.

Picturehouse, on the other hand, managed to acquire, in its short history, some form of identity as a 'tastemaker' with its release of arthouse films, especially non-US ones.[74] Titles such as *Pan's Labyrinth* and *La Vie en rose* both proved commercially successful and brought the division kudos and awards, suggesting that Picturehouse might have had a future at a time when WIP seemed to be in decline following Gill's exit. This was especially the case, as Picturehouse maintained a small degree of profitability, despite a string of underperforming homegrown films supplied primarily through HBO Films. However, the problems with HBO and especially the end of New Line Cinema as a distinct producing-distributing organisation within Time Warner made Picturehouse particularly vulnerable. Given its low profit margins, Warner Independent's failure to assert itself in the marketplace and the overall economic climate, Time Warner chose to kill two birds with one stone and closed them both. In this respect, their contributions to specialty film, and American independent film more specifically, were minimal compared to the other third-wave divisions.

## Case Study: *Criminal*
## (Gregory Jacobs, 2004, Warner Independent Pictures)

Even for its President, the establishment of Warner Independent Pictures was, in part, 'a response to keeping filmmakers like Steven Soderbergh at the studio who want to make both big and smaller movies'.[75] In partnership with George Clooney, Soderbergh had set up the production company Section Eight in 1999 at Warner Bros. with a view to making films 'as cheaply as possible in exchange for minimal creative interference' from the studio.[76] With Warner Bros. interested in attracting filmmakers who could deliver prestigious Oscar-worthy projects and with Section Eight agreeing to carry a very low overhead cost in exchange for creative freedom, the deal seemed to be beneficial for both parties.

Following the success of the company's first two productions (*Ocean's Eleven* and *Insomnia*), which had huge commercial appeal and involved the participation of some major Hollywood stars, the studio accommodated their third production, *Welcome to Collinwood*, which was a loose remake of the critically acclaimed 1958 Italian crime film *I Soliti Ignioti* [*Big Deal on Madonna Street*] (M. Monicelli). Featuring an ensemble cast of primarily character actors (William H. Macy, Luis Guzmán and Sam Rockwell) and a brief cameo from Clooney, the film had little commercial appeal. Warner had little experience in the distribution and marketing of small films, and *Welcome to Collinwood* proved a major failure at the US box office, ranking last in the studio's releases for the year with a gross of a little over $300,000. Following this performance Warner passed on other Section Eight specialty films, including films directed by Soderbergh and Clooney themselves (*Full Frontal* and *Confessions of a Dangerous Mind*, respectively), which ended up being released by Miramax. However, it retained the right to distribute other Section Eight titles with more commercial appeal.

The establishment of WIP allowed Section Eight to stay with Warner, as its specialty division would be in a position to use distribution and marketing practices that were more appropriate for low-budget independent films. It did not take long for the production company and the new specialty distributor to get down to business. *Criminal* became WIP's third release, following *Before Sunset* and *We Don't Live Here Anymore*, and was the first of four Section Eight titles to be distributed by the division, with *The Jacket*, *Good Night, and Good Luck* and *A Scanner Darkly* to follow. Interestingly, *Criminal* was a remake of the Argentinian con game film *Nine Queens*, which Warner Independent's rival, SPC, had distributed in the US market in 2002, but which had not found the commercial and critical success that other films from Latin America countries experienced in the early 2000s (see Case Study in Chapter 5). Anticipating that a US version would prove more commercial, Section Eight purchased the remake rights for the film in February 2003, with a view to making it the company's first picture to be scripted and directed by Gregory Jacobs, Soderbergh's long-serving first assistant director.

For WIP the film seemed to be an excellent proposition. The clear generic qualities of *Criminal* made it a much more commercially appealing title than its first two releases, despite the fact that Section Eight cast the film with familiar character actors John C. Reilly and Diego Luna, rather than full-blown Hollywood stars. On the other hand, the emphasis of con artist and con game films on questions of character psychology and the workings of the human psyche had made them a staple of indie filmmaking in the US, despite an equally prominent focus on suspenseful plotting that tends to be a characteristic of popular mainstream cinema. With films like *Confidence* (J. Foley, 2003) and *The Spanish Prisoner* becoming hits for Lions Gate and SPC, respectively, Warner was happy for the $10 million-budget *Criminal* (co-financed with 2929 Entertainment) to be released by its specialty label.[77]

As a remake of *Nine Queens*, *Criminal* is unusually faithful to the original. The basic storyline of two conmen working together for the day and being drawn to the sale of a replica of an extremely valuable collector's item to a rich businessman, before all is revealed to be a con set up by the younger of the two, is the same as in the original, with the exception of some details that have no particular effect on the construction of the narrative (the pair consists of an American and a Mexican, Richard and Rodrigo; instead of a sheet of stamps they are trying to sell a replica of an extremely valuable bank note; and a few other details). However, unlike *Nine Queens*, the narrative of which takes place in Buenos Aires but which works in such a way as to exclude images that are clearly identifiable as Argentinian,[78] *Criminal* emphasises locality throughout via location shooting in, and clear mention of, well-known areas in Los Angeles. This allows *Criminal* to break away from the nondescript Latin American background of the original and to situate its plot in the more recognisable world cityscape of Los Angeles.

*Criminal*'s biggest difference from *Nine Queens*, however, lies in the former's lack of critique of the society it represents. While *Nine Queens* frames all confidence games that form part of and structure its narrative as direct effects of the chronic corruption that has permeated all aspects of life in modern Argentina, *Criminal* is not interested in pointing a finger at US society and the levels of corruption that have also permeated it. Instead, corruption is constructed in strictly individual terms, suggesting that it is a characteristic of some 'bad apples' rather than a defining element of American society. This is seen clearly in the penultimate scene, when Richard goes to a bank to cash his cheque. While, in the original, Marcos is confronted with a collapsed financial institution that is the product of the 'real' financial crisis Argentina faced in the late 1990s and early 2000s, in *Criminal* Richard goes to a bank that has no such problems. What is problematic is the actual cheque he is trying to cash, which turns out to be counterfeit and leads to his arrest. *Criminal*, then, does not move to engage with the kind of social and political issues that are raised by *Nine Queens*. On the other hand, by casting a young Mexican actor as a protagonist and the mastermind behind the con and by 'allowing' him to participate in the formation of the heterosexual couple with a white female partner that closes the narrative, the film offers a particularly progressive take on race and gender politics in the US during the first term of the ultra-conservative administration of George W. Bush. In this respect, it is not just a genre film lacking political positioning.

Despite its progressive message, however, the film found little appeal at the box office. The lack of established stars, competition with three other

> specialty films that opened in the same weekend and, perhaps, its reluctance to tell the *Nine Queens* story in new ways affected its box-office success. With a final US gross of slightly less than $1 million, *Criminal* became a significant box-office failure for both Section Eight and Warner Independent. The two partners had to wait for *Good Night, and Good Luck*, in 2005, to celebrate a hit.

## NOTES

1. See The Numbers (http://www.the-numbers.com/market/Distributors/); accessed on 2 June 2011.
2. King, *Indiewood USA*, 216–29.
3. Unless otherwise stated, all figures for this chapter were taken from IMDb (www.imdb.com); accessed on 2 June 2011.
4. Hernandez, Eugene, 'Warner Bros. Unveils Specialty Division with Mark Gill at the Helm', *Indiewire* (8 August 2003), http://www.indiewire.com/article/warner_bros._unveils_specialty_division_with_mark_gill_at_the_helm; accessed on 1 June 2011.
5. Dunkley and Rooney, 'HBO Draws a Fine Line', 15.
6. Barry Meyer, Chairman and Chief Executive Officer of Warner Bros. Entertainment, and Alan Horn, President and Chief Operating Officer, were quoted in 'Warner Bros. Entertainment Names Mark Gill President of Newly Created Warner Independent Pictures', *Business Wire* (7 August 2003), n/a.
7. Bloom, David, Claude Brodesser, Cathy Dunkley et al., 'Facts on Pacts 2003', *Weekly Variety* (28 April 2003), 12.
8. Mohr, Ian, 'Federbush, Bing Join New WIP Unit', *Hollywood Reporter* (14 August 2003), 3.
9. 'Warner Bros. Entertainment', n/a.
10. Dunkley, Cathy and Jonathan Bing, 'Classics Click at Warners', *Daily Variety* (8 August 2003), 1.
11. Ibid.
12. Davis, *Far from Heaven*, 16.
13. Rooney, David, 'Warner Independent on Cold-blooded Trail', *Daily Variety* (8 September 2003), 19.
14. Ibid., 5 and 19.
15. Mohr, Ian, 'WIP Scores First Pickup at Sundance', *Hollywood Reporter* (22 January 2004), 1.
16. Kit, Borys, 'Wood Sparks Role in WIP's "Illuminated"', *Hollywood Reporter* (19 March 2004), 3.
17. Dunkley, Cathy, 'Warner Independent Pictures', *Daily Variety* (8 September 2004), S22.
18. Brodesser, Claude, 'Niche Pics Stoke Summer Heat', *Weekly Variety* (8 March 2004), 53; Snyder, Gabriel, 'Niche Pics Feel a Pinch', *Daily Variety* (2 July 2004), 1.
19. Snyder, 'Niche Pics', 11.
20. Dunkley, 'Warner Independent Pictures', S22.
21. Ibid.
22. Lowry, Brian and Jill Feiwell, 'Oater Floats Globes' Boat', *Daily Variety* (14 December 2005), 1.

23. Harris, Dana and Cathy Dunkley, 'Distribs Pair for Jacquet's "Journey"', *Daily Variety* (24 January 2005), 18.
24. James, Alison and Pamela McClintock, 'Penguins Feather Warners' Nest', *Weekly Variety* (15 August 2005), 7.
25. Chattaway, Peter, '*March of the Penguins*: A Review', *Christianity Today* (24 June 2005), http://www.christianitytoday.com/ct/movies/reviews/2005/marchofpenguins.html; accessed on 1 June 2011.
26. 'Mark Gill, Warner Independent Pictures President, to be Closing Keynote Speaker at 2005 MAVC', *Business Wire* (17 October 2005), n/a.
27. McClintock, Pamela, 'Warner Independent Pictures; Domestic Distribution Report', *Daily Variety* (7 September 2005), A22.
28. Tzioumakis, Yannis, 'From the Business of Cinema to the Business of Entertainment: Hollywood Cinema in the Age of Digital Technology', in *American Cinema in the Digital Age*, ed. Robert C. Sickels (New Haven, CT: Greenwood, 2010), 27.
29. Hernandez, Greg, 'More Than 300 Laid Off at Warner; Independent Unit Takes Hit', *Daily News* (Los Angeles) (3 November 2005), n/a.
30. Harris, Dana, 'WIP Plucks "Duck" for U.S.', *Daily Variety* (6 June 2005), 5.
31. McClintock, Pamela, 'Warner's March of the Exec', *Daily Variety* (4 May 2006), 1.
32. Robinov was quoted in 'Warner Bros. Entertainment', n/a.
33. McClintock, Pamela, 'WIP's Going All the Way', *Daily Variety* (22 September 2006), 4.
34. Kay, Jeremy, 'Polly Cohen Installed as New Warner Independent Chief', *Screen Daily* (9 May 2006), http://www.screendaily.com/polly-cohen-installed-as-new-warner-independent-chief/4027094.article; accessed on 2 June 2011.
35. Ibid.
36. Fleming, Michael, 'Warners Arm Tends "Garden"', *Daily Variety* (22 September 2006), 1.
37. McClintock, Pamela, 'Specialty Biz Looking for Liftoff', *Daily Variety* (3 January 2008), 53.
38. Harris, Dana, 'Redrawn Lines Making a Mark', *Daily Variety* (16 September 2004), 1.
39. Fritz, Ben and Ian Mohr, 'Time Warner Has Indie Spirit', *Daily Variety* (24 March 2005), 8.
40. Molloy, Claire, *Memento* (Edinburgh: Edinburgh University Press, 2010), 13.
41. Mohr, Ian, 'Domestic Distribution Reports: Picturehouse', *Daily Variety* (7 September 2005), A24.
42. Ibid.
43. Mohr, Ian, 'Picturehouse Revs Up Specialty Biz', *Weekly Variety* (25 July 2005), 14.
44. 'HBO / New Line Cinema Name Joint Venture Picturehouse', *PR Newswire* (13 May 2005), n/a.
45. Ibid.
46. Mohr, 'Picturehouse Revs Up Specialty Biz', 14.
47. Brooks, Brian, 'Bob Berney's New Gig - Picturehouse - Launched in Cannes; Slate and Staff Unveiled', *Indiewire* (13 May 2005), http://www.indiewire.com/article/bob_berneys_new_gig_-_picturehouse_-_launched_in_cannes_slate_and_staff_unv/; accessed on 2 June 2011.
48. Harris, Dana, 'Berney Banks *Factotum*', *Daily Variety* (25 May 2005), 4; Thompson, Anne, 'Picturehouse Making History', *Hollywood Reporter* (20 June 2005), n/a.
49. Thompson, Anne, 'Picturehouse Wins Altman's "Companion"', *Hollywood Reporter* (31 October 2005), n/a.

50. Berney was quoted in Zeitchik, Steven, 'Picturehouse: Fare is Out There', *Daily Variety* (1 October 2006), 10.
51. Mohr, Ian, '"Prairie" Finds Companion', *Daily Variety* (31 October 2005), 1.
52. Thompson, 'Picturehouse Wins', n/a.
53. Bing, Jonathan, 'Talk's Not Cheap to Word-of-Mouth Marketers', *Daily Variety* (30 May 2006), 2.
54. De La Fuente, Anne-Marie, 'Labyrinth Finds its Way to $6 million at Picturehouse', *Daily Variety* (24 January 2006), 26.
55. Goldstein, Gregg and Anne Thompson, 'Picturehouse Grows "Rose" in U.S. Soil', *Hollywood Reporter* (26 May 2006), n/a.
56. Zeitchik, Steven and Gabriel Snyder, 'Picturehouse Grooves to "Cantante" Moves', *Daily Variety* (18 September 2006), 1; and Goldstein, Gregg, 'Picturehouse Acquires "Cantante" Rights', *Hollywood Reporter* (16 September 2006), n/a.
57. Zeitchik, 'Picturehouse', 16.
58. Goldstein, Gregg, 'Picturehouse Shifts its Foundation', *Hollywood Reporter* (10 January 2008), 4.
59. Ibid., 21.
60. Hayes, Dade, 'Picturehouse', *Daily Variety* (8 September 2008), n/a.
61. Goldstein, Gregg, 'Knocked Down but Not Out', *Hollywood Reporter* (7 January 2008), 45.
62. McClintock, Pamela, 'Niche Pics' Glut Check', *Daily Variety* (8 September 2008), A19.
63. McClintock, Pamela, 'Specialty Slide', *Daily Variety* (10 September 2009), A17.
64. Ibid.
65. The figures for *Spider-Man* were taken from BoxOffice Guru, http://www.boxofficeguru.com/072108.htm; accessed on 1 May 2011.
66. Motion Picture Association of America, *Theatrical Market Statistics 2009*, http://www.mpaa.org/Resources/091af5d6-faf7-4f58-9a8e-405466c1c5e5.pdf; accessed on 2 June 2011.
67. Kit, Borys and Gregg Goldstein, 'Niche is Ditched at Warners', *Hollywood Reporter* (9 May 2008), 26.
68. Goldstein, Gregg, 'Hey, Buddy, Can You Spare a Dime?', *Hollywood Reporter* (29 August 2008), S4.
69. Wray, Richard, 'Jobs to Go as New Line Cinema Merged into Warner Bros', *The Guardian* (29 February 2008), http://www.guardian.co.uk/business/2008/feb/29/useconomy; accessed on 2 June 2011.
70. Abramowitz, Rachel, 'Indie Picturehouse Tries to Stay in the Big Picture', *Los Angeles Times* (7 May 2008), E4.
71. Barnes, Brooks, 'To Reduce Costs, Warner Brothers Closing 2 Film Divisions', *New York Times* (9 May 2008), n/a.
72. Abramowitz, Rachel, 'Warners Shuts 2 Divisions', *Los Angeles Times* (9 May 2008), E1.
73. McNary, Dave and Dade Hayes, 'Warner Slams Door on Specialty Pix', *Daily Variety* (9 May 2008), 19.
74. Abramowitz, 'Warners Shuts 2 Divisions', E11.
75. Gill, quoted in Dunkley and Bing, 'Classics Click', 15.
76. McLean, Thomas J., 'Section Eight Goes Up in Smoke', *Daily Variety* (13 October 2006), A2.
77. Holson, Laura M., 'Actor-Director Team Finds Freedom but Not Profit', *New York Times* (17 January 2005), http://www.nytimes.com/2005/01/17/business/worldbusiness/17iht-clooney.html; accessed on 2 June 2011.

78. Shaw, Deborah, 'Playing Hollywood at its Own Game? Bielinsky's *Nueve Reinas*', in *Contemporary Latin American Cinema: Breaking into the Global Market*, ed. Deborah Shaw (Plymouth: Rowman & Littlefield, 2007), 72.

# Index

*About Schmidt* 202
*Across the Sea of Time* 115
*Adaptation* 118, 202
*Adjuster, The* 77
*Adventures of Sebastian Cole, The* 161
*Afraid of the Dark* 90
*African Queen, The* 56
*After the Rehearsal* 48
*Alambrista!* 31
*All about My Mother* 120
*All the Real Girls* 120
Allen, Woody 98, 190
Almodóvar, Pedro 74, 120, 121, 125, 185
Altman, Robert 35, 92, 93, 94, 214
*Amadeus* 69
*Amateur* 115, 136
*America's Heart and Soul* 205
American film industry 14, 44, 65, 66, 71, 77, 87, 89, 93, 112
American Film Marketing Association 137
*American in Paris, An* 23
American independent cinema/film 1, 2, 3, 4, 5, 6, 7, 8, 9, 12, 13, 14, 15, 16, 18, 27, 32, 35, 38, 44, 47, 49, 53, 59, 60, 61, 62, 71, 76, 79, 88, 116, 137, 160, 171, 178, 179, 188, 220; *see also* contemporary American independent cinema; American indie cinema/film; independent film: movement; indie cinema/filmmaking; indiewood
American independent film canon/canonical title 5, 9, 16, 71, 76, 90, 98, 104, 115, 133, 150, 167, 188, 189,
195; *see also* independent film: canon/canonical titles
American indie cinema/film 9, 15, 177; *see also* indie cinema/film
American International Pictures 65
American Playhouse 136
*American Splendor* 101, 201, 202
*Among Giants* 141
*Amongst Friends* 94
*Amores Perros* 126, 184
Ancillary markets 33, 34, 39, 74, 94, 103, 122, 156, 169, 194, 218
*And the Ship Sails On* 48
*And Your Mother Too! (Y Tu Mamá También)* 126
Anderson, Paul Thomas 166
Andrew, Geoff 80
*Angel* 48
*Angel at My Table, An* 90
*Anniversary Party, The* 100
*Another Country* 68, 70
*Antarctica (Nankyoku Monogatari)* 58
*Antwone Fisher* 144, 145, 200
*Anywhere but Here* 140
AOL 101, 102, 199, 201
AOL Time Warner 201
*Apostle, The* 180
Arbus, Diane 213
*Around the Bend* 204, 205
Art cinema 11, 27, 32, 126
Arthouse cinema/film 3–4, 9, 25–7, 29–31, 33–6, 38, 44–8, 51–2, 55–6, 65–70, 73–5, 78, 88, 94–5, 100, 110, 113–15, 122, 126, 134, 143, 150, 156–61, 164, 169, 171, 185, 187, 201, 208, 211–12, 219–20

film market 4, 9, 25, 27, 30, 51, 55, 67, 95, 110, 115
major arthouse film markets 70
non-US 25, 31, 34–5, 44–6, 70–1, 78, 88, 110, 125–6, 157, 161, 171, 220
Artisan 11, 140–1, 146, 157, 181
*As You Like It* 213, 216
*Ash Wednesday* 150, 185
Association of Independent Video and Filmmakers 32
*Astronaut Farmer, The* 209
*At First Sight (Coup de foudre / Entre nous)* 36
Atlantic Releasing Corporation 74
*Atonement* 191, 216
*Austin Powers* 219
authorship 8, 10, 80
*Auto Focus* 120, 122
Avenue Pictures 74, 91, 92
*Awfully Big Adventure, An* 96

*Babel* 158, 166, 167, 168, 169, 171, 173, 208
*Babette's Feast (Babette's Gaestebud)* 73
*Baby, It's You* 38
*Baghead* 110, 194
*Ballad of Little Jo, The* 93, 94
*Balls of Fury* 191
*Banger Sisters, The* 143, 144, 145, 146, 154
*Barcelona* 94, 104, 105
Barker, Michael 26, 67, 76, 78, 109, 111, 116, 123, 124, 159
*Barton Fink* 167
Baumbach, Noah 167, 192–5
Bay, Michael 185, 187
Beatles, The 50
*Beautiful Girls* 145
*Before Sunrise* 204

*Before Sunset* 204, 205, 221
*Being John Malkovich* 182
*Being Julia* 123
*Bend it Like Beckham* 146, 164
*Beneath* 165
Bernard, Tom 26, 67, 77, 78, 109, 111, 113, 116, 118, 124, 159
Berney, Bob 201, 211, 212, 213, 214
Bertolucci, Bernardo 25, 46, 134, 136, 147
*Betrayal* 56
Bielinsky, Fabian 125
*Big Chill, The* 62
*Big Deal on Madonna Street (I Soliti Ignioti)* 221
*Billy Elliot* 182
*Birth* 102
Biskind, Peter 73, 160
*Black Hole* 166
*Black Snake Moan* 165
*Black Swan* 133, 149
*Blood and Wine* 134, 138
*Blood Simple* 167
Bloom, Marcie 75, 77, 109, 111, 116, 159, 174
*Bob the Gambler (Bob le flambeur)* 46
Bonne Pioche 206
*Bootmen* 154
*Bowling for Columbine* 172
Boyle, Danny 134, 141, 144
*Boys Don't Cry* 133, 134, 141
Bravo 94
*Breaking the Waves* 180
*Bride of Chucky, The* 187
*Bride of the Wind* 161
*Brideshead Revisited* 51
*Bridge on the River Kwai, The* 56
*Britannia Hospital* 35
British Zenith Pictures 91
*Brokeback Mountain* 177–8, 188–9, 191, 204, 214
*Brothers McMullen, The* 133–6, 150–2, 188
*Brown Sugar* 144–6, 154
Buena Vista France 206
*Burn After Reading* 192
Burns, Edward 135–6, 150–2, 162, 182, 185
Bush, George W. 173, 222

*Cabaret Balkan (Bure Baruta)* 161
Calley, John 116, 124
Camarzin, Mel 163
*Camille Claudel* 75, 83
Cammack, Ben 50
Canal Plus 76
Canby, Vincent 29, 80
*Capote* 110, 123, 124
Capote, Truman 204
*Careful, He Might Hear You* 58
*Carmen* 68, 72

*Case 39* 170
Cassavetes, John 57, 150
Castle Rock 104, 204
CBS 163, 206
*Celluloid Closet, The* 115, 172
*Chan is Missing* 3, 71
*Chaos (Kaos)* 37
*Chasing Amy* 137
*Chicago* 202
*Chilly Scenes of Winter* 34
*Chinese Coffee* 154
*Choose Me* 48
*Chosen, The* 55
*Chumscrubber, The* 213
Cinecom 3, 4, 73, 75, 90, 92
Cinema 5 Distributing 25, 27, 32
*Cinema of Outsiders* 160
Cineplex 74
Cinevista 75
*Circle of Deceit (Die Fälschung)* 32
*Civilization* 124
classics arms *see* classics divisions
classics divisions 4–10, 15–16, 26, 30–1, 35, 37–40, 45, 47–9, 51–5, 59, 61, 65–7, 69–70, 75–8, 87–9, 97, 102, 110–12, 115–16, 125, 135, 139, 145, 156, 157, 160, 163, 166, 199
first wave 7, 93
second wave 9; *see also* specialty divisions: second wave of
*see also* specialty divisions
*Clearing, The* 147, 205
*Clerks* 151
Clooney, George 127, 167, 203, 206, 206, 221
*Closer You Get, The* 154
*Cock and Bull Story, A* 213
Coen, Joel and Ethan 167
Cohen, Polly 209
*Cold Mountain* 16
*Colonel Redl (Oberst Redl)* 70, 72
Columbia 3, 9–10, 13–14, 27, 44–9, 60–2, 65, 109, 111, 113, 116, 124, 156, 186
Home Entertainment 111
Pictures 111, 119, 139
Pictures Entertainment 111
TriStar Home Video 93
Tristar Pictures 116
Comcast 192
*Come Back to the Five and Dime, Jimmy Dean, Jimmy Dean* 92
*Comfort and Joy* 54
*Confessions of a Dangerous Mind* 221
*Confidence* 126, 222
*Constant Gardener, The* 188
contemporary American

independent cinema/film/ US independent cinema/ film 2–7, 12, 14, 16, 32, 44, 60, 79, 142, 171, 179, 188
convergence 10, 17, 149, 152
*Coraline* 190
Corman, Roger 26, 27, 32
*Cousin Bette* 140
*Cousin cousine* 45
*Crash* 189
Craven, Wes 148, 190
*Crazy Heart* 133
*Criminal* 16, 127, 205, 221–3
*Crouching Tiger, Hidden Dragon* 119–21, 123–5, 145, 162, 182–3
*Crumb* 115
*Cry Wolf* 188
*Crying Game, The* 95, 134, 138
*Cutter's Way* 29–31, 54
*Cyrano de Bergerac* 75, 83
*Czlowiek z Zelaza (Man of Iron)* 35

*Damn Nation* 166
*Damsels in Distress* 105
*Dancer in the Dark* 100
*Dancing in Water (Hey Babu Riba)* 73
*Danton* 44, 47, 75
*Danzón* 114
*Darjeeling Limited, The* 133, 148
*Das Boot* 45–6
De Palma, Brian 26–7
*Dear Diary (Caro Diario)* 94
*Death and the Maiden* 94, 184
*Death Game* 5
*Death of an Angel* 57
*Deconstructing Harry* 98
*Deep End, The* 144
*Defiance* 170
*De-Lovely* 205
*Denise Calls Up* 115, 151
*Desperately Seeking Susan* 66
Deutchman, Ira 4, 7, 18, 26, 41, 88–90, 92, 95, 103, 104
*Devil in the Flesh (Diavolo in Corpo)* 73
Diller, Barry 8, 181–2
*Dim Sum: A Little Bit of Heart* 71
Dimension Films 9, 98, 118, 143, 166, 187–8, 190
Dinerstein, David 157, 159–61, 166
*Dirty Dancing* 73
*Dirty Shame, A* 102
Disney 9, 10, 13, 16, 88, 103, 114, 117, 118, 133–5, 147, 156, 168, 175, 180, 186, 205–6
*Diva* 33, 45
*Diving Bell and the Butterfly, The* 216
DNA Films 147

*Do the Right Thing* 2, 80–1
Dolby Stereo Sound System 50
Dolgen, Jonathan 158, 163
Domingo, Plácido 52
Doumanian, Jean 120
*Down by Law* 72, 79–80
*Dozens, The* 31
*Draughtsman's Contract, The* 35
*Dreamchild* 55
*Dreamers, The* 147
*Dreaming of Joseph Lees* 141
Dreamworks SKG 170
*Drugstore Cowboy* 8, 91
*Duck Season (Temporada de Patos)* 207

*East West (Est ouest)* 119
*Easy Rider* 61
*Eating Raoul* 44, 55
Ebert, Roger 90
*Education, An* 124
*Edward II* 91–2
*Eight Men Out* 66
*8 Women (8 femmes)* 185, 193
*El Cantante* 215
El Deseo 185
*El Laberinto del Fauno (Pan's Labyrinth)* 201, 215, 218, 220
*El Mariachi* 151
*El Norte* 3, 137
*Election* 11
*Elephant* 101, 201, 210
*Emperor's Journey, The (La Marche de L'empereur)* 206
*Empire Records* 200
*End of the Line* 5, 72
Endeavor Talent Agency 166
*Enduring Love* 163
*English Patient, The* 117
*Eternal Sunshine of the Spotless Mind* 177, 185–6
Eugenides, Jeffrey 161
*Eureka* 36
*Europa, Europa* 76
*Europeans, The* 5
*Even Cowgirls Get the Blues* 93–4
*Every Word is True* 204
*Everything is Illuminated* 204

*Fabian* 32
*Factotum* 213
*Fahrenheit 9/11* 147, 172
*Far from Heaven* 177–8, 184–5, 202
*Fargo* 181
*Fast Food Nation* 148
*Father of the Bride* 23
*Feeling Minnesota* 96
Fellini, Federico 25, 48
*Fight Club* 11, 12, 140
Film Entertainment Group 58
*Filmmaker Magazine* 18
Filmways 65
Fine Line Features 7–10, 15, 18, 26, 81, 87–105, 109–10, 112, 114–15, 117, 135, 138–41, 156–7, 159, 165, 171–2, 180, 187, 199–202, 208, 201–11, 216
Fine Line Theater 94
*Fiorile* 94
First Run Features 3
Focus Features 6, 10, 15, 16, 81, 88, 123, 125, 147, 150–1, 163, 165, 166, 171, 177–80, 183–95, 202, 203, 208, 210, 212, 214, 216, 220
    International 183–4, 190–1
*Fog of War, The* 110, 121, 172
*For Your Consideration* 206
Forster, E.M. 75, 111, 112
*Four-Eyed Monsters* 194
*Four Feathers, The* 147
*Four Friends* 60
*400 Blows, The (Les Quatre cents coups)* 26, 27
*Four Weddings and a Funeral* 138, 181
Fox 55–9, 98, 135–6, 139, 141, 143, 146, 148, 156
    Animation Studios 140, 144
    Atomic 148, 166, 188
    Filmed Entertainment 140, 142, 144
    Inc. 58
    2000 140, 142, 144
    *see also* Twentieth Century Fox
Fox Searchlight 6, 10, 12, 15, 88, 96, 115, 117, 123, 125, 133, 134–53, 156–9, 163–6, 169, 171, 177, 179–80, 182, 186, 189, 191–3, 200, 203, 205, 208, 210, 212, 214, 216–17, 220
*Frankie Starlight* 96
Frears, Stephen 71
Freston, Tom 163, 164
*Frida* 202
Friedman, Rob 158, 159
*Friends with Money* 123
*From Mao to Mozart: Isaac Stern in China* 32, 171
*Full Frontal* 221
*Full Monty, The* 117, 134, 138–41, 145–7
*Full Moon in Paris* 70
*Funny Games* 210
*Funny Ha Ha* 194
*Fur* 213

*Gabriela (Gabriela, Cravo e Canela)* 36
*Gal Young 'Un* 26, 31
*Gangs of New York* 16, 202
*Garage Days* 146
*Garden of the Finzi-Continis, The* 116
*Garden State* 147, 164
*Gas Food Lodging* 114
Gaumont 45–9, 62
General Electric 189, 192
*Genocide* 35
*Get Real* 161
*Gift, The* 157, 161, 163, 164
Gigliotti, Donna 67, 75
Gill, Mark 203, 207, 208, 209, 220
Gilula, Stephen 134, 142–3
*Girl Fight* 118
*Girl on the Bridge, The (La Fille sur le pont)* 161
*Girl 6* 136–7
*Girl with the Red Hair, The (Het Meisje met het Rode Haar)* 35
*Gods Must Be Crazy, The* 48, 55, 58–9
Goldcrest Films 68
Gomery, Douglas 14
Gondry, Michel 185
*Good Girl, The* 144
Good Machine 119, 151, 178, 180–3
    International 183
*Good Marriage, A (Le Beau Mariage)* 32, 67
*Good Night, and Good Luck* 201, 206, 220, 221, 223
*Good Thief, The* 146
*Good Will Hunting* 11, 117, 142
*Goodbye, Children (Au revoir, les enfants)* 72
Gore, Al 172–3
*Gosford Park* 182
*Gospel* 55
*Governess, The* 118
*Goya in Bordeaux* 118
*Grace is Gone* 216
Gramercy Pictures 96, 140–1, 180–1
*Grass Harp, The* 96
*Grease 2* 60
*Great Raid, The* 147
*Great Wall, A* 71, 82
*Green Ray, The (Le Rayon vert)* 70
Grey, Brad 166
*Grey Fox, The* 35, 36
Greenberg 192–5
*Grifters, The* 8
Guber, Peter 116
Guggenheim, Davis 171–3
*Gummo* 98
*Guys, The* 185
*Gymslip Lovers* 5

*Hail, Mary (Je vous, salue, Marie)* 48
*Hairspray* 87
*Hamlet 2* 192, 193
Handmade Films 68
*Hanna K.* 52
*Hannah Takes the Stairs* 194

*Happiness* 180
*Hard Day's Night, A* 50
Harrison, George 68
Hartley, Hal 8, 90, 91, 119, 136
Haynes, Todd 182, 184, 216
HBO 10, 34, 39, 101–3, 114, 165, 186, 199, 201, 210–13, 215–16, 218–20
Films 210, 212, 213, 215, 216, 218, 219, 220
Showcase 114
*Head over Heels* 34
*Heartland* 2, 5, 26, 31, 55
*Heat and Dust* 52
*Heaven's Gate* 34
*Hedwig and the Angry Inch* 100
*Help!* 50
*Henry Fool* 119
Hernandez, Eugene 166
*Hidden, The* 87
*Hills Have Eyes, The* 148
*His Dark Materials* 219
Hitchcock, Alfred 49, 54, 59
*Hitcher, The* 191
*Hito Hata: Raise the Banner* 31
Hollywood
 film industry 1, 2
 majors/studios/major studios 1, 2, 5, 7, 8, 9–11, 13, 15, 32, 30, 53, 55, 59, 65, 79, 87–8, 97, 133, 148, 156, 178–9, 205
 Renaissance 26, 92
*Hollywood Reporter* 18, 70, 99, 115, 117, 139
Holmlund, Chris 102
*Home at the End of the World, A* 204, 205
*Home Movies* 26
Home Shopping Network 181
*Hoop Dreams* 94, 95, 172
Hope, Ted 151
Horizon Films 68
Horn, Alan 219
*Hot Fuzz* 191
*Hours, The* 202
*House of Flying Daggers* 123
*House of Games* 66
*House of Mirth* 118
*House Party* 87
*Howards End* 75–8, 111–13, 118, 120, 124
*Hulk* 183
*Human Stain, The* 147
*Hurlyburly* 99
*Hustle & Flow* 164–6

*I Heart Huckabees* 147
*I Was a Teenage Zombie* 68
*Ice Storm, The* 138
Idei, Nobuyuki 116
IFC Films 202, 212
*I'll Sleep When I'm Dead* 163
*Imaginary Heroes* 123
IMAX 115

*Imposters, The* 134
*In America* 144, 146
*In Cold Blood* 204
*In the Company of Men* 110
*In the Valley of Elah* 209, 210, 220
*Inconvenient Truth, An* 167–8, 171–3
*Incredibly True Adventure of Two Girls in Love, The* 96
Independent Feature Project 6, 32, 47, 74
independent film
 canon/canonical titles 3, 5, 9, 16, 71, 76 , 90, 98, 104, 115, 133, 150, 167, 188, 189, 195; *see also* American independent film canon/canonical titles
 companies 3, 137
 distributors 3, 4, 10, 11, 33, 51, 61, 68, 71, 73, 74, 77, 78, 91, 93, 101, 135, 164, 180
 market 3, 4, 5, 30, 31, 65, 66, 115
 movement 2, 4, 32, 55, 79
 producers 3, 4, 14, 56, 94, 120, 182, 209
 production 2, 38, 93, 178, 201, 211
Independent Film Channel 122
Independent Film Importers and Distributors of America 25
Independent Film Project 116
indie cinema/film 1, 8–11, 13, 15, 53, 88, 94, 96, 103, 110, 114, 119, 142, 149, 150, 151, 171, 177, 178, 188, 195, 199, 201, 213, 222; *see also* American indie cinema/film
*Indiewire* 18, 166
indiewood 1, 10–12, 15–16, 110, 125–6, 140, 142, 148–50, 157–60, 163, 165–7, 169–71, 173, 177–9, 182, 184–9, 191–5, 200–6, 208, 213–14, 217, 219–20; *see also* American independent cinema
*Indochine* 114, 119
*Infamous* 209
*Inglourious Basterds* 12
Insdorf, Annette 2–4, 26, 32, 81
*Inside Job* 124
*Insomnia* 203, 221
*Intimate Relations* 138
*Intimate Strangers* 163
*Into the Wild* 167–8, 171
*Intolerable Cruelty* 167
*Invisible Circus, The* 100
Island / Alive 3

*Jacket, The* 205, 221
*James Joyce's Women* 55

*Jane Austen Book Club, The* 124
Janus Films 27
Jarmusch, Jim 72, 79–81, 91
*Jean de Florette* 72, 75
*Jeffrey* 77
*Jesus of Montreal (Jésus de Montréal)* 75, 83
*JFK* 13
*Joe and Maxi* 31
*Johnson Family Vacation* 147
*Joshua, Then and Now* 57–8
*Jules et Jim* 26
*Julius Caesar* 23
*Juno* 12, 133, 134, 148, 149, 152, 169, 216
JVC 79, 81

Katz, James L. 51, 53, 54
Kaufman, Charlie 185
Kerkorian, Kirk 23, 34
*Key Exchange* 58
Kidman, Nicole 102, 167, 213
*Kids* 188
*Kids Are All Right, The* 178
*Kid Stays in the Picture, The* 184, 185
Killer Films 203, 204, 213
King, Geoff 1, 11, 151, 179, 186
*King Lear* 70
*Kingdom Come* 143, 144
Kino International 25, 26
*Kinsey* 147
*Kipperbang* 6
*Kirlian Witness, The* 31
*Kiss of the Spider Woman, The* 3, 48, 71, 73
*Kissing Jessica Stein* 144
*Kissing on the Mouth* 194
*Kit Kittredge: An American Girl* 216
*Kite Runner, The* 168
Kline, Kevin 140, 214
Kluge, John 78, 111
Knight, Peter 190
Krim, Don 25
*Kung Fu Hustle* 123
Kurosawa, Akira 25, 70, 76
Kwit, Nathaniel 26

*La Dolce Vita* 25
*La Notte* 25, 32
*La Traviata* 44, 52
*Ladykillers, The* 167
Laika Productions 190
Landmark Theater Corporation 143
*Last Battle, The* 48
*Last Days* 213
*Last Days of Disco, The* 105
*Last King of Scotland, The* 148
*Last Metro, The (Le Dernier Metro)* 27, 29, 31–3, 42, 44–5, 75
Lavoe, Héctor 215
Law, Lindsay 136–7, 139–41, 153

# INDEX 231

Le Divorce 146
Le Vie en Rose 215, 220
L'Eau des collines 72
Lee, Ang 119–20, 136, 138, 183, 191
Lee, Spike 2, 72, 80, 123, 134
Lennon, John 50
Leopard, The 57
Lesher, John 158, 166–8, 172
Let Him Have It 90
Levitt-Pickman 4; see also Pickman Films
Levy, Emmanuel 152, 160
Liaison Films 185
Lianna 4, 35, 38–40
Libra Films 33
Life and Times of Rosie the Riveter, The 31
Life Goes On (La Vie continue) 46
Life is Beautiful (La Vita è Bella) 100, 119
Lili Marleen 31
Limbo 118
Linde, David 178–9, 183–4, 187, 189–90
Linklater, Richard 6, 134, 144, 204, 206
Lions Gate /Lionsgate 11, 140, 141, 146, 181, 184, 189, 222
Little Miss Sunshine 133, 148–9, 152
Little Odessa 96
Lives of Others, The 124
Living in Oblivion 9, 115
Lola 31, 33
London Kills Me 90
Lone Star 40, 110, 115, 118
Looking for Comedy in the Muslim World 207
Looking for Richard 137
Lopert Pictures 25, 27
Lord of the Rings, The 100, 102, 201–2, 212
Lost in Translation 177, 185, 187
Love and Other Catastrophes 138
low-budget genre production 87, 118
Lust, Caution (Se, Jie) 191

macro-industrial approaches to media industry studies 18
Mad Hot Ballroom 164–5, 172
major independents 16, 145, 150, 177, 186, 187, 212
majors see Hollywood: majors
Mamet, David 14, 100, 111, 117, 119
Man from the Snowy River, The 55, 56, 59
Man of Flowers 58
Man Who Knew Too Much, The 54
Manon des sources 72

March of the Penguins 172, 206–7, 209, 220
Margot at the Wedding 167
Maria, Full of Grace 102, 210
Marvin and Tige 57
M.A.S.H 92
Maurice 75, 111
MCA 49, 51–2
Mean Machine 157
Mechanic, Bill 134, 142, 153
Medavoy, Mike 33, 70, 111
media convergence see convergence
media industry studies 17
Memento 188, 211
Men with Guns 118
Merchant-Ivory 5, 52, 73, 75, 77, 111–12, 146
Merritt, Greg 152
Merry Christmas 123
Merry Christmas Mr Lawrence 52, 54
Metromedia Entertainment Group 77
  International Group 77–8
Metropolitan 87, 89–90, 104–5
MGM (Metro Goldwyn Mayer) 12, 23–4, 34–7, 78, 205
  Festival 23, 24
  Home Entertainment 78
MGM / UA 34–7, 205
MGM / UA Classics 36–7; see also United Artists Classics
Mi Vida Loca 114
micro-industrial approaches to media industry studies 18
Midsummer Night's Dream, A 140
Mighty Heart, A 167
Milk 177–8, 192
Milou in May (Milou en mai) 75–6, 83
mini-majors 16, 37, 66, 112
Minority Report 204
Miramax 6–12, 16–18, 55, 65, 81, 88, 95–6, 98, 103, 109–10, 114–17, 119, 124, 133–5, 141–2, 145–7, 150, 153, 156–8, 166–9, 171, 177–80, 183, 185–7, 189–90, 193, 202–3, 216, 221
Miss Parker and the Vicious Circle 94
Missing 46
Mongol, The 213, 215
Monogram 14
Monsieur Hire 75, 83
Monster 211
Monster in a Box 92
Month in the Country, A 73
Moon in the Gutter, The (La Lune dans lecaniveau) 47
Moonlighting 50–1, 69
Moonves, Leslie 163
More American Graffiti 60

Morita, Akio 116
Morris, David Burton 47, 60–1
Mother and the Whore, The (La Maman et la putain) 26
Mother Night 96
Motion Picture Association of America 169, 218
Motion Picture Patents Company 32
Motorcycle Diaries, The (Diarios de Motocicleta) 126, 186, 193
MTV 163, 165, 166
  Films 165, 170
Mumblecore films 193–5
Murdoch, Rupert 58, 146
Murrow, Edward R. 206
My Beautiful Laundrette 71, 73
My Big Fat Greek Wedding 17, 18, 187, 202, 212
My Dinner with André 3
My Father's Glory (La Gloire de mon père) 76
My First Mister 161
My Life as a Dog (Mitt Liv so Hund) 73
My Life in Ruins 150
My Mother's Castle (Le Château de ma mère) 76
My Own Private Idaho 7, 90–1, 93
MySpace 148, 165
Mystery Train 75, 79–81, 83, 91
Mystic Pizza 73
Myth of Fingerprints, The 117–19

Naked 94
Naked in New York 93
Napoleon 50
Napoleon Dynamite 133, 147, 164–5
Nashville 92
National Geographic 206
National Velvet 23
NBC 189
  Universal 190, 192
Neal, Kelly 54
Needham, Gary 149, 178, 189
neo-indie (companies) 66, 104
Never on Sunday 25
New Line Cinema 7, 9–10, 16, 65–6, 74, 78, 87, 89–95, 97–100, 102–3, 135, 145, 150, 156, 177, 185, 187, 199–202, 210–12, 216, 218–20
New Queer Cinema 91
New World Pictures 26–7, 32, 74
New York Film Festival 33
New York, New York 31
New York Times 29, 80
New Yorker Films 3, 31–3, 71, 115
Newmarket Films 11, 101, 157, 201, 211–13

News Corporation 146, 148
niche
　audiences 8, 10–11, 29, 178
　distribution 37–8, 49, 52, 109, 117, 219
　distributors 117, 122, 124, 181, 204
　film market 50, 54, 78, 110, 114–15, 124, 220
　filmmaking 122, 182
*Nicholas and Alexandra* 56
*Nicholas Nickleby* 204
Nichols, Bill 173
Nickelodeon 164–5
　Movies 170
*Night on Earth, A* 91–2
*Nightmare on Elm Street, A* 7, 87
*Nine Queens (Nueve Reinas)* 16, 120, 125–7, 205, 221–3
*No Country for Old Men* 158, 167–9, 171, 194, 202, 216
*North Star, The (L'Étoile du nord)* 35
*Northern Lights* 2, 26, 31
*Nothing Lasts Forever* 36
*Notorious* 150
*Notorious Betty Page, The* 213
*Nowhere* 98

*Ocean's Eleven* 203, 221
October Films 8, 11, 115, 140–1, 156, 180–1
*Omen, The* 214
*Once Were Warriors* 96
*One Deadly Summer (L'Été meurtrier)* 52, 54
*One Hour Photo* 144
*Opposite of Sex, The* 119
Ordesky, Mark 88, 98–100, 102, 201
Orion Classics 5– 9, 15, 26, 36–7, 39, 61,65–78, 80, 82, 89, 91, 109–12, 114, 125, 138, 159
Orion Pictures 24, 65–6, 77–8, 89, 111
　Home Entertainment 75
*Orphan, The (Orfanato)* 215
*Oscar and Lucinda* 138

*Painted Veil, The* 206
*Palindromes* 149
*Paradise Road* 138
Paramount 10, 13, 38, 49, 58, 77, 98, 116, 156–9, 162–4, 166–8, 170–1, 180–1, 202
　Worldwide Acquisitions Group 170
Paramount Classics 10, 15, 98, 116, 140, 157, 158, 159, 160–8, 171–3, 178, 180, 182, 208, 214
Paramount Insurgent 188
Paramount Vantage 10, 15, 158, 168–71, 173, 179, 191, 208,

214–15, 219
*Parole Officer, The* 147
Participant Productions 172, 206
Pasolini, Uberto 138–9, 147
*Passion* 35
*Passion of the Christ, The* 211
*Pauline at the Beach (Pauline à la plage)* 67, 68, 70
PBS 91, 136
*Pecker* 99
Perren, Alisa 8, 17–18, 96, 110
*Persona* 25
*Phat Girlz* 148
*Photographer, The (Le Point de mire)* 46
*Piaf (Piaf: The Early Years)* 44, 55
*Pianist, The* 179, 184, 185, 202
*Piano, The* 95
Pickman Films 3–4; *see also* Levitt-Pickaman
Picturehouse 10, 15, 88, 103, 199, 200–2, 210–16, 218–20
*Pie in the Sky* 97
Pinter, Harold 56
Pixar 190, 214
platform release 9, 45–6, 52, 69, 89, 92, 119, 145, 152, 169, 173, 200, 206, 216
Platinum Dunes 185, 187, 190
*Player, The* 8, 13, 92–3
*Please Give* 110
Polanski, Roman 94, 179, 184
*Polish Wedding* 140
*Pollock* 121
Polygram
　Entertainment 76, 93, 181
　Filmed Entertainment 180–1
*Possession* 184, 185
*Postman, The (Il Postino)* 95
*Pot Luck (L'Auberge espagnole)* 146
Poverty Row 14
*Prairie Home Companion, A* 214, 215
*Prairie Wind* 165
Prestige Films 10
*Pride & Prejudice* 188
*Privates on Parade* 68
*Proof* 91, 147
*Promise, The (Wu Ji)* 207
*Puberty Blues* 52
*Puffy Chair, The* 194
*Pulp Fiction* 10–11, 13, 95, 116, 145, 188
*Purple Haze* 44, 47, 49, 60–2

quality independent cinema/films/titles 3, 5, 8, 10, 31, 67–8, 99, 101, 186
quality indie blockbuster 96, 110, 133
*Quiet American, The* 202
*Quills* 140, 154

Rabe, David 99
*Rachel Getting Married* 124
*Rage in Harlem, A* 8
*Rain without Thunder* 77, 82
*Raise the Red Lantern (Da hong deng long gao gao gua)* 77
*Ran* 70
Random House 190
*Rapture, The* 90, 92
*Real Women Have Curves* 101, 211
*Rear Window* 54
Redford, Robert 147, 203
Relativity Media 192
Renzi, Maggie 39
*Repo Man* 44, 54, 59
Republic Pictures 14
rerelease market 23, 30–1, 44–6, 49–51, 54, 57, 59, 116, 156
*Reservation Road* 190–1
*Reservoir Dogs* 8
*Return of the Secaucus Seven* 2–3, 26, 31, 33, 38–9
*Reuben Reuben* 7
*Revolutionary Road* 170, 194
*Rhapsody in August (Hachi-gatsu no Kyôshikyoku)* 76
Rice, Peter 134, 141–2, 146, 154
Rich, B. Ruby 91
*Richard III* 137
*Ringer, The* 147–8
*Ripley's Game* 101
*Rita, Sue and Bob Too* 3
RKO 24
*Road, The (Yol)* 46
Robinov, Jeff 208
*Rock School* 213
*Rocket Science* 215
*Rocky Horror Picture Show, The* 69
Rogue Pictures 118, 166, 185, 187–8, 190–2
Rohmer, Eric 32–3, 67–8, 70, 77
*Room with a View, A* 73, 75, 89, 111–12
*Rope* 54
*Roseanna's Grave* 98
Rothman, Tom 135–7, 145
Rudin, Scott 194
*Run Silent, Run Deep* 46
Russell, David O. 94, 147, 166

*Sacrifice, The (Offret)* 71
*Safe* 9, 110, 115, 119, 137, 182
Samuel Goldwyn Company, The 3, 8, 11, 26, 73, 77, 115, 135–7
*Savages, The* 148, 216
*Saving Grace* 100
*Saving Private Ryan* 150
*Say Amen, Somebody* 35, 171–2
Sayles, John 35, 38–40, 115, 118, 120
*Scanner Darkly, A* 201, 206, 209, 220, 221

Schamus, James 151, 178–9, 182–3, 187, 189–1
Schatz, Thomas 18
Schreger, Charles 45, 48, 60
Screen Gems 98, 111, 118, 143, 202
*Screen International* 18, 53
*Scrubbers* 68
*Sea Inside, The (Mar Adentro)* 102
Seagram 179, 180–2
*Second Chance (Si c'était à refaire)* 31
*Secret Agent, The* 137
*Secret Diary of Sigmund Freud, The* 57
*Secrets and Lies* 180
Section Eight 127, 203, 206, 221–3
*Seed of Chucky, The* 187
*sex, lies, and videotape* 6–8, 13, 73, 80–1, 87, 89–90, 109, 139, 149
*Sexy Beast* 144
*Shakespeare in Love* 11, 117, 142, 187
*Shape of Things, The* 186
*Shaun of the Dead* 187
Shaye, Robert 87
*She Hate Me* 123
Shenson, Walter 50
*She's Gotta Have It* 3, 72
*She's the One* 137, 150, 152, 182
*Shine* 97, 103, 139
*Shooting Fish* 140
*Short Cuts* 8, 93–4
Showtime 34, 39, 94, 122
*Sidewalks of New York* 150, 162
*Sideways* 133, 147, 214
*Silk* 215
SimEx-Iwerks 115
*Simpatico* 99
*Simple Men* 91–2
Skouras Pictures 73, 74
*Slacker* 76
*Sleeping Dictionary, The* 101
*Slumdog Millionaire* 133, 149
*Smilla's Feeling for Snow* 138
*Snow Angels* 210
Soderbergh, Steven 6, 73, 80, 127, 142, 203, 221
*Soft Fruit* 154
*Somewhere* 92
*Son of Rambow* 169
Sony 9, 65, 77, 78, 109, 111–12, 115–17, 121, 124–5, 135, 158–9, 186, 212, 218
   Pictures Classics Large Format 115, 116
   Pictures Entertainment 111, 113, 116, 118, 124
Sony Pictures Classics (SPC) 9, 13–16, 26, 40, 77–8, 88, 96, 109–27, 133, 135, 140, 141, 150, 153, 156–60, 162–3, 169, 171–2, 180, 191, 205, 208, 212, 215, 220–2
*Sotto…Sotto* 48
*Spanish Prisoner, The* 13–14, 118, 126, 222
*Spanking the Monkey* 94
specialty/specialised film 7, 13–15, 18, 33–5, 50, 54, 58–9, 73, 75–6, 80, 89, 92, 94–5, 99, 103, 124, 210, 212
   business 219
   distribution 14, 33, 36–7, 50, 54, 56, 71, 70, 78, 92, 103, 135, 138, 215
   divisions shakeout 124, 133, 150, 170, 192
   market 3, 4, 14, 18, 29, 45–7, 51, 55, 57, 65, 72–5, 77, 80, 87, 93, 109, 111, 125, 133, 136–7, 139, 146–7, 150, 152, 157, 171, 184, 186–7, 193, 199, 209
   sector 90, 94, 124, 139, 141–3, 152, 156
specialty divisions/film divisions/film labels 7, 9–10, 12, 15–18, 48, 57, 65, 76, 81, 89, 96, 102–3, 116, 118, 122, 141, 146, 158, 161, 166–7, 171, 178, 180–3, 186, 189, 191, 193, 199–201, 206–10, 212, 218–21
   second wave 16, 65, 87, 109
   third wave 12, 16, 57, 88, 118, 123, 125, 133, 163, 171, 211, 220; *see also* third wave studio labels
   *see also* classics divisions; stand-alone
*Spellbound* 172
Spelling Entertainment 93
*Spider-Man 3* 218
Spiegel, Sam 56
Spirit Awards 116, 169
*Squid and the Whale, The* 195
Stand-alone companies/distributors/independent companies/mini-major/producer-distributor 3–5, 7, 11, 13, 16, 39, 58, 65–6, 87, 93, 112, 115, 140, 146–7, 157, 163, 165, 180, 182, 188, 193, 202, 205, 208, 211, 217
*Star Maps* 134, 138
*Starter for Ten* 215
Starz Encore 186
*State and Main* 100
*Stealing Beauty* 136–7
Stiller, Ben 194–5
Stillman, Whit 94, 104–5
*Stone Boy* 57
*Storytelling* 101

*Stranger than Paradise* 3, 79
*Strangers Kiss* 69
*Strangers, The* 192
*Streamers* 4, 35, 92
Studio Canal 185
Studio divisions 4–7, 10–11, 13, 18, 53, 60, 93, 116, 122, 150, 152, 157, 159, 161, 163–4, 166, 169–71, 177–8, 181, 188, 194, 200, 202, 205, 208, 212, 217–18; *see also* classics divisions; specialty divisions
*Sugar Cane Alley (Rue cases nègres)* 70
Sundance
   Film Channel 122, 137
   Film Festival 13, 97, 101, 110, 135–6, 138, 144, 151, 161, 164–5, 172, 204, 206
   Film Institute 6, 57, 94, 99–100, 167
Sundance-Miramax era, the 6, 7, 12
*Sunday in the Country, A (Un Dimanche à la campagne)* 36
*Sunshine* (D. Boyle) 148
*Sunshine* (István Szabó) 157, 161–2
*Sunshine State* 120
*Super Size Me* 172
*Super Spook* 5
*Super Troopers* 144
*Surviving Picasso* 200
*Swoon* 91–2, 137
*Sylvia* 37, 185
Szabó, István 70, 157, 161

*Tale of Springtime (Conte de printemps)* 77
*Talk to Her (Habla con Ella)* 120–1, 125
Tarantino, Quentin 6, 8, 10, 188
*Teenage Mutant Ninja Turtles* 7, 87
Tender Loving Care Films (TLC Films) 58
*Thank You for Smoking* 148
*That's Entertainment!* 23–4
*There is No Word* 209
*There Will Be Blood* 158, 167–9, 171, 173, 194, 202
*Thin Red Line, The* 140
*Thing About My Folks, The* 213
*Third Miracle, The* 118
*Thirteen Conversations about One Thing* 120
*This World, Then the Fireworks* 77
Thompson, Anne 169
*Three Kings* 11, 200
*Threshold* 55
*Ticket to Heaven* 32
Time 199

Time Warner 88, 97–8, 101–3, 117, 156, 199–202, 204, 207, 210–12, 215–16, 219–20; *see also* Warner
*To Want to Fly (Volere Volare)* 91
*Too Beautiful for You (Trop belle pour toi)* 75, 83
Top-rank independent producers 56
Total Film Group 161
*Traffic* 11–12, 142, 162, 182
*Traffik* 142
Transamerica 23–4, 34, 65
*Trees Lounge* 77
*Trekkies* 156–7, 161, 172
*Trick* 99
Trimark 140
*Trip to Bountiful, The* 71
Tri-Star Pictures 111, 113, 116
Triumph Films 15, 45–9, 51, 55, 59–62
*Tropic Thunder* 195
*Trouble With Harry, The* 54
Truffaut, François 27, 30–1, 33, 46, 173
*Trust* 90, 106
*Trust the Man* 148
*Tuck Everlasting* 31
Turner Broadcasting System (TBS) 9, 94–5, 97, 103, 156, 199, 199
*Twelfth Night* 96
Twentieth Century Fox 3, 10, 44, 48, 55, 57–9, 63, 134–6, 140–2, 144–5, 153, 181, 214
Entertainment 56
*see also* Fox
Twentieth Century Fox International Classics (TCFIC) 15, 54–7, 63, 112
Twentieth Century Fox Specialized Film Division (TCFSFD) 57
*21 Grams* 179, 184–6
*28 Days Later* 134, 144, 146, 147
2929 Entertainment 206
*Two Girls and a Guy* 140

UGC-Fox Distribution 136
*Unbelievable Truth, The* 90
*Under the Volcano* 5, 52–4, 56
*Unforgiven* 13
*Union City* 31
Union Générale Cinématographique (UGC) 119, 136
United Artists 3, 14, 23–7, 30–1, 33–4, 36, 47, 50, 65, 67, 110
United Artists Classics (UA Classics) 3–5, 15, 18, 24, 26–40, 44–5, 47, 49, 51, 54, 61, 67, 69, 71, 78, 90, 92, 110, 118, 125, 159, 171–2
Universal 2, 3, 5, 10, 13–14, 44, 48–55, 59, 65, 81, 118, 156, 178–84, 186, 189–93, 200
Focus 180, 182–3
Motion Picture Group 51
Special Projects 54
*see also* NBC: Universal; Vivendi: Universal
Universal Classics 5, 10, 15, 49–56, 59, 69
US film industry *see* American film industry
US independent film market *see* independent film: market
USA Film and Video Festival 47, 60, 61
USA Films 11, 140–2, 146, 162, 180–4
USA Networks 180–2
*Ushpizin* 213
*Usual Suspects, The* 181
Utley, Nancy 134, 141–3

Vachon, Christine 203, 204
*Van, The* 138
Van Sant, Gus 90–1, 93–4, 101, 213
*Vanity Fair* 185–6
*Variety* 18, 25, 37, 68, 93, 100, 143, 165, 189, 190, 192, 205, 212, 216
*Vera Drake* 102
*Veronika Voss (Die Sehnsucht der Veronika Voss)* 31, 33
*Vertigo* 54
*Very Long Engagement, A* 205
Vestron 73–4
Viacom Entertainment 156, 158–9, 163–5, 170
*Virgin Suicides, The* 157, 161
Vitale, Ruth 88, 95, 98, 157, 159–62, 164, 166
Vivendi 179, 182
Universal 177, 179, 182–3, 189

Wai, Wong Kar 147
*Waiting for Guffman* 115, 118
*Waitress* 148
Wajda, Andrzej 35, 46–7
*Waking Life* 144, 206
*Waking Ned* 134, 140
*War at Home, The* 31
Warner 10, 13, 24, 97, 170, 179, 192, 199, 201–5, 207–9, 218–22
Bros. 10, 24, 27, 97, 104, 180, 186, 199–200, 204, 207–9, 219, 221
Bros. Entertainment Group 203–4
Bros. Festival 24
*see also* Time Warner
Warner Independent Pictures (WIP) 10, 15–16, 127, 165, 199–210, 213, 215–16, 220–1, 223
*Waterland* 91–2
*We Don't Live Here Anymore* 204, 205, 221
Weaver, Sigourney 135, 138
Weinstein (brothers), Bob and Harvey 124, 147, 169
Weinstein Company, The 147, 216
*Welcome to Collinwood* 221
*Welcome to the Dollhouse* 9, 110, 115
*Wetherby* 37
*Whale Rider* 211
*Where is Marlowe?* 161
*Where's Poppa?* 31
*Where the Green Ants Dream (Wo die grünen Ameisen träumen)* 68
White, Michael 69
*Whiteboyz* 141
*Widows' Peak* 94
*Wild at Heart* 13
Wildwood 20
Wilinsky, Barbara 25
*Winged Migration* 121
*Wings of Courage* 115
*Wings of Desire (Himmel über Berlin)* 74
*Winslow Boy, The* 111, 117, 119
*Winter Solstice* 165
*Woman Next Door, The (La Femme d'à côté)* 31
*Woman on Top* 154
*Woman's Tale, A* 77
*Women, The* 215
*Women on the Verge of a Nervous Breakdown (Mujeres al Borde de un Ataque de Nervios)* 74
Wozniak, Victoria 61
Wyatt, Justin 16, 102, 177

*You Can Count on Me* 161, 164
Young, Neil 165

Zentropa Films 100
*Ziggy Stardust and the Spiders from Mars* 57
Ziskin, Laura 140

EU representative:
Easy Access System Europe
Mustamäe tee 50, 10621 Tallinn, Estonia
Gpsr.requests@easproject.com

www.ingramcontent.com/pod-product-compliance
Lightning Source LLC
Chambersburg PA
CBHW062214300426
44115CB00012BA/2058